DECOLONIZING
ETHNOGRAPHY

DECOLONIZING ETHNOGRAPHY

Undocumented Immigrants and New Directions in Social Science

CAROLINA ALONSO BEJARANO / LUCIA LÓPEZ JUÁREZ
MIRIAN A. MIJANGOS GARCÍA / DANIEL M. GOLDSTEIN

Duke University Press   Durham and London   2019

Designed by Courtney Leigh Baker
Typeset in Minion Pro and Avenir by CGI

Library of Congress Cataloging-in-Publication Data
Names: Alonso Bejarano, Carolina, [date] author. | López Juárez, Lucia,
author. | Mijangos García, Mirian A., author. | Goldstein, Daniel M.,
[date] author.
Title: Decolonizing ethnography : undocumented immigrants and new
directions in social science / Carolina Alonso Bejarano,
Lucia López Juárez, Mirian A. Mijangos García, and
Daniel M. Goldstein.
Description: Durham : Duke University Press, 2019. | Includes
bibliographical references and index.
Identifiers: LCCN 2018042313 (print) | LCCN 2018060919 (ebook)
ISBN 9781478004547 (ebook)
ISBN 9781478003625 (hardcover)
ISBN 9781478003953 (pbk.)
Subjects: LCSH: Anthropology—Methodology. | Ethnology—Methodology. |
Eurocentrism. | Critical pedagogy. | Racism in higher education. |
Education, Higher—Social aspects. | Education and globalization. |
Decolonization. | Marginality, Social—Developing countries.
Classification: LCC LC191.98.D44 (ebook) |
LCC LC191.98.D44 A46 2019 (print) DDC 378.008—dc23
LC record available at https://lccn.loc.gov/2018042313

Cover art: Illustration and hand lettering by Peter Quach. Courtesy
of the artist.

(*opposite*): Figure FM.1. Photo by Daniel M. Goldstein.

Para nuestro querido Evandro, Q.E.P.D.

Contents

June 17, 2014

one of this day i will find the opportunity to become a president of usa.
opss back to real life, well life is toff in this country usa,
since i come to this country to leave the american dream
so far only leaving by nightmares, so they say going to be easier
    don"t worry,
but they never say to do worry to learn english.
do worry to have a legal green card
do worry to pay high price for rent your own habitate
do worry etc.etc.etc . . .
so it is not easier i like to go back to my country wich is brazil . . .
but right now in brasil we have . . . poverty all over.
hospital has no good management people are dieng.
scholls fall a part,has no teacher ,money in people pocket only
    for the rich ones.
i fell bad because right now am leaving in usa . . .
i hope one day everything get in place.

Preface

"Are you scared about Trump?" Carolina asked Mirian.

It was December 2016, and Donald Trump had recently been elected president of the United States. Carolina and Mirian were in a restaurant in downtown New Brunswick, NJ. They were warm inside the restaurant but it was raining heavily outside.

Mirian looked at Caro for a long time without replying. Then she asked, "Are *you* scared, *nena*?" Caro admitted that she was, and not just for herself but also for so many people she loves. "People like you," Carolina told Mirian. Mirian said that, to the contrary, she was not more afraid than she already had been. "I am here to stay. *Ahora nos toca organizarnos aún más porque la ilegalidad no es sólo un problema de nosotros los indocumentados*" [Now it's time to organize even more because illegality doesn't only affect us, the undocumented immigrants]. She smiled at Caro, who found comfort in Mirian's kind eyes.

Earlier that day Mirian had spoken to Carolina's Latino Studies class about her life as an undocumented woman organizer from Guatemala. She told the students about working long days, having a work accident, and becoming an ethnographer and activist in the immigrants' rights movement. She told them about her daughter who she has not seen in many years, about civil disobedience and being in jail, and about her work as a singer and songwriter. She sang one of her songs for the class, about the need for immigration reform, and told students about the relationship between art and activism.

It was important for Caro to bring Mirian to talk about her work in class that day, only a few weeks after the election, because the debate around immigration was at the core of Trump's presidential campaign. As poet Nicholas

Powers noted, "He won with a metaphor. He won with the image of a wall" (Powers 2016). Mirian's story, as well as her approach to activism, recognizes that this metaphorical wall excludes many of us—and not just those of us who are not U.S. citizens.

Much has happened in terms of immigration policy and political rhetoric around immigration since we officially closed our four-year ethnographic project in August, 2015. Despite the fact that the Obama administration's "deportation machine" was operating at full force during our research and remained unrivaled by the deportation efforts of any previous adminis-tration, it was not yet the era of Donald Trump and the open and state-sanctioned hateful rhetoric toward immigrants from the Global South and people of color in general. Under President Trump, the policy of the Obama administration that prioritized the deportation of immigrants with criminal records has been replaced by a "zero tolerance" policy in which everyone—especially nonwhite folks, from toddlers to naturalized citizens—is subject to incarceration and deportation.

This book is based on ethnographic research conducted in a New Jer-sey town between August 2011 and August 2015, when the policing and ha-rassment of immigrants in the United States was relatively less intense than it would become under the Trump administration. As we go to press, the modified "Muslim Ban" has been upheld by the Supreme Court; immigrant families are being jailed by executive order; thousands of immigrant children have been separated from their families, and many of them remain detained or lost in the system despite a judicial order mandating immediate reunifica-tion; a new Denaturalization Task Force is targeting naturalized citizens for deportation; the administration is attempting to end the Deferred Action for Childhood Arrivals (DACA) program that gives some protection to un-documented immigrants who came as minors . . . The list goes on and on.

Based on our findings, in these pages we stress the rights that undocu-mented immigrants have in this country. We advocate for undocumented people to engage with the justice system and to adopt direct action strategies in defense of their dignity and rights. And we contend that ethnography can be a tool for undocumented people in these struggles. Lucy and Mirian, the two undocumented authors of this book, continue to follow this program despite the increased risk for folks with their immigration status. In writing this book with Carolina and Daniel they are asserting their right to think freely, to speak publicly, and to exist in the United States. We recognize, however, that the stakes have changed since we researched and wrote our book as a call for action, at a time when a Trump presidency seemed improbable at best. In the current era of regular ICE raids in courtrooms across the country, it is becoming increasingly difficult for undocumented immigrants to engage with the justice system to defend their rights as workers and as people. The same can be said about direct action strategies that may result in people's arrest and subsequent deportation.

But people, both documented and undocumented, are also responding to the Trump administration's immigration policies in the massive way that we imagine in this book, and that we believe is necessary to bring about any immigration reform in this country. As Mirian suggested above, people are beginning to realize that the surging sexism, racism, and authoritarianism of the Trump regime harms all of us—citizens and noncitizens. For instance, "Abolish ICE" has become a mainstream idea, as protesters flood the streets and occupy buildings in outrage, especially after seeing and hearing footage of immigrant children being held in cages by immigration officials. In a context of increased policing and demonization of immigrants—particularly immigrants of color—but also of increased public awareness and engagement with the struggle for immigrants' rights, we believe our book to be a timely contribution to the movement for the recognition of the humanity of all people. As Lucy says, today, in the midst of the rise of White Nationalism as a policy of state in the United States, "we have to keep struggling against our oppression. Like in the times of Martin Luther King, when you had to risk something to get something. The history of decolonization continues."

Acknowledgments

This book would not be possible without the collaboration of countless people in the place we call Hometown. We thank all those who shared their stories with us, in particular the members of "Casa Hometown" and its director, Rita Dentino, who made invaluable contributions to this project and from the beginning welcomed us with open arms. Others to whom we are indebted include Lauren Dempsey, Tony Dentino, John Leschak, Sima Milgraum, Juan Reyes, Jorge Torres, Roberto Vaca, and friends at Unidad Latina en Acción, and Teresa Vivar at Lazos América Unida. We also thank the many undocumented friends whose names we cannot include, owing to the criminalization of undocumented immigrants in the United States.

The feedback from our two anonymous reviewers was indispensable to shaping the arguments made in these pages. Angela Stuesse in particular provided valuable feedback and engagement with our ideas. Other academic friends and contributors to whom we give our thanks include Ulla Berg, Linda Bosniak, Janice Fine, Alyshia Gálvez, Peter Guarnaccia, Ursula Rao, and Jasmin A. Young. Jeremy Friedman read the final draft of the book and offered invaluable edits and feedback, and Peter Quach made illustrations for us, which we included throughout the book and cover. We are grateful to Gisela Fosado and her staff at Duke University Press for their patient and skillful work on this project. Thanks also to the administrative staff in the Department of Anthropology at Rutgers University, particularly Ginny Caputo, Shelly Harden, and Jovani Reaves, for logistical support throughout the research process.

This material is based in part upon work supported by the National Science Foundation under Grant Number 1324234. Any opinions, findings, and conclusions or recommendations expressed in this material are those of the authors and do not necessarily reflect the views of the National Science Foundation. Preliminary funding was provided by the Russell Sage Foundation. Sections of chapter 3 originally appeared in Daniel M. Goldstein and Carolina Alonso-Bejarano, 2017, "E-Terrify: Securitized Immigration and Biometric Surveillance in the Workplace," *Human Organization* 76 (1): 1–14.

Carolina thanks the administrators and faculty of the Departments of Latino and Caribbean Studies and Women's and Gender Studies at Rutgers University, her two academic homes. In particular, her work has been inspired by the mentoring and encouragement of Carlos U. Decena, Robyn M. Rodriguez, Yolanda Martinez-San Miguel, Nelson Maldonado-Torres, Ed Cohen, Drucilla Cornell, Elizabeth Grosz, Marisa Fuentes, Jasbir K. Puar, and Daniel M. Goldstein. Throughout her years teaching at Rutgers, Caro has encountered many students who have reflected with her upon the topics discussed in this book. Special thanks go to Jamie King, an undergraduate student and native of Hometown, who worked as her research assistant on her dissertation project. The intellectual and emotional support of Martha Lucía Bejarano Marín, Jorge Ernesto Alonso Muñoz, Jasmin A. Young, Peter Quach, Jeremy Friedman, Stephen Seely, Max Hantel, Stina Soderling, Miriam Tola, Kendra Boyd, Jesse Bayker, Nafisa Tanjeem, Rosemary Ndubuizu, Alexandra Demshock, Mónica Ramón Ríos, Carlos Labbé, Marlita Greenwald, Tiana Hayden, Malav Kanuga, Efraín Rozas, J. Brager, Enmanuel Martinez, Amanda Kaplan, the H(e)art House Collective, Nelson de Witt, Juliana Devis Durán, David Lababsa, Huem Otero, María Paula Vela Valdez, Juan Felipe Rodriguez Bueno, Nicolás Cáceres Daza, Daniel Casallas Noguera, Ana María Zuluaga Prada, Daniel Calderón Ardila, Adriana Gómez Unda, Ana María Canal, and Carolina de Angulo Sanz has been invaluable for Carolina, who also thanks her family for supporting her every step of the way. She forever stands in solidarity with Lucy, Mirian, and Daniel, *sus compañeros de viaje etnográfico*, who shared with her the experience of doing fieldwork while trying to be a better ally to undocumented folks.

Lucy thanks God and the Juquila Virgin for giving her life and allowing her to write this book. She also thanks Caro and Daniel for inviting her and Mirian to be the bridge, allowing them to learn many stories that touched their hearts. Finally, Lucy thanks her husband and her children for their support and understanding.

Daniel would like to thank his students, colleagues, and friends in and around Rutgers University, who have constantly supported him in his work and personal life. Huge thanks and appreciation to Lucy, Mirian, and Carolina for making this project possible.

Mirian thanks God for giving her the gift of writing and singing songs, and also for giving her the privilege to migrate to this beautiful country and meet wonderful people. She is grateful for her parents on Earth, Pedro Mijangos and María Santos García, and for her two children, Nick Segura Mijangos, who first brought her to this country for his mountain biking competition, and Kimberly Segura Mijangos, who at age twelve supported Mirian in her decision to come to the United States. Her brothers and sisters have also always been there for her. She thanks the organization Casa Hometown for the support and sisterhood she has found there. Don Eugenio and his wife, Aracely, have offered Mirian unconditional support in times of anguish. Don Narciso and his wife, Teresa, were the ones who took her to Casa Hometown when she thought that no lawyer would help her, and Juan Reyes was the first person to welcome her into the organization. Rita Dentino and her husband, Tony Dentino, took Mirian into their beautiful home when she had nowhere to go, and they fought for her life. Sima Milgraum, Mirian's lawyer, also fought for her. The help of John Leschak and his family has been invaluable for Mirian, as was the help from the doctors at Central State Hospital in New Jersey. Mirian also thanks her friends from the Domestic Workers Alliance. Her friend Lucy López was her companion in the field and in the fight for immigrants' rights. Daniel Goldstein, her maestro, took the time to instruct Mirian and help her in this very special project. Doctora Carolina, her friend and maestra, was a great collaborator in doing the fieldwork and writing this book. Finally, Mirian thanks you, the reader, for reading our book.

Introduction

In 1991, Faye Harrison and her colleagues published a slim volume of essays calling for the decolonization of anthropology.[1] With postmodernist, feminist, and political-economic approaches dominating the discussion of what might constitute a critical anthropology for the twenty-first century, the scholars of "the decolonizing generation" (Allen and Jobson 2016) put forward a different agenda. Perceiving a crisis in both the discipline and the world at large, Harrison and her colleagues looked beyond the Western intellectual canon for their inspiration while envisioning ways in which anthropology might become an instrument for advocacy and progressive social change. They posed questions that addressed anthropology's colonial past and its continued relevance to contemporary anthropological practice.[2] "Can an authentic anthropology emerge from the critical intellectual traditions and counter-hegemonic struggles of Third World peoples?" Harrison asked. And, "How can anthropological knowledge advance the interests of the world's majority during this period of ongoing crisis and uncertainty?" (Harrison 1991b, 1–2).

In the twenty-first century, these questions remain unanswered, their urgency undiminished. The world today continues to present profound challenges that frame anthropological practice: savage inequalities of income and opportunity, sustained by an unbridled capitalism; intractable racism, sexism, xeno- and homophobia, woven into the very fabric of our social institutions; senseless and seemingly endless war; an ever-expanding prison-industrial complex; political corruption and police brutality. Add to this a pervasive feeling of insecurity—a precariousness born of the rapid concentration of wealth in the 1 percent, planetary climate change, and a permanent War on Something (terror? opioids? immigrants? Take your pick)—and you have our society circa the 2020s.

How has anthropology responded to this reality?

The discipline's trajectory has been long and convoluted. Born in the colonial era as part of the broader Enlightenment project of discovering the unknown, early anthropologists studied the peoples of the lands then colonized by Europe and the United States. For much of its history, anthropology—like the other social sciences and related fields—understood itself to *be* a science, basing its conclusions on supposedly objective research and dispassionate analysis while ignoring the obvious political realities in which its work was embedded. In the 1960s and 1970s, some anthropologists—including women, people of color, and anthropologists from the Global South—began to criticize the objectivist stance, questioning the possibility of objectivity itself and shifting the field away from a concern with grand questions of human development toward more focused, problem-driven studies (Pels 1997, 2014). They also called into question anthropology's colonial legacy, drawing attention to the field's origins in and, at times, collaboration with the project of colonial rule (Asad 1973; Stocking 1993). Anthropology—"a child of Western imperialism" (Gough 1968, 12; see also Forte 2014, 2016)—became historicized and often critical, aiming not merely to understand society but to denounce its inequities and cruelties.

These critiques led to significant and enduring changes in the discipline. Anthropologists today are more attuned to the roles of power, history, and political economy in shaping cultural realities and to the relationships between large-scale, often global problems and the local worlds of the people and institutions they study. Feminist anthropology has been influential in making gender-based formations and inequalities central to the study of cultures and societies worldwide and in challenging the power imbalances that exist within all forms of social life, academia included. Feminist and postmodern anthropologies have also inculcated an awareness in anthropologists of their own roles in producing the knowledge they write about, including attention to the author's racialized and gendered "positionality" and the power relations that underlie the ethnographic process itself.[3] Applied or "practicing" anthropologists, meanwhile, look to use ethnographic knowledge to make change in the world, taking the discipline's methods and findings and putting them to work in an effort to improve the lives of others.[4]

Nevertheless, mainstream anthropology—what some critics (Restrepo and Escobar 2005, 100) have called "dominant" anthropology—has yet to engage fully with the decolonial challenge. Despite years of critique and the many changes in its theory and method, anthropology, like other social sciences, remains plagued by what we identify here as the *coloniality* at the heart of the anthropological project (see chapter 1). In its theory, dominant anthropology remains Eurocentric, even as many individual anthropologists in their work struggle against Eurocentrism and its consequences. In its methodology, dominant anthropology continues to endorse a model of scholarship in which the lives of cultural others constitute the legitimate objects of scholarly inquiry and to practice forms of research that distribute power upward, from those being studied to those doing the studying. We call this entire configuration *colonial anthropology*. This strain of anthropology has dominated the discipline, in both its academic and applied forms, from its founding to the present day.[5] Anthropology's unwillingness or inability to come to terms with its coloniality limits its possibilities as a field of both academic and applied research. And, we contend, unless anthropologists fully reckon with its implications, the discipline will become steadily more irrelevant, unable to engage meaningfully with the problems that confront us in a world shaped by coloniality. In this book, we argue that a new kind of mainstream anthropology can emerge from an engagement with decolonial theory and methodology, an engagement that characterized the project described in the chapters that follow.[6]

At the same time, however, this characterization is not meant to be monolithic—colonial anthropology may be dominant, but it is not all-encompassing. If anthropology remains colonial, it is a coloniality that, like other regimes of power, is fractured and fraught with contradiction, containing spaces that afford the possibility of transformation. Within the dominant paradigm, many scholars—uncomfortable with the inequities of colonial anthropology and the discipline's academic/applied rupture—have developed approaches that challenge the field's disconnection from the world while maintaining its intellectual insights and critical edge. These approaches appear under different labels, each with its own characteristic adjective, though they sometimes overlap and compete. The "action" anthropology of Sol Tax, for example, was an early attempt to bridge the academic/applied rift while challenging the power of the researcher, goals shared and developed by those who do "Participatory Action Research" (e.g., Fals Borda 2001; Reason and Bradbury 2008; Smith 2015). Others have similarly developed "collaborative" or "participatory" research methods to involve local people in the work of ethnography and to advance their particular concerns (e.g., Hale and Stephen 2014; Hemment 2007; Lassiter 2008; Reiter and Oslender 2014). "Engaged," "activist," and "militant" anthropologists have called for a more explicitly political approach to research design and method that makes common cause with the struggles of those with whom ethnographers work.[7] Feminist, Black, indigenous, and queer anthropologists have issued similar calls, locating activism and engagement as centerpieces of their intellectual and liberation work.[8] Many anthropologists have endorsed a "public" scholarship that includes everything from direct action to cultural critique;[9] "world" and "native" anthropologists have challenged hegemonic modes of understanding and pushed to open the field to non-Western theorists and perspectives (e.g., Jones 1988; Lins Ribeiro 2014; Lins Ribeiro and Escobar 2006; Restrepo and Escobar 2005). Similarly, anthropologists interested in what has been termed the "ontological turn" have asked how indigenous ideas can converse with Western philosophy and have called for an anthropology that works for the "permanent decolonization of thought" (e.g., Viveiros de Castro 2009, 13). Each of these anthropologies represents an important challenge to the colonial variety; each represents a response to Harrison's call for anthropologists to "accept the challenge of working to free the study of humankind from the prevailing forces of global inequality and dehumanization and to locate it firmly in the complex struggle for genuine transformation" (Harrison 1991b, 10; see Berreman 1968). Many of these approaches have inspired the project described in this book.

But powerful counterforces are at work in the academy. Those of us looking to go beyond the limits of the dominant paradigm soon encounter resistance from the centuries-old investment in the colonial-academic project. The academy is structured to defend the colonial approach to scholarship and to privilege those who collaborate to maintain it. These values are reinforced by the culture of audit and accountability now rampant in the neoliberal university (Overing 2006; Shore and Wright 1999; Strathern 2000). Graduate training programs and career ladders reward academic publication, grant-getting, and, to a lesser extent, classroom teaching, all of it quantified and ranked within a disciplinary hierarchy in which such work is the only value worth pursuing. Conservative voices discourage us from questioning our own authority and exploring too far outside the academy, contributing to the lingering sense of powerlessness that we believe many younger anthropologists feel. Those of us who wish to use our work to advance a cause or address a different public often find ourselves without the time or resources to do so, our advisors and colleagues encouraging us to keep our focus on academic work—which, they insist, is "what we do best." Women, scholars of color, queer and indigenous people, and native anthropologists interested in nontraditional scholarship face additional hurdles in the white public space of dominant anthropology (Brodkin, Morgen, and Hutchinson 2011), our very identities seeming to underscore the lack of detachment or "rigor" that skeptics find in anti-colonial research. The embodied experiences of field researchers, particularly of women and scholars of color, are deemed inappropriate for the polite conversation of the academy (Berry et al. 2017). Other forms of engagement are sometimes thought to cheapen one's academic profile, to reflect badly on one's professional ambition, or to interfere with one's ability to produce "objective" scholarship. In our experience, students in particular express doubts about the field's willingness to allow them to combine their academic and activist goals, and they question their decision to pursue anthropology in the first place. They express confusion when confronted with the diversity of counter-dominant movements and fail to recognize themselves among the adjectives. "Am I an 'engaged' anthropologist?" they wonder. "I don't see myself as an 'activist.'" "What the hell is a 'public' anthropologist?" And so on.

For instance, not long ago Daniel and Carolina were invited to speak about their immigration research to a graduate seminar at a prestigious university, in an anthropology department not known for a particular interest in academic engagement or activism. The conversation quickly turned to political and ethical issues and the possibility of using anthropological knowledge to advance the causes one cares about. Many students in the seminar expressed concerns about this, but one student in particular stood out. In her first year of graduate school, she was planning to conduct dissertation fieldwork in the town where she had grown up and so felt deeply obligated to use her research to assist her informants—in her case, these included her family and friends—in their local travails. This student was struggling to find a way to do this, to find the relevance of her inquiries to the lives of the people she studies. She was also deeply anxious about the possible professional and social consequences of her work: that her university might not accept her research as proper anthropology; that she might not ever be able to get an academic job because her work might be seen as insufficiently conceptual or abstract; or, alternatively, that her friends at home might ostracize her for making abstractions out of their suffering. And she was worried that, for all these reasons, anthropology might not be the right discipline for her.

Centering Alternative Anthropologies

This book has multiple audiences and agendas, one of which is to explore the rights of undocumented immigrants in the United States. But it also addresses academics, ethnographers, and social scientists, including students and professionals like those described above, who seek to do more with anthropology than just interpret the lives of others, building their careers by fueling the academic machine. It is meant for those who—despite the long history of critically engaged anthropology and the many achievements of those who have come before—continue to doubt their abilities and seek permission to pursue their goals. We believe that these anthropologists are dissatisfied with colonial anthropology's position vis-à-vis the contemporary world and its problems, in which the suffering of others is a subject of intellectual analysis but not typically of informed action.[10] They are not content within the narrow confines of academia and its normative limits on what counts as legitimate scholarly work, but the usual forms of applied anthropology leave them hungry for theory and political engagement. These scholars are troubled by the dominant anthropology, in which they recognize the power imbalances that exist between themselves and the people who are the objects of their research (and between themselves and their professional mentors; see chapter 3). Many social scientists today continue to enjoy the intellectual work of academia yet are searching for ways to engage the world without retracing the colonial footsteps of their ancestors. Their fieldwork brings them into close relationships with individuals and communities caught in dire struggles for dignity and survival in a world of brutal and enduring injustices, and they are outraged by the situations they encounter.[11] Some researchers—including Black, Latinx,[12] LGBTQ, working-class, and indigenous scholars—come from communities with intimate experience of these struggles and find the academicization of suffering intolerable. Many scholars are uncomfortable with cultural analysis or "critique" amid profound social violence.[13] The questions of the decolonizing generation remain relevant to this impulse: Many scholars are still asking Harrison's question, "How can anthropological knowledge advance the interests of the world's majority during this period of ongoing crisis and uncertainty?" (Harrison 1991b, 1–2).

In recounting our work with undocumented people in New Jersey, we describe a theory and a method for those looking not only to join scholarship with social engagement and political activism but to challenge the coloniality of anthropology itself. Inspired by earlier generations' efforts to decolonize anthropology and building on the many advances made by colleagues practicing activist, feminist, world, and collaborative anthropologies (among others), this book builds on and extends previous counter-dominant approaches to explore the possibility of remaking the problematic ideologies and relationships that underlie ethnographic practice more generally. To do so, the book draws on the literature of the "decolonial turn," a move within ethnic, area, and cultural studies that recognizes the colonial nature of Western thought and scholarly inquiry and attempts to transcend it.[14] In that vein, we argue that anthropology's enduring *coloniality* (a concept we explore more fully in chapter 1) limits its possibilities and potential, inflicts harm on the very people it seeks to understand, and alienates a generation of students hoping to use the tools of anthropology to impact the world. Countering this requires scholars once again to take seriously calls to *decolonize* ethnographic research—to reexamine its history, reinvent its present, and reimagine its future.

Central to our discussion is the methodological reassessment that decolonizing requires. The colonial within anthropology is perhaps most evident in the practice of ethnographic field research, long the discipline's most distinctive feature. Of course, some anthropologists "study up," focusing their attention on powerful people and institutions; others work in settings and among groups to which this observation may not apply (Nader 1972). But by and large, anthropology is known for studying the poor, the marginalized, the indigenous, the powerless. To collect its data, ethnography relies on the disparities of power, position, and access inherent in the fieldwork relationship, disparities that reflect the logics and structures of earlier colonial formations. Colonial anthropology is made possible by the historical relations that have subjected the many to the domination of the few, positioning some within the academy to be able to study and know and intervene in the lives of those located without. Whether understood as disinterested and value-neutral or as attentive to identity, position, and power, research—the techniques by which authoritative knowledge is produced—as traditionally conducted in the academy remains a situated practice, grounded in ways of thinking and doing characteristic of the West, unreflexively infused with Western power, and perpetually reinscribing Western forms of knowledge, representation, and authority (see Smith 2012). Colonial anthropology deploys the tools of ethnography to know the lifeworlds of others without contributing to those worlds or allowing their inhabitants to become full actors in or beneficiaries of the research process. The colonial strain of ethnographic research is extractive. It cracks open the oysters of other people's lives and harvests the rich goo within. It brings this material back to the university, the factory wherein it deploys further tools—what it calls "theory," sets of ideas that are nearly always the products of Western thought—to process raw materials from abroad and render them suitable for Western consumption. In the academic-capitalist machine, the university department remains the place of absolute privilege to which most—even most

Ph.D.-carrying anthropologists—are denied access. The power to know is restricted to those who are fortunate enough to speak and write from that place of dominance.[15]

To decolonize anthropology (or, for that matter, any of the social sciences) is to decenter the academic project as it has been historically understood, recentering it on committed social praxis—"the instrumentalization of liberating intellectual production" (Gordon 1991, 156)—in its various forms. This requires more than just "giving back" to those whom anthropologists have studied,[16] more than "engagement" in some general sense.[17] It requires ethnographers to recognize the privilege their colonial heritage bestows and to dismantle the subject/object dichotomy on which all modern science is founded. It asks them to take seriously "'lateralist' approaches to theory" (Boyer and Howe 2015; see also Maurer 2005), what is sometimes called "theory from below" or "theory from the south" (Comaroff and Comaroff 2012a), to understand and prioritize local conceptions of local realities, rather than just running those realities through the interpretive machinery of elite European social theory. It requires anthropologists to write in different ways to address multiple publics—not only the usual scholarly readership or even wider audiences of educated readers, but publics that include anthropological subjects themselves. It asks ethnographic researchers to acknowledge the privilege and power that come with assuming the Western academic's authoritative stance and to adopt a posture of humility and solidarity in recognizing injustices and taking part in combating them. In doing so, it frees scholars and researchers from convention, allowing them to open themselves to the possibility of learning *from* others, rather than merely learning *about* them (Jones and Jenkins 2008).

A decolonial methodology takes a different point of departure to arrive at a different set of endpoints. It is anti-objectivist, not in the classic sense of objectivity in which the anthropologist is exhorted to remain aloof from her object of study in order to understand the truth of an ethnographic reality. Rather, the decolonial approach is anti-objectivist—or, in another sense, anti-objectificationist—in that it asks ethnographers to regard their study populations not as objects, but as fully equal subjects capable of becoming their own ethnographers. Instead of being the ones who know, in other words, anthropologists can allow their historical objects to take control of the research process and to benefit from the power that knowledge confers. This means putting the instruments of ethnographic research in the hands of local people so that they may produce knowledge about themselves, for themselves.[18]

Anthropologists, we are suggesting, can use the very tools of the discipline not merely to study and represent those whom a previous generation called "the Other," or even to advocate on their behalf, but to join with those in struggle so that they may become scholars of their own lives and communities. Ethnographic research, its instruments and methods, can be used not only by professional scholars to study subordinated peoples. Ethnography can be a tool of self-knowledge for the marginalized, and by enabling them to better understand and articulate their condition, it can contribute to popular struggles for liberation. Coincidentally, such an approach can lead to better, richer ethnographic data, emerging from the engaged and embodied participation of local collaborators in the research process (Juris 2007). To the extent that this approach inverts the relations of power and privilege that have always characterized ethnographic work, it can begin to quiet the ghosts of anthropology's coloniality and make ethnography an instrument of subaltern self-empowerment.

Given the diversity of adjectives from which to choose, we describe our research in this book as a form of activist anthropology, though it has much in common with other approaches mentioned previously as well. Ultimately, we hope to see the emergence of new counter-dominant anthropologies that incorporate and embrace the lessons of activist, engaged, feminist, indigenous, collaborative, decolonial, world, and other critical predecessors. When these alternative anthropologies move from the fringes to the center of the canon, the fruits of the discipline will be available to the many, not only to the privileged few. Anthropology will offer a toolset that the oppressed can themselves adopt for their own political and intellectual projects. It will be a discipline that can fully respond to the challenge of using ethnographic knowledge to advance the interests of the world's majority in these times of relentless crisis, uncertainty, and peril.

Decolonizing Research on Undocumented Immigrants

The importance of decolonizing anthropology should be apparent to ethnographers working with undocumented people in the United States. The situation of the undocumented—the consequences that illegalization, exploitation, and violence enact on their bodies, families, and lives—is clear and compelling. Under these circumstances, merely researching and writing academically about undocumented people seems profoundly immoral. To do so is to participate in the same abusive systems that produce migrant vulnerability in the first place. Like the machines that disfigure migrant bodies on the farm and in the factory—like the machine of global capitalism that consumes human labor to generate wealth for privileged others—ethnographic research about immigrants can be a machine, the lives and experiences of its objects serving as raw material to fuel the academic engine. In our New Jersey fieldwork, we—like many other researchers of undocumented lives[19]—felt compelled to work with local people to fight back against the predicaments in which they were enmeshed. We didn't simply want to extract data, but to use what we learned to throw a monkey wrench into the workings of both the U.S. deportation regime and the academic-capitalist machinery of scientific research.

To that end, in August of 2011 Carolina and Daniel—the academics on the research team—began a project in activist anthropology that aimed to join the work of ethnography to the struggle for undocumented workers' rights. The project was to study how the "securitization of immigration" in the United States was impacting undocumented people living in one small New Jersey town. Two years later, Lucy and Mirian joined as research assistants. In time, we came to focus more specifically on the effects of immigrant securitization on undocumented workers, as these were manifest through such workplace abuses as wage theft and work accidents. We also worked as activists, collaborating with two local community organizations advocating for the rights of the undocumented. The details of the project are discussed in chapter 3.

None of us anticipated that our collaboration would require us to take a new perspective on ethnographic research, one that we are here calling "decolonial." Over the course of two years after joining the project, Lucy and Mirian evolved from research assistants to collaborators to full-fledged ethnographers while continuing to work as activists for immigrant rights and immigration reform. In the process, they took the work of ethnography and activism—two linked yet parallel elements in the project's original conception—and fully integrated them, such that the ethnographic research became indistinguishable from the activism. As they conducted research about work accidents and wage theft, Mirian and Lucy not only learned about and collected data on these problems. They also used the research encounter to inform injured workers of their rights, to deliver services directly to them, to exhort them to become active in demanding benefits under the law, and to recruit them to join a local immigrant rights organization. At the same time, the knowledge they gained through research made them more effective activists. Through interviewing and participant observation, Lucy and Mirian developed broader and deeper perspectives on workplace abuses than what they knew from their own experiences or from talking in isolated and unsystematic ways with victims of abuse. These efforts contributed to an expanded understanding for all of us on the research team. Armed with data to support our claims, we could argue more forcefully for the rights of undocumented workers while empowering those workers to take up their own defense.

We describe this research as decolonial for several reasons. For one, it was Mirian and Lucy who took control of the research process and made ethnography into something more than an academic exercise. Already activists for immigrant rights, Lucy and Mirian found in ethnography a powerful tool to enhance their ongoing activism and to create new spaces in which they could work to activate others. They also experienced powerful personal changes as they became more comfortable in their role as activist anthropologists, gaining increased confidence and a greater sense of efficacy in their own lives. Similarly, Carolina and Daniel also grew as scholar/activists: Through their engagement with Lucy, Mirian, and the undocumented community of Hometown, they encountered their own assumptions about field research, theorizing, and collaboration and attempted to grapple with them. The data the project generated were rich and carefully documented, a much more robust source for academic analysis and writing than ordinary fieldwork methods would have provided. Perhaps most importantly, the project demonstrated the utility of ethnography as a tool for self-empowerment, public advocacy, and personal transformation, both for professional scholars and in the lives and communities of those historically identified as anthropology's Others.

Another important decolonial finding to come from this research—one discussed in more detail in chapter 4—is that ethnographic subjects can themselves be the source of theory, rather than merely the objects on which theory acts. In this project, we observed the emergence of an *undocumented activist's theory of undocumentation*—what might be called an "emic" or native understanding of what it means to be undocumented and an activist in the twenty-first-century United States. We call it "undocumented activist theory," for short. It is a theory of the nature of undocumentation, what it means, its causes and appropriate responses to it, as developed by undocumented activists themselves. It is a theory that stands in contrast to those of academics, who emphasize structural explanations that represent undocumented immigrants as the suffering subjects of immigration policy and the objects of critical scholarly analysis (Robbins 2013). Undocumented activist theory recognizes these structural problems but identifies the lack of unity among the undocumented as a factor contributing to their inability to demand the rights that are their due as workers and human beings. Such a theory constitutes a set of ideas that demand to be taken seriously as theory, not dismissed as a misreading or a folk notion. Nor is it static: In chapter 4 we track the ways in which undocumented activist theory developed and changed as Lucy and Mirian joined their activism with ethnography and learned more about themselves and their community. Undocumented activist theory is the product of those who create it: people who lack the requisite passport into the lofty academic realms from which authorized theory flows, but who are deeply engaged in resisting injustice and fostering reform and who are struggling to make sense of their experience. By daring to theorize, the undocumented people in this book challenge the global division of knowing that we criticize as an expression of colonial power. Taking undocumented activist theory seriously is another decolonial move that this project—and this book—undertakes.

Arjun Appadurai has called research a *right*. The right to research is "the right to the tools through which any citizen can systematically increase the stock of knowledge which they consider most vital to their survival as human beings and to their claims as citizens" (Appadurai 2006, 168). This is a powerful insight, though it is limited by Appadurai's insistence on citizenship. As our New Jersey fieldwork demonstrates, research is a valuable tool for noncitizens as well, including the most marginalized and illegalized people in society.[20] In recognizing ethnographic research as an instrument of self-discovery, community advocacy, and collective struggle, we find that as ethnographers we already possess unique resources to contribute to the causes we care about. What we learned from our New Jersey project is that ethnography—the skills it provides, the methods it employs, the stance it requires, and the knowledge it produces—can be a powerful instrument in political activism and a productive force for positive social change. By offering the tools of research to our friends in the field, we become *their* collaborators as they work to demand their rights and to denounce injustice more effectively, and in doing so we can contribute to their struggles for social and political reform.

A Decolonized Publication

This book is coauthored by four people from different backgrounds and perspectives, an unlikely team of activist-researchers who embarked on an ethnographic project to learn what they could about undocumented workers and, in the process, learned something about ethnography itself. Daniel was the project's principal investigator, a designation bestowed by the National Science Foundation, which funded the majority of the research. Carolina (aka "Caro"), at the time a graduate student in Women's and Gender Studies under Daniel's supervision, had never previously studied anthropology or practiced ethnographic research. Lucy and Mirian were residents of the place we call "Hometown," in central New Jersey. Undocumented immigrants from Mexico and Guatemala, respectively, Lucy and Mirian had never heard of anthropology or ethnography before the start of field research.

At the beginning, Daniel was the teacher, Carolina the student, and Mirian and Lucy the employees or research assistants. But over the two years in which we worked together, Mirian and Lucy also became the teachers, demonstrating the true potential of a decolonized methodology for both scholarly learning and political praxis. They seized the opportunity to do ethnographic research, making it into a critical tool in their struggle for immigrant rights and recognition. Mirian and Lucy turned our ethnographic work into a vehicle for their activism and the knowledge we produced an instrument for more effective advocacy. The results were transformative. By the end of our project, ethnography had changed them and they had changed ethnography.

The question of authorship is a complicated one for a decolonized anthropology. Typically ethnographers, like many if not all researchers, work collaboratively in the field, albeit within established hierarchies of authority. But anthropology is unlike many other sciences in its insistence on the single-authored ethnography—lab-based sciences, for example, typically assign authorship to all the various contributors to a project.[21] This is probably a relic of the discipline's colonial past, in which the intrepid "Lone Ethnographer" set out by "himself" to document the unknown (Rosaldo 1989). So, even today, when the time comes for writing up the research the scholar assumes sole authorship of the final product. This is part of the extractive nature of the traditional research enterprise, in which "writing" equates only with the act of inscription, rather than with the whole range of activities that preceded that act and made it possible. A decolonized anthropology must recognize the contributions of those collaborators in the field who were integrally involved in data collection and with formulating the ideas that are put down in writing. At the same time, however, the act of inscription should not be underestimated. Sitting down and writing a book is an immensely difficult task, requiring strict dedication of time and energy to bring the project to fruition. Scholars must share authorship with their fieldwork collaborators, but they also deserve recognition for the effort they invest in producing the text out of the fieldwork experience. Determining authorship is thus a task not without contradictions. It requires us to make tough, politicized choices.

This book is coauthored by four people with different backgrounds, all of whom participated in the field research and activism on which this book is based. Daniel coordinated and managed the project and its many components and participated in the research and activism that comprised the project's daily work. In writing, he sat down daily at the keyboard to craft the majority of this text. Carolina, whose work analyzes the relationship between decolonial feminist theory and the production of immigrant "illegality" in the United States, also wrote several sections of the book and provided edits and comments for the other sections, which we later discussed and incorporated. She also did the archival research that informs our description of Hometown and selected and translated many of the fieldnotes included in this book. Mirian and Lucy, in addition to coproducing much of the data on which the book is based, were active in discussing the themes of the book and the stories it tells; they reviewed the chapters, making comments and suggestions that were incorporated into the final draft. Carolina, Mirian, Lucy, and Daniel together wrote chapter 5, which includes a play that dramatizes Mirian's work accident and the lessons learned from it.

Determining authorship also raises the question of pseudonyms. Anyone writing about the undocumented has to take care in disguising people's identities, for obvious reasons. But does it make sense to give authorial credit to someone identified by a false name? Yes and no. On the one hand, undocumented people are very familiar with pseudonyms and often use them in their own lives. Many workers acquire fake identities in order to work, borrowing or buying the Social Security numbers of others so that they can be hired "legally" (see, e.g., Horton 2015). Other people use false names to hide from the police, an abusive ex-partner, a creditor, or a criminal gang. Some of these names can be quite creative. One of the *jornaleros* (day laborers) in Hometown calls himself "James Bond"; another has adopted the sobriquet "Vicente Fernandez," in honor of the famous Mexican *corrido* singer, and laughs because *gringos* don't get the joke. A good friend named "José" once pulled Daniel aside before a meeting to say that most people in town know him as "Tony," and so Daniel shouldn't be surprised if he heard him addressed that way. Another friend, whom some people called "Carmelita" and others "Juana," one day admitted to Caro that her real name was Magda. And so on.

While it would not be inconsistent, then, to credit an undocumented author using a pseudonym, it also defeats the purpose of acknowledging that individual's contribution to the book. In the end, that is why Lucy and Mirian elected to identify themselves by their real names. They are proud of the work they did on the project and want to be credited for their role in producing this book. They want to be able to give copies to their children and to friends in town and back home, to show that they have done something important and unexpected in coauthoring a book in the United States. They balance this pride, of course, with a certain trepidation in revealing themselves fully before the public and the law, especially in this moment of intensified hatred and policing of immigrants in the United States (see the preface). The four of us had extensive discussions about this prior to publication. Daniel and Caro thought it better to use only Mirian and Lucy's first names in listing authorship, but Mirian and Lucy felt differently. As Mirian put it, in an email to Caro on November 10, 2017: "I want my last names to be used [in the book]: because in the first place I am not afraid to have them appear there and also because for me it is very important that my children and my grandchildren and great-grandchildren see it, so it serves as an example for them." Lucy said something similar, in an email of November 15, 2017: "I have decided to use my [real] name, because it is time to come out of the shadows. Now is the time for a change, and besides that, I do it to inspire many other people to arm ourselves with courage [*armarnos de valor*]." The strength of these women and their commitment to the values of dignity, defiance, and social activism (discussed later in this book) are clear from their words. Though Caro and Daniel remained concerned about the decision to publish real names, they deferred to Lucy and Mirian. However, as a group we agreed not to use photographs that would put real faces together with real names. Instead, we commissioned drawings from the artist Peter Quach, another longtime friend and collaborator, which appear throughout the book to illustrate its various themes. Where necessary, some personal details have been altered to provide protection from possible legal repercussions.

The chapters of the book tell the story of the research process while introducing readers to the problem of work-related injuries and abuses and how they impact the lives of undocumented workers. Chapter 1 explores the meaning of coloniality, begun in this introduction, in more detail. In particular, it considers the implications of what has been called the "decolonial turn" for anthropological research and how this and related ideas can help anthropologists to move away from their historically produced coloniality and toward a new perspective on theory and method. In chapter 2, we offer an account of the personal and professional histories of the four coauthors of this book, describing our journeys toward decolonizing ethnographic research, to provide readers with the perspectives we each brought to the project and how the ethnographic research intersected with our own activist goals. Then, in chapter 3, we turn to a discussion of the research problem and setting—the vulnerabilities facing undocumented workers in Hometown, NJ—and how our research team came together to confront these issues. The decolonial methodology and approach to undocumented theory that emerged in the course of the research process is explored in chapter 4. At the end of the research, the four of us authored and performed a one-act play about work accidents, which we understood to be part of our ongoing efforts to make our research public and productive for local residents, including the people who served as participants in the research. This play appears as part of chapter 5. Originally written in Spanish, we present the text of the play here in both Spanish and English (with a translation by Carolina). In the conclusion, we return to the question of what it means to decolonize anthropology and why we believe it is so critical for the future of ethnographic research.

One conclusion that might be drawn from the anti-colonial critiques made in this book is that anthropology is on its deathbed, or should be—indeed, others both within and outside of anthropology have made this very claim (e.g., Mafeje 2001; Magubane and Faris 1985). We disagree among ourselves as to whether or not anthropology as a discipline can ultimately enact a decolonial social science (see the conclusion), but we all agree that the decolonial turn can signal a new beginning for ethnographers everywhere. Though the book contains a strong critique of anthropology as traditionally practiced, it is, in the end, a hopeful expression of all that ethnographic research can and should be as we move forward into the future.

COLONIAL ANTHROPOLOGY
AND ITS ALTERNATIVES

Anthropologists have long been critics of sexism, colonialism, racism, inequality, and capitalist exploitation, especially in the sites and contexts in which they practice ethnographic research. And yet anthropology remains a colonial discipline, a reality that shapes its theories and methods and limits its possibilities for engaged political action. Exploring this reality and pointing the way toward alternatives are the aims of this chapter.

Anthropology emerged as a scientific discipline during the colonial era, when Europeans were consolidating their control over the non-Western territories that they had subjugated to their rule. The people of these territories became anthropology's objects of analysis, and anthropology became the discipline in the Western scientific academy dedicated to the study of non-Western peoples. Within the emerging social sciences, anthropology laid claim to the "primitive" world as its intellectual turf, occupying what has been called the "savage slot" in academia and ceding the study of the modern or "civilized" to other fields (Trouillot 1991). Critical to this project was the ethnographic method, including the techniques of participant-observation through long-term field research, which enabled anthropologists to access the insiders' perspectives on their own societies. Scholars debate anthropology's contributions to colonial rule, with some calling it the "handmaiden of colonialism," created merely to serve colonial interests, a charge that others reject (Lewis 2013). But whatever service they may have provided colonizers, anthropologists benefited more from colonialism than the colonial powers did from anthropology. Colonial domination of non-European others made the world safe for anthropological fieldwork: With the natives violently "pacified" and their territories opened for exploration, anthropologists could readily move in to local indigenous communities and set up shop (Asad 1979, 91–92). The colonial power structure enabled Europeans to safely observe and participate in the lives of non-Europeans, to establish the long-term, intimate relations that became the basis for and the hallmark of ethnographic fieldwork.

Yet, rarely if ever did anthropologists of the colonial era mention the fact of colonialism or its possible impacts on the people they studied. Although they worked with people whose lives were lived under the shadow of colonial rule, their own practice made possible by that rule, anthropologists wrote as though they were studying a world apart, their objects living in original societies untouched by outside influence. As Talal Asad observed, this blindness to—or willful ignorance of—the colonial context was widespread and persisted well into the twentieth century: "It is not a matter of dispute that social anthropology emerged as a distinctive discipline at the beginning of the colonial era, that it became a flourishing academic profession towards its close, or that throughout this period its efforts were devoted to a description and analysis—carried out by Europeans, for a European audience—of non-European societies dominated by European power. And yet there is a strange reluctance on the part of most professional anthropologists to consider seriously the power structure within which their discipline has taken shape" (Asad 1973, 14–15).

Anthropologists have since become much more aware of their discipline's colonial origins, and anthropology in general has become more critical and political. A so-called crisis of anthropology came in the 1970s, when the formal end of colonialism in most of the world shattered "the optimistic scientific disciplinary confidence" of the past (Stocking 2001, 320) and anthropologists' claims to universal, generalizable knowledge about human culture became untenable. New concerns, new theories, and new methodologies began to take hold. Ethnographers began to denounce the conditions of inequality and disempowerment that many of their friends and collaborators in the field experienced, offering powerful critiques of the racist, sexist, capitalist formations that characterized their fieldsites. Feminist anthropology, meanwhile, gained greater influence as its long-standing concerns with gender, sexism, and sexuality, and of gendered and racialized power more generally, moved closer to the center of anthropological attention. Many anthropologists were influenced by postcolonial theory, becoming critical of the effects of European colonialism—and of subsequent programs, including neoliberal capitalism—on the societies that they studied. Such concepts as "community," "development," even "culture" became explicit targets of critique as anthropological analysis became global, historical, and concerned with power at the most local of sites.[1] Anthropology had its postmodern turn, during which scholars interrogated the discipline's claims to knowledge and found them wanting, calling into question the very possibility of scientific objectivity. In the late 1980s and early 1990s, as part of what is sometimes referred to as the "writing culture" moment, anthropologists began to deconstruct ethnography's authorial techniques and to experiment with new forms of ethnographic expression, often including their subjects' voices in their texts and recognizing the anthropological self as an actor in the social world being depicted (Clifford and Marcus 1986; Marcus and Fischer 1986). Feminist anthropologists, their earlier efforts at literary experimentation neglected or derided, critiqued the writing culture project's attempt to include "other voices" as a co-optation rather than a truly dialogical innovation (Abu-Lughod 1991; Behar and Gordon 1996; Visweswaran 1994).[2] More recently, collaborative, activist, and engaged forms of research emerged as efforts to make anthropology more productive for the peoples under study and more ethically sustainable for anthropologists themselves.

Yet, despite its concern with power, injustice, and inequality, including its critique of its own colonial past, dominant anthropology—like all academic disciplines—remains part of a larger colonial project. From a decolonial perspective, this is the case not merely because of anthropology's emergence within the era of *colonialism* but because of its inherent *coloniality*. For contemporary scholars and students, it is less relevant to ask whether early anthropologists colluded with colonizers to facilitate colonial rule than it is to examine the inscription of coloniality in anthropology's DNA. To understand this claim, in this chapter we explore the idea of coloniality and the role that science—including so-called soft sciences like anthropology—have played in maintaining it.

It is impossible in one small book to provide a comprehensive summary of the extensive, interdisciplinary scholarship on colonialism and postcolonialism, or the so-called decolonial turn.[3] Nor can we delineate the variations within the colonial project stemming from the different national origins of the colonizers, the cultures of the colonized, or the specificities of the colonial encounter in different world regions. Nor is that necessary for our argument. The idea of "the colonial" here does more than reference the events of a particular historical period. Rather, we use "the colonial" and "coloniality" to mark an entire structure of racialized and gendered power and social inequality within which ethnographic research has been, and continues to be, conducted; decolonizing is the process of undoing that inequality, of exposing and dismantling ethnography's deep coloniality. Thus, in what follows we describe a theoretical framework for remaking colonial anthropology, employing some of the insights gained from a reading of feminist theory, indigenous critique, and the decolonial turn, which we consider to be underutilized resources for decolonizing anthropology. (Throughout, the more technical aspects of the discussion can be found in the endnotes.) We then assess anthropology and its history, reviewing its colonial origins and the formation of its dominant variety in the twentieth century, exploring the coloniality inherent in traditional anthropological practice. This section is followed by a look at some alternative approaches—including feminist, collaborative, world, and activist anthropologies—that represent precedents for pushing back against colonial anthropology. Those approaches inspired our own project, which we discuss in more detail in the chapters that follow.

Anthropology, Coloniality, and the Politics of Knowing

DECOLONIAL FEMINIST THEORY

In the most general sense, the colonial era can be said to have begun with the voyage of Christopher Columbus to the "New World" in 1492. It lasted into the mid-twentieth century, by which time most colonized lands had become independent nations. But centuries of political, economic, and cultural rule by Europeans and U.S. Americans over the rest of the world's peoples left their mark on the way all people continue to live, act, and think. Decolonial theory represents an effort to examine and challenge the many ways in which colonial experience is embedded, not just in people's everyday lives, but in scholarly efforts to understand those lives and to write about them.

World history, for example, has traditionally been written from the perspective of the West, for a Western audience, focusing on Western accomplishments. Until relatively recently, when non-Western people appeared in these histories it was as savage others standing in the way of civilization's "progress" and the unfolding of the West's manifest destiny. Early social scientists, concerned with contemporary realities more than historical ones, produced similar stories, with non-Western people understood as evolutionary precursors to modern Europeans, living relics of the past who might, with proper guidance, someday attain the Europeans' level of civilization. Western

"Man" was taken for granted as representing the fundamentally human, and Western experience was equated with human experience, universal and all-encompassing (Wynter 2003).

By the mid- to late twentieth century—as the colonial era was finally ending in most of the world, with the formation of independent nations out of formerly colonized territories—the hegemony of the Western perspective was being questioned, significantly by non-Western scholars who rejected the universalist posture of Western historiography and science. The interdisciplinary field of postcolonial studies drew scholarly attention to the West's construction of itself through its colonial encounters with non-Western others. For postcolonial scholars like Gayatri Spivak, Edward Said, and Homi Bhabha, the West (the "occidental") and the non-West (the "oriental") were not fundamental opposites but deeply intertwined and mutually constitutive (Said 1978).[4] The world, in other words, is not merely the story of the modern West, nor history solely the product of Western expansion and its impacts (Bhambra 2014).[5] Postcolonialists argued instead that the idea of "the West" itself was a product of colonial engagement with the colonized, as colonizers encountered difference and, in the process, invented themselves and imagined their own inherent superiority (Said 1978, 1993).[6] Postcolonial scholars inserted other histories, other narratives into the historical record, calling on the experiences of the subjugated (the "subaltern") to diversify and problematize the universalist narrative of the West.[7] But these postcolonial insights came with a caveat: In the process of writing about the subaltern, Spivak warned, scholars must be cautious about "speaking for" them, introducing a concern with the politics of representation into the postcolonial conversation (Spivak 1988; see also Spivak 1999).[8] Spivak and other feminist scholars criticized academics who pretended to give voice to the oppressed, seeming to allow the subaltern to speak for themselves while obscuring the power and privilege that permitted academics to author such accounts.

Decolonial theory shares some basic premises with postcolonial and subaltern studies, especially in its effort to see Western experience not as a universal project of Europe but as a particular one of engagement between Europe and the colonial world.[9] But decolonial theorists reject postcolonial studies' reliance on works of European philosophy, drawing instead from, and continuing the work of, non-Western, colonized writers and intellectuals.[10] Decolonial theory reaches beyond the academy to valorize the knowledges of the colonized—ways of thinking that colonizers tried to suppress or destroy[11]—and calls attention to the work of thinkers (indigenous and Black people, among others) not ordinarily recognized as such within the Western canon.[12]

Most significant for our discussion is decolonial theory's distinction between *colonialism* and *coloniality*. Colonialism is a system of political, economic, and cultural domination in which one nation or people establishes sovereignty over another. Coloniality is what endures, long after the formal systems of colonial rule have disappeared.[13] It includes structures of and ideas about race, gender, and sexuality characteristic of colonialism and is animated by its logics of rationality, heteronormative patriarchy,[14] white supremacy, and Eurocentrism. For cultural theorist Nelson Maldonado-Torres, coloniality refers to the enduring patterns and systems that emerged during the colonial era and that continue to define cultural meanings, economic organization, social relations, and knowledge production: "Thus, coloniality survives colonialism. It is maintained alive in books, in the criteria for academic performance, in cultural patterns, in common sense, in the self-image of peoples, in aspirations of self, and so many other aspects of our modern experience. In a way, as modern subjects we breathe coloniality all the time and every day" (Maldonado-Torres 2007, 243).

Sociologist Aníbal Quijano observes that coloniality "is still the most general form of domination in the world today, once colonialism as an explicit political order was destroyed. It doesn't exhaust, obviously, the conditions or the modes of exploitation and domination between peoples. But it hasn't ceased to be, for 500 years, their main framework" (Quijano 2007, 170; see also Quijano 2001). Or, as Ranajit Guha puts it, "The colonial experience has outlived decolonization and continues to be related significantly to the concerns of our time" (Guha 2001, 41–42).

Examples of coloniality in contemporary society abound. To mention but one, take the prevalence of white Western standards of female beauty—lightness of skin, straightness of hair, thinness of nose, and so on—in many places, both within and outside the West (Bryant 2013; Svitak 2014). Non-Western women purchase skin lighteners, hair straighteners, and other cosmetics in an effort to approximate the Eurocentric ideal, while global popular culture valorizes that ideal through entertainment, advertising, beauty pageants, and the like (Cohen, Wilk, and Stoeltje 1995; Goldstein 2000). The persistence of these beauty standards—established in colonial times and existing well beyond the end of colonialism in most of the world—demonstrates the coloniality of beauty today. Importantly, however, conformity with Western ideals is not universal: Women in many societies (including Western women of color) have challenged white Western standards, valorizing the beauty of non-Western and nonwhite features, often through organized movements, education and ad campaigns, and documentary films (Feminist Africa 2016; Sefa-Boakye 2015; Steele 2016). This fact points to another element of coloniality: It is not uniform and all encompassing, but often fragmented and contains spaces for resistance (see figure 1.1).

Decolonial theory takes seriously the role of race in the colonial project. The concept of race was critical to the founding and maintenance of all colonial institutions, beliefs, and behaviors. Racist assumptions about the natural superiority of the European over the non-European served to organize the entire colonial framework of rule, what Quijano calls the "colonial matrix of power."[15] Colonized peoples were defined within the racist colonial matrix as savages, "the ultimate locus of inferiority," reduced to the category of natural objects and so inherently governable by the civilized.[16] As Boaventura de Sousa Santos et al. observe, the non-Western person was "constituted as an intrinsically disqualified being, a collection of characteristics that were markers of inferiority towards the power and knowledge of the West and, thus, available for use and appropriation by the latter" (Santos, Nunes, and Meneses 2007, xxxv). Being inherently inferior to the European forms of knowledge and belief, non-Western forms could be replaced—by force, if necessary—with colonial understandings. This was a critical dimension of colonialism that complemented its exploitive, extractive side with a "civilizing mission" intended to uplift the non-European through education, religion, and reform. Christianity, European language, Western styles of dress, of sexual modesty, of personal deportment—all of these and more were presumed to be superior to the local varieties and so would replace them. "Race" located native inferiority in the body of the colonized, destining nonwhites to servitude and abuse. Intellectual ability was also supposed to coincide with race: Colonizers viewed themselves as capable of rational thought, colonized peoples as only able to respond to base urges and emotions.[17] Those unable to think for themselves, consequently, were considered disposable—rapeable, killable fodder for colonial armies and factories and farms (Mbembe 2003).

Feminist decolonial theorists further complicated these insights by applying them to considerations of gender, sex, and sexuality. If race was introduced in the colonial context as a way to identify the colonized as radically different from the colonizer, gender was an equally important system for drawing such distinctions, both between colonizer and colonized and within those groups as well. Feminist decolonial scholar María Lugones calls this the "modern/colonial gender system" (Lugones 2007). In contrast to the

FIGURE 1.1. Members of Casa Hometown march in support of immigrants' rights; May 1, 2013. Illustration by Peter Quach.

Christian civilizing mission, which had as its ostensible aim the conversion of savage others into modern Christians, the modern/colonial gender system had a different if unspoken mission: to further dehumanize the colonized. As with race, Lugones says, gender operated in the colonial context to establish contrasts between Europeans and natives. Within the European gender system, "woman" is characterized by her passivity, domesticity, and sexual purity; she is responsible for the reproduction of race and capital and the maintenance of the bourgeois family (see Stoler 1989a, 1989b.). In this role she is subordinate to "man," who in turn is strong, heterosexual, and Christian, fit for public life and political rule. Within the ruling class, the gendering of white women subordinates them to patriarchal authority, within the home and in public life, both domains also prescribing a normative heterosexuality.[18] Meanwhile, Europeans judged the colonized to be more beast than human, their bodily behaviors "promiscuous, grotesquely sexual, and sinful" (Lugones 2010, 743). As with race, colonizers viewed the colonized as violating European gender norms, thus requiring their subordination and control. Colonized men, for example, were regarded as sexual predators, a menace especially to white women by virtue of their out-of-control sexuality. As such, colonizers viewed dark-skinned men as needing strict policing, humiliation, and monitoring by white colonial men to keep them in line.[19] In these analyses, Lugones and other feminist decolonial scholars call attention to the intersectionality of race and gender, their coconstitution and mutual perpetuation (McClintock 1995; see also Alexander and Mohanty 1997; Crenshaw 1989; Etienne and Leacock 1980; Lugones 2012; Minh-ha 1989; Mohanty 1988). Many anthropologists have provided contemporary and historical examples that illustrate the theories described here, including the ways in which the colonial matrix of power contained resources that the colonized could use to challenge their subordination. For example, Sally Engle Merry's work on the colonization of Hawaii provides an excellent illustration of the ways in which race and gender were key factors in the restructuring of Hawaiian culture, politics, and economy, accomplished through changes in the legal system implemented by U.S. colonizers.[20]

For all its utility, decolonial theory has been limited by its focus mainly on the humanities. Postcolonial and decolonial theory has emerged largely from the work of cultural studies scholars, including historians, literary theorists, and philosophers, most of whom rely on texts as the basis of their analyses. This approach has led to many valuable insights, some of which have been discussed previously. But one may wonder about the adequacy of an exclusively text-based field to achieve the goals that decolonial theorists have set for themselves. Anthropologists and other social researchers may be skeptical as to how, for example, reflections on the seventeenth-century writings of the Andean chronicler Guaman Poma (Mignolo 2011b) serve to achieve the decolonial goal of "halt[ing] the practices of domination and exclusion in the world-system" (Dussel 1998, 19).[21] Anthropologists should be intrigued by the decolonial effort to think "from a subaltern perspective," from the viewpoint of those historically marginalized and subordinated (Mignolo 2002; see also Anzaldúa 1987). But at what point does the desire to think from the perspective of subalternity become another act of ventriloquism, the same kind of privileged representation to which feminist scholars have alerted us?[22] Without sustained dialogue with and full engagement in the lived reality of those labeled *subaltern*, can scholars presume to understand their perspectives, much less to think or speak from them? This is perhaps what Bolivian intellectual and activist Silvia Rivera Cusicanqui has in mind when she critiques the decolonial project as another form of colonialism, incapable of unsettling long-standing forms of political and social inequality: "Without altering anything of the relations of force in the 'palaces' of empire, the cultural studies departments of North American universities have adopted the ideas of subaltern studies and launched debates in Latin America, thus creating a jargon, a conceptual apparatus, and forms of reference and counterreference that have isolated academic treatises from any obligation to or dialogue with insurgent social forces" (Rivera Cusicanqui 2012, 98).

Decolonial theory has sometimes aggregated subaltern people in a way that neglects diversity among oppressed peoples and erases differences between geographical locations. This is the case in decolonial observations about Latin America, where "the subaltern" tend to be lumped together as a single entity, culturally and historically homogenized. Decolonial theory pushes us to attend to the interactions of race, place, class, and gender as discursive categories that shape past and present social relations in the region; yet, as Kiran Asher observes, "Latin American people and places are assumed as categories of analysis rather than parsed" (Asher 2013, 839), the great diversity in the region ignored in favor of homogenizing claims about subaltern consciousness, practice, and thought. Ultimately, this approach can universalize a particular experience, repeating the mistake of the universalizing Western perspective it explicitly rejects. It can also reproduce an ideology of indigenism, the attribution of a cultural purity and originality to an imagined indigenous or subaltern subject (Simpson 2014).

Perhaps for these deficiencies, decolonial theory has not found much of a foothold in the social sciences. But the need for decolonization of the social sciences remains, and despite its limitations, decolonial theory offers some powerful tools for taking apart and reassembling contemporary anthropology.

MODERN SCIENCE AND ETHNOGRAPHIC COLONIALITY

Within the colonial matrix of power, modern science served as the instrument by which Europeans advanced their comprehension of the world.[23] As Europe extended its tentacles of economic exploitation and political and cultural domination, science was the tool by which the world could be made knowable to the European mind and white, male supremacy rendered as natural and inevitable. Modern science was established on the same universalist framework as colonialism, in which the European was the only fully human being and hence the only possible subject capable of exercising agency and possessing knowledge; all others, being inferior by nature to the European, could only be the objects of "his" knowledge. Scientific knowledge served a variety of functions for the European, helping him to know, understand, and therefore govern and control the world that surrounded him (see Haraway 1991). A range of technoscientific fields—including philology, ecology, telecommunications, and medicine, among others—served not only to advance European domination of colonized others; science and technology were staged to elicit admiration from the colonized and so to affirm the appropriateness of colonial rule. "As part of the civilising mission," notes Suman Seth, "science played two contradictory roles in colonial discourse, at once making clear to the 'natives' the kind of knowledge that they lacked (which omission justified colonialism itself), and holding out the hope that such knowledge could be theirs."[24] Such a promise, of course, could never be realized, due to what Europeans believed to be the inherent mental deficiencies of the colonized. Quijano notes that under colonialism, the knower/known, subject/object relationship obstructed the possibility of communication and shared knowledge production between Western and non-Western peoples (Quijano 2007). Collaboration, in other words, was impossible in the colonial context. The basic paradigm of Western science recognized the Westerner as subject and the non-Westerner only as object, capable of being known but never knowing in her own right.

The aim of Western science thus became, as Santos puts it, "knowledge-as-regulation": Scientific knowledge accumulated to establish a mastery of the world, following a trajectory from ignorance, which is understood as a form of disorder, to knowledge, understood as order (Santos 1995, 25). But science, then and now, does more than know the unknown—it also works to delegitimize other, nonscientific forms of knowledge. Only modern/colonial science can be a legitimate means of knowing; non-Western systems of knowledge and belief are discredited in the scientific model, dismissed as unsystematic, irrational, and false. Modern science produces a "monoculture of knowledge," in which science serves as the sole measure of truth (Santos 2006, 17). Other forms of knowing that do not fit the scientific monoculture are rendered nonexistent in a process that Santos calls "epistemicide": "Nonexistence is produced," he says, "whenever a certain entity is disqualified and rendered invisible, unintelligible or irreversibly discardable" (Santos 2006, 15–16). This sense of nonexistence, of invisibility, is also fundamental to the colonial racial hierarchy, at one time a scientifically valid system of human classification; though no longer considered scientifically true, race nevertheless continues to operate as part of Western coloniality, erasing that which does not fit its criteria of worthiness. "What is invisible about the person of color," Maldonado-Torres says, referencing African American novelist Ralph Ellison, "is its very humanity" (Maldonado-Torres 2007, 257).

This basic relationship has changed little from the colonial era to the present and to this day characterizes social science research in the colonial mode. The formative logic of the colonial ethnographic research relationship prescribes a stance of dominance and subordination between those doing the research and those who are its objects. It is grounded in the notion, rarely reflected upon, that "scientists have the 'right' (and ability) to intellectually know, interpret, and represent others" (Cannella and Manuelito 2008, 49). In its early days, anthropological research entailed rendering all that was different and other about the non-European knowable to the West; occupying the space of rationality and superiority, the anthropological participant-observer became the knowing subject par excellence. Ethnographic research was—and still is—based on a unidirectional subject/object knowledge transfer, in which information flows from (knowable) object to (knowing) subject, with the latter able to represent that information to others of its kind.[25] The power in such a relationship lies with the one who knows, a neat reflection of the coloniality within which such relations are constituted. This imbalance is reproduced in the research process, in which the one who knows also calls the shots. In the dominant variety of ethnographic research, the researcher decides what questions are to be investigated and what is important and unimportant in the data she collects. The researcher chooses the methods to be used and decides when to use them. The researcher analyzes the data using theory, ideas drawn from the scholarly canon, which in dominant anthropology is remarkably narrow and Eurocentric. The research complete, the researcher decides what to write about the data collected, how to write it, and for whom.[26]

The objects of anthropological research, meanwhile, have little role to play in this process beyond being providers of "unprocessed data" (Comaroff and Comaroff 2012b, 114). Dominant anthropological research is extractive because it effectively mines local terrain for rich nuggets of raw data, which it then exports and refines (Goldstein 2012; Lins Ribeiro 2014). In both the colonial and postcolonial contexts, the parallels between extractive research and other industrial processes are evident and easily recognized as a form of capitalist production in the transnational mode. As Jean Comaroff and John Comaroff put it, non-European peoples "are treated less as sources of refined knowledge than as reservoirs of raw fact: of the minutiae from which Euromodernity might fashion its testable theories and transcendent truths. Just as it has long capitalized on non-Western 'raw materials' by ostensibly adding value and refinement to them" (Comaroff and Comaroff 2012b, 114). In dominant anthropological research, the objects of research play no role in defining the research questions and experience little to no benefit as a result of it. In the end, the foreign researcher can build a career from this work and enjoy a comfortable middle-class Western lifestyle, while those who provide the raw materials for research remain in the conditions in which the anthropologist first encountered them.

Similar ideologies and practices can be found in other forms of social research—for example, in applied research guided by a humanitarian logic.[27] This kind of research aims to "help" formerly colonized peoples, enabling them to "develop" or rescuing them from the chains of "cultural tradition." Even though these researchers today are often "well-meaning, hardworking, middle-class missionaries, liberals, modernists, and believers in science, equality and progress," quite distinct from the "rapacious bandit-kings" of the colonial era (Nandy 1989, xi), contemporary humanitarianism bears the coloniality of the European civilizing mission. Humanitarian researchers may be attached to NGOs or foreign governments, whose research aims are modernist, developmentalist, or religious, undertaken with the intent of saving the benighted native. They may be university-based academics, whose goals are more nebulous but whose work is somehow seen as contributing in a general way to "humankind." Even activist and engaged scholars, if they are not careful, can slip into the mode of "helping" those with whom they collaborate, a condescension that serves the ego of the bourgeois subject more than it does the ostensible objects of assistance.

Social researchers may have some understanding of the colonial history of the people and places they study, but they are often unable or unwilling to perceive the coloniality that structures their own relationship to their fields, their employers, and their research objects. This coloniality in turn frames ethnographic writing, which masks the modernizing masculine liberalism that persists in the humanist research project. This represents another potential pitfall for engaged and other anti-colonial anthropologists, who embrace critique without actually destabilizing their own privilege. The ethnographies produced under these conditions can embody what Mary Louise Pratt calls *anti-conquest*: "The strategies of representation whereby European bourgeois subjects seek to secure their innocence in the same moment as they assert European hegemony. . . . The main protagonist of the anti-conquest is a figure I sometimes call the 'seeing man,' an admittedly unfriendly label for the white male subject of European landscape discourse—he whose imperial eyes passively look out and possess" (Pratt 1992, 9; see also Coronil 1996; Restrepo and Escobar 2005).

No wonder, then, that for many non-Western people, especially indigenous people, "research" is an imperial tool, part of an unbroken chain of domination extending from colonial times to the present (Biolsi and Zimmerman 1997; Deloria 1969). Just as they have long resisted colonial domination, formerly and currently colonized peoples may resist the research process and its coloniality, which they recognize all too clearly as racist and extractive. Of central importance here is Western science's dismissal of all ideas that do not conform with its logic, a stance that is profoundly alienating to those cast as the objects of the scientific gaze.[28] Linda Tuhiwai Smith does not use the concept of coloniality, but her critique of what she calls "research through imperial eyes" contains a similar recognition; research, Smith says, is:

> an approach which assumes that Western ideas about the most fundamental things are the only ideas possible to hold, certainly the only rational ideas, and the only ideas which can make sense of the world, of reality, of social life and of human beings. It is an approach to indigenous peoples which still conveys a sense of innate superiority and an overabundance of desire to bring progress into the lives of indigenous peoples—spiritually, intellectually, socially and economically. It is research which from indigenous perspectives "steals" knowledge

from others and then uses it to benefit the people who "stole" it. Some indigenous and minority group researchers would call this approach simply racist. (Smith 2012, 58)

For Smith and other indigenous researchers, racism is manifest in the research process when they are made to serve as the objects of discovery for knowing white outsiders (Restrepo and Escobar 2005). Being the objects of research is insulting to their history and dignity as a people and denies them agency in the study of their own lives. "The objects of research," Smith says, "do not have a voice and do not contribute to research or science. . . . An object has no life force, no humanity, no spirit of its own, so therefore 'it' cannot make an active contribution" (Smith 2012, 64).

Although her critiques are made of research in general, for Smith and other indigenous writers anthropology remains "representative of all that is truly bad about research" (Smith 2012, 11). Despite the good will of many contemporary anthropologists,[29] they remain "the academics popularly perceived by the indigenous world as the epitome of all that is bad with academics" (Smith 2012, 70). This is not a new observation, unfortunately: Smith's writing echoes that of other native scholars who have long regarded anthropology as the worst kind of hypocritical, self-interested exploitation.[30]

ALTERNATIVE ANTHROPOLOGIES

Also true, however, is the fact that many ethnographic research subjects, indigenous and otherwise, are aware of the power of research to represent the "truth" of people's lives, and they desire a hand in shaping it. Earlier, we described how coloniality can be seen to contain spaces for its own dismantling, and so it is with colonial anthropology. Increasingly, the objects of anthropological research are talking back, demanding a role in and control over research about them and their societies and a say in deciding the uses to which it will be put. Indigenous approaches to research, advanced by Smith and other indigenous scholars, try to counter the coloniality of the research relationship; as Kim TallBear puts it:

> If what we want is democratic knowledge production that serves not only those who inquire and their institutions, but also those who are inquired upon (and appeals to "knowledge for the good of all" do not cut it), we must soften that boundary erected long ago between those who know versus those from whom the raw materials of knowledge production are extracted. Part of doing this is broadening the conceptual field. . . . It is also helpful to think creatively about the research

process as a relationship-building process, as a professional network-ing process with colleagues (not "subjects"), as an opportunity for conversation and sharing of knowledge, not simply data gathering. Research must then be conceived in less linear ways without necessar-ily knowable goals at the outset. (TallBear 2014, 2; see also West 2016)

Against the colonial approach to research outlined in the previous sec-tion, concerned anthropologists have themselves developed new approaches and techniques for making the research relationship a mutually productive one. In doing so, anthropologists have not only introduced new fieldwork methodologies, but have also expanded the discipline beyond its traditional concerns. For a long time and in a variety of ways, scholars have pushed back against anthropological coloniality, complicating the picture of a dis-cipline entirely collusive with the colonial project. The research we discuss in the next few chapters was influenced by these nondominant approaches, and this book is an argument for their broader application in the wider discipline.

In terms of influence, feminist anthropology represents the most long-standing and the most thorough challenge to dominant anthropology. Since the very beginnings of the discipline, some women anthropologists have employed different approaches to research and writing that challenged the normative scientific style and have often been denigrated for doing so, their work dismissed as unserious or nonobjective (Stocking 2001; see Hurston 1935, 1937; Mead 1928). Feminist scholars have argued for the inclusion of women, their concerns, and labors within the scope of ethnography, con-tending that anthropological understanding of the world is incomplete without attention to women and gendered forms of social ordering (e.g., Rosaldo and Lamphere 1974; Weiner 1976; Wolf 1972). In doing so, feminist anthropologists have made questions of power, inequality, and difference legitimate topics of scrutiny, while challenging the objectivist stance of dominant anthropology. Persuasively, they have argued for an approach that acknowledges the "positionality" of the researcher, her gendered and identity-based location vis-à-vis the people and subjects she studies.[31] Femi-nist anthropologists have called out the implicit male bias of the field, forc-ing a reconsideration not only of what anthropologists study but how they go about their practices of fieldwork, analysis, and writing. Nevertheless, white, Western feminist anthropologists have also been criticized for failing to recognize their own positionality and for maintaining hierarchical rela-tionships with their (nonwhite) research subjects (Abu-Lughod 1990; Behar

1996; Visweswaran 1988). For many, especially feminist anthropologists of color, these questions remain unresolved in the discipline, even for those practicing more explicitly activist forms of research (Berry et al. 2017).

Another counter-dominant approach can be found in collaborative ethnography. Developed in response to the "irrelevance of many academically positioned interpretations" to the people being studied and the power imbalance inherent in the traditional researcher/researched relationships, collaborative ethnography aims to include local consultants in every phase of the research process, from inception through publication (Lassiter 2005, 11). Anthropologist Luke Eric Lassiter has documented the history of collaboration in anthropology, tracing it to the very origins of the discipline. Lassiter makes an important statement about ethnographic methodology in his assertion that collaboration is fundamentally about morality: Ethnography, he argues, cannot be purely extractive, nor can anthropologists assume for themselves the authority to speak for others while erasing the role others play in the production of ethnographic knowledge (a problem whose origins can be found in the work of such early luminaries as Malinowski and Boas).[32] Instead, Lassiter argues, "Doing a more deliberate and explicit collaborative ethnography revolves first and foremost around an ethical and moral responsibility to consultants—who are engaged not as 'informants,' but as co-intellectuals and collaborators who help to shape our ethnographic understandings, our ethnographic texts, and our larger responsibility to others as researchers, citizens [sic], and activists. Constructed in this way, collaborative ethnography is first and foremost an ethical and moral enterprise, and subsequently a political one; it is not an enterprise in search of knowledge alone" (Lassiter 2005, 179).

Community-Based Participatory Research (CBPR), or Participatory Action Research (PAR), has been less influential in anthropology than in other disciplines, but these approaches contain many elements that are relevant to decolonizing anthropology. Building in part on the earlier work in "action anthropology" of Sol Tax and drawing on non-Western theorists like Paolo Freire and Pablo González Casanova, PAR rejects the idea of science as the objective production of universal truth, disconnected from any social reality. Instead, PAR advocates argue for the need to recognize researcher bias and bring a "moral conscience" to scientific research (Fals Borda 2001, 29). According to Orlando Fals Borda, this requires researchers to "decolonize ourselves"; though he doesn't use the concept of coloniality, Fals Borda argues that we need "to discover the reactionary traits and ideas implanted in our minds and behaviors mostly by the learning process" (Fals Borda

2001, 29). Fals Borda and other PAR scholars envision a role for social scientists as crusaders for economic development and social justice in their fieldsites. But more importantly for us—and like both collaborative and world anthropologists—Fals Borda argues for dissolving the boundaries between the academy and the world, authorizing research subjects themselves to be part of the knowledge-production process. And, like Appadurai's "right to research" (mentioned in the Introduction) (Appadurai 2006), Fals Borda states, "The common people deserve to know more about their own life conditions in order to defend their interests, than do other social classes who monopolize knowledge, resources, techniques and power; in fact we should pay attention to knowledge production just as much as the usual insistence on technical production, thus tilting the scales toward justice for the underprivileged" (Appadurai 2006; see also Fals Borda 1979).

From a "world anthropologies" perspective, all Western theory and research take for granted a Eurocentric epistemology—that is, a mode of thinking specific to and representative of the West (Escobar 2007). Within this mode—constituting what Arturo Escobar and his colleagues have called "dominant anthropologies"—all that is different from the West is rendered knowable to the West through the lens of Western social science, and only those situated within Western academic institutions are capable of producing this knowledge. This results in a marginalizing of all ideas and perspectives generated outside the West and has led to a vast inequality between U.S. and European academic institutions and those of the non-Western world. A world-anthropologies approach tries to change this situation by thinking about social reality from outside the Western paradigm, from the perspective of those on the fringes of modern life and capitalist prosperity. It calls attention to the work of non-Western thinkers and writers by encouraging international dialogue and publications. Most importantly to our analysis is world anthropologies' goal of decertifying expert knowledge, or "decolonizing expertise" (Restrepo and Escobar 2005, 114). Restrepo and Escobar have declared world anthropologies to be an "un-academic project," aiming to dissolve the boundaries between the academy and the rest of the world. By doing so, anthropologists can recognize the validity of other, non-Western, nonacademic forms of knowledge and realize that anthropology's "subjects can be knowledge-producers in their own right."[33]

Many of these themes have found their way into activist anthropology, which Shannon Speed defines as "the overt commitment to an engagement with our research subjects that is directed toward some form of shared political goals" (Speed 2008, 215). This definition is deliberately broad, allowing plenty of room to accommodate a variety of approaches, including those mentioned earlier. Activist anthropologists practice collaboration, including their fieldwork "subjects" in the planning, conduct, and publication of the research. Activist anthropology tries to engage multiple audiences, both within and outside the academy, believing that political and scholarly activity joined together can be mutually productive for both researcher and researched (Hale 2008). As we discussed in the book's Introduction, activist anthropology represents the thematic subdiscipline with which we most identify and provided the framework for developing and, at least initially, executing our research project on immigration in central New Jersey.

The picture that emerges from this brief review is one of complexity and complication. Anthropologists, though sometimes demonized as "the epitome of all that is bad with academics," have become increasingly conscious of the inequities embedded in the dominant mode of research practice and have been active in trying to create new ways of doing their work. In doing so, feminist, indigenous, world, collaborative, and activist anthropologists have all strived, in varied and not always effective ways, to remake the research relationship in the field, while also making their work beneficial to their research subjects. Their methodologies and philosophies offer guidance for how the decolonization of anthropology might proceed.

Conclusion: The Way Forward

Westerners will never (except in make-believe) be able to act the role of savages opposite those whom they once dominated. For when we Westerners cast them in this role they existed for us only as objects—whether for scientific study or political and economic domination. —CLAUDE LÉVI-STRAUSS, "Today's Crisis in Anthropology." UNESCO Courier 11 (1961): 12–17

To say that anthropology is a colonial discipline is more than saying that it contains "vestiges" of the colonial past or enjoys a vague colonial "legacy" owing to the history of its formation and development. Bland assertions of colonialism's "lingering" pervasiveness, of colonialism as an abstraction unlocalizable in practices and structures, are insufficient. Such language lacks the precision required to identify the specific ways in which the colonial is present in the contemporary, to recognize how it manifests in daily life and in the work of anthropology and other social sciences. Talk of a "colonial legacy," as Ann Stoler has noted, "makes no distinctions between what holds and what lies dormant, between residue and recomposition, between a weak and a tenacious trace. Such rubrics instill overconfidence in the knowledge that colonial history matters—far more than it animates an analytic vocabulary for deciphering how it does so" (Stoler 2008, 196). Railing against colonial legacies, in other words, may make liberal academics feel better about themselves for being historically grounded and politically astute without requiring them to actually admit how colonialism colors their own research and writing. As scholars and human beings, we must do more than merely "critique" the injustices that surround us and our work; as Silvia Rivera Cusicanqui (2012, 100) puts it, "There can be no discourse of decolonization, no theory of decolonization, without a decolonizing practice" (see also Sandoval 2000).

To recognize and move beyond colonial anthropology, then, we must do more than just acknowledge the discipline's colonial origins. We must, in fact, design new theories and methods—take an entirely different intellectual stance—to transcend what we have identified here as anthropology's basic coloniality. Thinking in decolonial terms upsets the colonial balance by inverting and subverting the power relations fundamental to ethnographic research and writing. It entails new orientations to anthropological theory, requires new forms of anthropological practice, and opens up new possibilities for academic careers. Efforts to decolonize anthropology can reinvigorate some older debates within the discipline and chart new courses for those wishing to break with outmoded ways of seeing and acting, to push the edges of what anthropology can be and do. Decolonizing is a way to address the problems we identify in this book's Introduction, to reconcile the apparent contradiction between academic and applied work and to challenge dominant anthropology's stance on what counts as "real" ethnographic research.

Thinking from a place of decoloniality—that is, from a place outside the academy, outside the West, from the global periphery—is something anthropologists are quite good at. It requires what Walter Mignolo (borrowing from the poet, thinker, and activist Gloria Anzaldúa) has called a kind of "border thinking"—that is, thinking from the perspective of those pushed to the fringes of capitalist prosperity and the modern world.[34] Enrique Dussel calls this "trans-modernity" (Dussel 2002), a project for looking at and thinking about the world "from its underside, from the perspective of the excluded other. Trans-modernity is a future-oriented project that seeks the liberation of all humanity."[35] To think decolonially is to "bring to the foreground the planetary dimension of human history silenced by discourses centering on modernity, postmodernity, and Western civilization" (Mignolo 2002, 61–62). It is to suggest the possibility of social transformation among the world's formerly colonized peoples as well as a shift in the priorities of academic labor. Decolonized scholarship, in Catherine Walsh's words, is "an intellectual production not aimed at individual accomplishment or limited to the confines of the academy, but rather at the *shared* need to confront the colonial-racist structures, systems, and institutions of society through a collective praxis" (Walsh 2007, 232; emphasis added). As the word *shared* suggests, decolonized work requires the involvement of all parties in the research process, a breaking down of the boundaries between academia and the world, and a full recognition of anthropology's so-called research subjects as thinkers and researchers in their own right.

Decolonizing anthropology, then, requires a shift in orientation and technique, the adoption of new perspectives on both theory and method, with the goal of enabling subalterns—those enduring objects of anthropological study—to decolonize knowledge practices as they become powerful actors in their own liberation. The following chapters explore our efforts to do just that.

JOURNEYS TOWARD DECOLONIZING

Shortly after receiving tenure at Rutgers University—feeling released from the constraints of the traditional, colonial research model—Daniel began to explore other possibilities, to push the boundaries of what research could be by incorporating other, more experimental elements into his work. These included activities that some, operating from a colonial perspective, would regard as forms of service. One morning, for example, following a departmental meeting in which he had mentioned this new work, a senior male colleague came into Daniel's office, closing the door behind him. In the strongest possible terms, he cautioned Daniel against getting involved in these alternative forms of research, which, he warned, would surely detract from Daniel's professional career. Better to leave these kinds of activities to the social workers, this colleague said, and focus our attention on scholarly research. That, he said, is what we do best.[1]

Professional anthropologists have a great deal of investment in the colonial research model. Research is the basis on which they construct their claims to knowledge and authority, the foundation on which they erect their professional and personal lives. Ethnographic research—including long-term participant observation, intensive interviewing, note taking, and fieldnote writing—is not easy work, requiring many sacrifices on the part of those who undertake it. Individuals with a commitment to traditional modes of research may have little patience for closely scrutinizing its politics and epistemologies. The suggestion that the way they do research needs to be rethought will likely make many people angry and uncomfortable.

But for a new generation of scholars discontented with the demands and restrictions that the colonial model imposes, such a call may feel liberating. Colonial research, grounded in the Enlightenment model of science, is a rather limited enterprise. It imposes standards of validity that disqualify a whole range of human endeavors from what can count as research. It demands a strict bounding of scholarship from other forms of work, producing the famous divide in anthropology between academic and applied research or, as is less often recognized, between scholarship and "service." A limited perspective on what counts as research leads to similarly limited forms of writing—academic essays and books, laden with jargon, perpetually citing the same authorities, speaking to a restricted audience of experts. We believe that many young anthropologists are drawn to the discipline for what they perceive to be its creative political potential, and the discovery that nonacademic forms of engagement may have to wait for their post-tenure release can be shocking and disappointing.[2]

This chapter examines the personal and professional histories of this book's four coauthors. It describes the different sets of experiences that comprise our backgrounds and provides context for understanding the perspectives we each brought to the research project, described in detail in the following chapters. We present these histories not as morality tales but as case studies: of the kinds of experiences scholars can have as they struggle against, and try to break free from, the constraints and limitations of colonial social science; and of the kinds of struggles that undocumented immigrants endure in living and working in the United States. That these very different struggles could coincide and become mutually reinforcing through a collaborative ethnographic project was, for us, remarkable and compelling, changing the ways all of us thought about our work, our values, and ourselves (see figure 2.1).

Undocumented, Unafraid: Mirian's Story

A snowy morning in February 2012. Caro and Daniel were at the muster zone talking to the *jornaleros* when Rita's car drove up. A woman with short black hair exited from the passenger side and greeted them in Spanish. She had a calm way about her, a soothing voice and gracious movements, though she held her neck and back rigid and straight. The three of them liked each other immediately. Mirian—for that is who she was—told Caro and Daniel that she had come to Hometown a few days prior, after having

FIGURE 2.1. The research team: Lucy, Caro, Mirian, Daniel, circa 2014. Illustration by Peter Quach.

worked elsewhere in New Jersey for three years. She was seeking help after having had an accident at work, and a friend had told her about Casa Hometown and the services it provides to the immigrant community. She was in a lot of pain—hence the rigid neck, which she couldn't move without sending agonizing flashes up and down her back and leg—but she was hopeful that she would find assistance in Hometown.

The ninth of thirteen children, Mirian was born on a ranch in a small town called Santa María Ixhuatan, in Guatemala. Her parents were farmers and ranchers who raised horses and cattle; her father was also a *comisionado*, the man responsible for keeping order in a town with no police presence. At age six Mirian started school in a nearby town, and by age twenty she had graduated college with a degree in accounting. By then her family no longer lived in Santa María Ixhuatan: During Guatemala's long civil war, her father's position as comisionado had brought him under suspicion as a collaborator with the military, and when the guerrillas came looking for him he sold their horses and cattle and moved his family to a village close to Guatemala City. After graduating, Mirian left home and moved to the capital, where she studied natural medicine, botany, and herbal healing at a local institute. She soon met and married a handsome young man with whom she had two children, both of whom loved mountain biking. But Mirian's husband liked to drink, and when he drank, he became violent. So eventually she left him and moved back home.

Mirian's four older brothers lived at her parents' ranch at the time of her return, but soon after one of them was disappeared—by the military or by the guerrillas, no one was sure. Fearing further violence, Mirian moved again, this time to Santa Catalina Pinula, a small rural enclave of mud houses close to her hometown. When she arrived she was struck by the poverty she found there. Many of the men had migrated to the United States, so the population consisted mostly of women, children, and the elderly. Women survived by doing agriculture on family fields, making long trips on foot to the nearest city to sell their produce. Mirian decided to organize them and, along with thirty-two women from the town, she created a cooperative business. The *Cooperativa Integral Agrícola Xincali* was a collective bakery where everyone rotated tasks and shared the profits. It was a big success, and Mirian worked there for eight years. During this time she met Alvaro, a mild-mannered farmer who treated her kindly. Shortly after they married, Alvaro decided to migrate to the United States to search for work.

In 2008, Mirian had the opportunity to go to California to accompany her son to a mountain biking competition, where he was participating as part of the Guatemalan national team. Being outside of Guatemala for the first time, Mirian realized how afraid she had been her whole life: Afraid of her ex-husband, who continued to harass her years after their divorce; afraid for her family and her children, for the quotidian violence with which they lived; afraid of being disappeared like her older brother. After returning home to Guatemala she kept yearning for that sense of safety she had experienced in the United States and wanted to go back. But Mirian knew of the dangers of crossing illegally: Shortly after her return from the competition, another one of her brothers died under mysterious circumstances while trying to cross the northern border. Mirian renewed her visa, and she returned to the United States. She left her children in the care of her mother, promising to send money as soon as she could.

At first she was terrified to be back in the United States. When she entered the country the immigrations officer asked her many questions and looked at her suspiciously, but eventually allowed her to enter. Her anxiety intensified after her tourist visa expired. Suddenly, she found herself without papers authorizing her to be in the U.S. She thought that every cop was going to recognize her and stop her, so she changed her appearance by cutting off her long black hair. Mirian traveled to New Jersey to join Alvaro, who had found work on a ranch caring for horses. Once there she tried going to a lawyer to get help applying for asylum for herself and her children, but rather than being helpful the lawyer questioned her dedication as a parent: If Guatemala is so dangerous, he asked, why did you leave your kids there? Discouraged, Mirian abandoned the idea of gaining legal status and joined Alvaro working on the horse ranch. Her sister, who had migrated to the United States previously, joined her there as well.

Mirian would later compare working at the ranch to being in prison. The gates to the compound were chained, and there were surveillance cameras everywhere to make sure no workers left the premises. Their supervisor, an undocumented Mexican man, and the horse trainer, a big Cuban guy, were strict with the rules. One rule in particular was constantly emphasized: "No leaving the ranch for any reason or we will think that you no longer want your job." The owner of the ranch, a wealthy white man who lived in New York City, operated a company store on the premises: He bought groceries and sold them back to his workers on the ranch, arguing that now they really had no reason to go outside the gates. At the time Mirian couldn't understand this restriction, but she came to realize that the ranch owner didn't want the authorities to learn that he was employing undocumented workers and that he was treating them more or less as slaves. Mirian didn't mind the rules at first: "I was so afraid to be outside the ranch and get caught by the police," she said, that she didn't even think of leaving.

For three years Mirian worked seven days a week, making $300 a week. She lived with Alvaro and her sister in a small trailer that belonged to the ranch, with no running water or bathroom facilities. She worked with ten other Latin American workers, responsible for the care of ninety-two horses. She had to be at work every day at 5:00 AM to walk the horses for their exercise, after which she would clean the main house, then walk the horses again. She liked to read with her sister after work. She also sang and wrote poetry, which provided her a way to express her fears and sorrows, her love of family, and her faith in God.

The day Mirian had her accident began like any other. She headed to the stables early in the morning and began walking one of the horses. She had walked that particular horse, an enormous brown gelding, many times before without a problem, but that morning something spooked him. Suddenly the horse slammed his body into Mirian, knocking her to the ground. She covered her face in terror as the panicked horse stepped on her back and right leg. The world seemed to come to a stop, Mirian only aware of the weight of the horse pressing her into the earth. At last the horse ran off. Mirian lay on the ground, weeping. No one could locate the supervisor, so eventually one of the other ranch workers defied the rules and took her to the hospital in a taxi. A doctor gave her a shot of something and instructions that she didn't understand and sent her back to the ranch.

The very next day Mirian was called back to work. As she tried to rise at 5:00 AM to walk the horses, she felt a bolt of lightning shoot from her foot to her head. It was impossible to put weight on her injured leg. She simply couldn't walk. Her sister walked her horses for her that day, but the supervisor had no patience for that arrangement: "Either you work," he said, "or you leave." Five days later, the wound in her leg had begun to fester, and Mirian realized she had to go to the ER as soon as possible. This time her husband drove her there in one of the ranch vehicles. When the hospital admissions person asked what had happened to her, Mirian told the truth. She was then asked for the phone number and address of her employer, so that the hospital could verify her insurance coverage. Soon a hospital staffer came to tell Mirian that he had called the number she provided but the owner of the ranch denied having any knowledge of Mirian or her accident. The owner even claimed he had no female employees. Mirian was puzzled, sure that there had been some sort of misunderstanding. An ER doctor gave her antibiotics for the infection in her leg and again sent her back to the ranch.

Upon her return, Mirian found the horse trainer waiting for her. He scolded her for going to the hospital on her own, and especially for giving out the ranch's contact information. A few days later a nurse sent by the hospital came to the ranch to clean Mirian's wound, but she was denied permission to enter the premises and had to leave without seeing Mirian. A couple of Mirian's friends from outside also came to visit her, but the trainer wouldn't let them in: "This is not a hotel," he told her. "This is private property and I will call the cops." The trainer called the owner, known to all the workers as the *patrón*. He came to see Mirian in her trailer. "You are really screwing up by attracting so much attention to the ranch," he said, menacingly. "Why did you tell the hospital you had a work accident? You should have told people you fell off your bicycle." Mirian responded that she didn't know how to ride a bike. The patrón, enraged, stormed out.

A week went by, and Mirian had to be rushed to the hospital again. This time she was sweating profusely and throwing up. In the hospital they cleaned her wound again and sent her back home. Again the trainer was waiting for her: "Do you understand how badly you've hurt us?" he told her. Mirian didn't understand. "*El patrón* is furious," the trainer said. "He would rather spend $100,000 to make you disappear than to let you tarnish his record with the insurance company." As in Guatemala, Mirian began to fear for her life, worrying that the patrón would murder her. Later that day the patrón came looking for her again, but the other workers helped her hide in the stables. The same night she escaped, climbing through a gap in the fence to freedom.

Mirian went to a friend's house, where she hid for two days. Her friend told her about Casa Hometown, a local workers' center and immigrants' rights advocacy organization, suggesting that perhaps they could help her. So Mirian went and met with Rita, the director of Casa Hometown, and Helen, a lawyer to whom Casa Hometown frequently referred injured workers. After hearing Mirian's story and seeing the wound she had on her leg, Helen told Mirian that she could sue her employer to force him to pay for her medical bills and compensation for lost wages. Mirian was surprised to learn that this was a possibility, given that she was undocumented, but Helen assured her that immigration status was not an issue for a worker's compensation case in the state of New Jersey. They signed a power of attorney, authorizing Helen to work on Mirian's behalf. Rita and Mirian hit it off right away, and, after hearing about the threat made against her life, Rita offered to let Mirian stay at her place until she got settled. For the first time in a long time, Mirian felt safe.

Mirian missed her children terribly. In her condition she was unable to work, so she could not continue to send money home to support the family she had left behind. Mirian bought a phone card and called her children every day. Her son was in college now, studying to become an engineer, and her daughter was in high school; but after Mirian's accident her son decided to migrate to the United States. He joined her in Hometown in November 2012 and now works there as a day laborer.

Mirian felt supported by Casa Hometown and its members. Helen eventually helped Mirian to win her court case against her employer, who was ordered to pay her back wages, his insurance company held responsible for her medical bills. Now, no longer fearing the retaliation of her former employer, Mirian began a protracted battle with the employer's insurance company and the medical establishment to receive proper care. For the next two years Mirian was in and out of the hospital. Sometimes she would have excruciating headaches; other times she would be up all night vomiting or wake to find blood in her urine. She visited the ER multiple times, but no doctor could identify definitively the cause of her problem. At first she was in physical therapy for the injured leg; later she began treatment for her right arm, which she couldn't raise above her shoulder. But her leg, back, and overall body pain persisted. With her disability payments running out, Mirian needed approval from a doctor to whom the insurance company referred her to grant an extension; this doctor refused to order an MRI, intimating that Mirian was faking her injury to dupe the insurance company. Nor would he give her a "can't work" letter, which would obligate the insurance company to extend her disability coverage. Finally, almost a year after her accident, Mirian (again with help from Casa Hometown) persuaded the doctor to order an MRI. It revealed that she had ruptured the fourth vertebra in her backbone and that it would require surgery to repair. Mirian had two operations over the next few months to try to correct the problem. Throughout the time of our research Mirian was regularly in pain. Though her symptoms have eased somewhat, she is in pain to this day.

One Anthropologist's Journey: Daniel's Story

Daniel's career trajectory in some ways reflects the path that anthropology itself has been traveling over the last several decades, as it has come to embrace an engaged, activist, and now—we argue—decolonial perspective. Like many young anthropologists, Daniel was trained in an academic anthropology that knew nothing of its own history of social engagement and political activism. A phenotypically white, heterosexual, cisgendered man, Daniel did his graduate studies in a department that had strong cadres of both academic and applied anthropologists, but the lines between and around them were clearly drawn. "Applied anthropology" meant working in "development," for the government or an NGO. Projects were contract-driven, their objectives dictated from the top down. Research was generally short-term (the "rapid rural appraisal" was state of the art) and focused on practical, material concerns like nutritional status, agricultural techniques, and household organization of farm families, while declining to ask critical questions about power and political economy. Even more progressive approaches, like the "Women in Development" or "Participatory Research" models that some were advocating, were framed by modernizing assumptions about the "developed" and "developing" worlds that few applied anthropologists at the time seemed to question. Like many of his cohort, in need of money for his studies, Daniel worked part time in an office that did applied research in arid lands studies, helping to edit a journal on farming systems research. When he first began doing ethnographic field research in the mid-1990s, Daniel knew nothing of activism or engagement as methodological possibilities. He went to Bolivia for his dissertation research with a purely academic agenda.

He was quickly disabused of that possibility. Quite understandably, the residents of Villa Sebastián Pagador—a poor, marginal, and largely indigenous *barrio* (neighborhood) on the outskirts of Cochabamba, Bolivia—had no interest in him or his research unless that research had some tangible benefit for them. All too accustomed to exploitive neocolonial relations with outsiders—including those from the state, NGOs, and international institutions concerned with their "development"—the people of Pagador instantly recognized academic anthropology as another extractive enterprise from which they had little to gain. Only when Daniel could persuade them that his work would have some return for them did they allow him to stick around and ask his impertinent questions.

Fortunately for Daniel's project, the leaders of the barrio were eager to have a book written about their situation and didn't mind if it was written in English. In Villa Pagador, Daniel had stumbled into a large-scale project of collective self-invention, an ongoing campaign of local identity production and publicity intended to counter the negative stereotypes that the powerful held about indigenous, rural-to-urban migrants. Recognizing that being seen (by politicians, NGOs, even international institutions like the World Bank) as an organized community active in its own self-help development projects could attract more outside assistance, the political leaders of Villa Pagador were very concerned to be represented publicly as unified, collaborative, and modern. The leaders envisioned the book that Daniel would eventually write as a contribution to local publicity, a way to put the name of Villa Pagador into the minds of millions of North American readers. (Barrio leaders greatly overestimated the size of the audience for anthropological texts.) Although quite distinct from an applied anthropology project, a concern with development—specifically, with how the subjects of development strategically position themselves as its worthy recipients—became a critical dimension of Daniel's research.

The requirements his Bolivian field consultants imposed as a basic condition of research taught Daniel his first lesson in decolonial ethnography: a willingness to put our research to work on behalf of our field consultants may not be an option, but a necessity for successful fieldwork. Were it not for his promise to write a book about the community, Daniel would not have been allowed to do research in Villa Pagador. This was a far cry from what the applied anthropologists he knew would imagine as development. It came from the ground up rather than the top down, expressing a desire identified from within the community itself. It recognized development not as the natural unfolding of human potential, but as a scarce resource for which local communities compete, with public identity or reputation as a key element in that competition. Daniel's work in Villa Pagador was definitely not applied anthropology. What it was still lacked, for him, an identifying label.

In the end, Daniel wrote the academic book that he had originally set out to write. That book offered an honest account of what he learned in the field, including the realities of local violence and the conflicts and competing agendas that existed at the heart of the local project of collective representation (Goldstein 2004). Daniel had fulfilled his promise to the barrio leaders: He had published a book, in English, about Villa Pagador. But in his heart, he felt that he had failed them. Although the book would present the barrio's name and its problems to a foreign audience, it would not contribute directly to their struggle for local improvements. Daniel didn't know what else he could do.

When he returned to Bolivia a few years later to begin a new research project, Daniel went with a different approach in mind. This time, from the beginning of the project he anticipated the requirement that his research bear some relevance to the concerns of the local people with whom he would be working. What's more, he intended from the outset for his work to be reciprocal, that he would find ways to make benefits flow directly from the project to the community. Having identified the barrio of Loma Pampa—another neighborhood situated on the farthest southern periphery of Cochabamba city—as the study site, Daniel immediately entered into discussions with barrio leaders about the work and its possible outcomes. That was how he met Don Miguel, the president of Loma Pampa and the man who would become his key consultant and closest friend in the barrio. Miguel helped Daniel to frame the broader questions of the research and introduced him to a range of people, both within and outside of Loma Pampa, to whom he and his team of research assistants could direct their inquiries.

Given its focus on security—perhaps the most critical problem facing residents of the chronically insecure barrios of Cochabamba—local people were very enthusiastic about the project, which they perceived as an effort to resolve the issues that plagued them. As this sort of work in the barrios is typically performed by nongovernmental organizations, Daniel and his team were perceived as an NGO whose principal purpose was to problem-solve. Their appeals to being a "strictly academic" research project went unheard, their claims to being mere researchers buried beneath the weight of people's expectations. And, truth be told, Daniel and his colleagues welcomed those perceptions, as they contributed to people's willingness to participate in the research. They were invited to meetings and into people's homes and thanked everywhere they went for their efforts to solve the problems of insecurity in the barrios. This was great for the research and for the researchers' egos, but Daniel's conscience nagged him. He wasn't really there to solve anybody's problems. Was he?

The only way to do what people seemed to want him to do—tackle the problems of insecurity, problems too big for them to resolve themselves—was to raise funds to implement a bigger project. So, together with his assistants and Don Miguel, Daniel and his team officially created an NGO. Subsequently, they applied for and received major external funding to design and implement projects to enhance access to justice and offer human rights training for people in Loma Pampa and surrounding neighborhoods. The results were mixed. As detailed elsewhere, embracing the NGO identity and accepting outside money transformed the project (Goldstein 2004). No longer doing "pure" research, the team now had the financing to undertake more ambitious efforts to help make the local community more secure by offering programs in law and human rights and providing legal alternatives to violence. But their NGO also had to contend with all the challenges that plague institutions of this type, including increasing hierarchy, internal conflicts, accusations of corruption, and extensive administrative duties and reporting requirements. Daniel became less a researcher than a project manager and began to feel a growing distance between him, the project, and the local community.

What had happened, Daniel realized in retrospect, was that in an effort to be more engaged he had allowed himself and the project to become more detached. As part of the worldwide nongovernmental industrial complex, the NGO they had created was now providing services to community members rather than working alongside them. These services responded to local needs and desires but came from the top down, incorporating a neoliberal, developmentalist logic that prescribed training and self-help in confronting intolerable, perhaps irresolvable, structural challenges. What began as a good-faith effort to fulfill his implicit promises to his interlocutors had evolved into public service, freighted with politics and contradictions. Although the work they did benefited local people in a variety of ways, its impacts were short-lived. The structures of inequality and injustice that framed local disempowerment remained unmoved. Exhausted and disappointed and stressed out by the infighting that had emerged among his collaborators, Daniel quit the NGO and left the project. Independently, he continued his research in Loma Pampa for another five years, but he no longer worked with the NGO he had helped to found or the project he had helped to fund.

Even before leaving the NGO, Daniel had begun working on a new project in Cochabamba, this time focused on insecurity in the Cancha, the city's enormous outdoor market where everyone shops and where many barrio residents work. Here, he developed two parallel projects with two groups of market vendors—the legal vendors who hold permanent stalls inside the Cancha and the illegal street vendors, or *ambulantes*, who sell in the streets and public spaces surrounding it. These groups of vendors are historically antagonists in the market, each facing their own forms of insecurity—from "delinquents," from the state, and from other vendors. Again working with some Bolivian research assistants but without the framework of an NGO, Daniel entered into discussions with the leaders of both groups to gain permission to do research and to determine how his work might be made to benefit them in their struggles to improve security in the market.

As in Villa Pagador, the market vendors made reciprocity a precondition for allowing Daniel and his colleagues research access to the market. In exchange for being allowed to conduct his academic research, Daniel promised to provide each of the two groups with which he was working with a book of their own, documenting their experiences of insecurity and presenting their case to the state for why their security needs should be met. Ironically, it was precisely because of Daniel's outsider status and scholarly credentials that the market vendors deemed him capable of writing these books. They required, they said, an "objective" account of their predicaments, one based on a "scientific" study of the facts of insecurity that they faced. So, over the course of the research period, Daniel and his team worked with members of each group of vendors to study these problems and, at the end, wrote and self-published a short book for each group, copies of which they freely distributed.

The work in the Cancha marketplace was unlike any of his previous research projects in Bolivia. By now, Daniel recognized what he was doing as a form of activist anthropology, a rubric he had only recently encountered. Unlike Villa Pagador—where he felt that he had failed to engage reciprocally with the community—or Loma Pampa—where he felt that he had mistakenly pursued a developmentalist, NGO route to reciprocity—in the Cancha Daniel responded by providing local collaborators with resources that they themselves requested and that emerged organically from the research process. Daniel and his research team worked alongside the vendors of the Cancha, putting their anthropological knowledge to work to assist them in their struggles. Their mutual collaboration was essential to the ethnographic research, enabling Daniel to subsequently author his own ethnographic narrative of his experience and the lessons learned about insecurity and informality in Bolivia (Goldstein 2016).

Over the course of three distinct research experiences, Daniel had moved from a traditional research practice to one that was more engaged and reciprocal. Each project had moved him along this trajectory, each community or group with which he worked requiring that he take certain steps in the direction of activism and advocacy in order for his research to be successful. And Daniel's perspective evolved. The old boundaries between academic and applied anthropology began to dissolve, replaced by an activist perspective that recognized the mutual reinforcement that reciprocity provided to research and that research could provide to activism.

These questions would evolve further as Daniel began to consider a new research project in the United States. Having long studied security issues in Bolivia, in 2010 Daniel became interested in the securitization of immigration in the United States, with a particular focus on undocumented communities in the state of New Jersey. Daniel's interest in this project, however, was more than intellectual. He was concerned with how immigration had come to be seen as a threat to national security in the U.S., one that apparently could be resolved only through heightened illegalization and deportation of immigrants, militarization of the border, and intensified policing of the internal spaces of the country. Daniel set out to understand how people in one New Jersey town were coping with the problems of living undocumented in a securitized context, with an eye to how anthropology might contribute to their struggles for rights, recognition, and a more secure life in the United States.

Daniel's first contacts in the community of "Hometown," New Jersey, were facilitated by Robyn Rodriguez, a colleague in sociology working on similar issues in the state. She accompanied Daniel to Hometown and introduced him to Rita, the director of Casa Hometown. Robyn also introduced Daniel to Carolina, who had recently begun the Ph.D. program in Women's and Gender Studies at Rutgers and who had worked for her as a graduate assistant. Though she had not previously studied anthropology, Caro showed an instant aptitude for ethnographic work, and she and Daniel began to contemplate a research project in Hometown.

Becoming an Organizer: Carolina's Story

Graduate students frequently participate in the research of their advisors and teachers, though they are rarely acknowledged for the critical role they play in the execution of a project. In the case of our activist research in Hometown, Carolina (Caro, as we call her) was much more than a research assistant. Her work on feminist decolonial theory and her experience as an activist and organizer were central elements of our project, making her an equal collaborator in the research (for further discussion, see chapter 3).

A native of Bogotá, Colombia, Carolina grew up in an affluent home. Observing the gross economic inequality that characterizes the city, at an early age Caro began to wonder what she could do to change the situation. At first her concerns centered mainly on class issues: Why did some people have more wealth than others? But soon she realized that it wasn't only about class. As a little girl she came to understand that there were some privileges reserved only for men, and she wondered why things were that way, too.

After graduating from high school Caro went to Sweden to live with her aunt and attend college. In Stockholm she learned about economic redistribution and feminism. She also encountered undocumented immigrants for the first time—the concept of immigrant "illegality" was not a part of Colombian political discourse at the time. Occasionally finding odd jobs to make some money, Caro worked with undocumented immigrants from South America and listened to their life stories and struggles, understanding the privilege she had as a visa holder. It was also in Sweden that Carolina became aware of her white privilege: while a dark-skinned Colombian friend was afraid of being attacked by racist skinheads, Caro felt no such fear, her skin color being no different from that of a white European.

After a year in Sweden Caro returned to Bogotá and enrolled in the university, where she studied political science and then law, having decided that she wanted to become a lawyer and "save the world." But during her time in law school her career plans changed. Caro became more interested in feminist theory and was disappointed with the slow pace of the legal system in protecting the rights of those in need. She worked as a researcher for the Gender and Law Institute at her university and cowrote her honors thesis on pregnant low-income teenagers' access to education. In 2008, when she completed her legal training, she decided that she didn't want to practice law. With the help of a friend and inspired by a biography of Simone de Beauvoir, she moved to Paris to work as an au pair.

During her time living in Paris Caro became friends with people active in the *Sans Papiers* movement, fighting for the rights of undocumented immigrants in France. She went to a march where she saw the police attack protesters who held their ground against the onslaught, and she felt empowered. In 2009, Caro's dear friend, another Colombian, found herself in visa trouble and soon became undocumented in Paris. Caro saw firsthand the fear that comes from living without papers, as her friend struggled to regularize her situation and avoid deportation. By that time Caro had decided that she wanted to become a gender studies professor and had moved to London to earn a master's degree in gender and social policy. As an immigrant herself she had become aware of the importance of a person's immigration status, especially when that status is unauthorized; so for her master's Caro dedicated herself to studies of U.S. immigration and the problems facing undocumented people, particularly undocumented women. She wrote her thesis on Arizona SB 1070's impact on undocumented Latinas' access to healthcare and became interested in the use of state and local legislation for purposes of immigration control.[3]

After arriving at Rutgers University in 2010 to pursue a doctoral degree in women's and gender studies, Caro discovered decolonial theory and began applying it to her other interests in feminism, immigration, and the law. She understood that studying the "production of immigrant illegality" (De Genova 2002) required that she become active in the immigrants' rights movement, so she joined an immigrants' rights organization in New Brunswick, NJ, and started visiting undocumented immigrants being held in the Elizabeth Detention Center. She continued to gain more understanding of her white privilege as a documented, gender-conforming Latin American and began wondering what that meant in terms of her research. Up to that point she had mostly studied white feminism and European philosophy. Her professors at Rutgers encouraged her to read beyond the Western philosophical canon, and she soon found herself diving into the works of Sylvia Wynter, Chela Sandoval, Gloria Anzaldúa, Aníbal Quijano, and Édouard Glissant. Race joined gender as a main lens through which she understood inequality and oppression in the world.

In fall 2011 Caro got involved in the protests against capitalism, corruption, and the state that came to be known as Occupy Wall Street. Having just moved to New York City, she began spending more and more of her time in Zuccotti Park in lower Manhattan, where a tent camp had been set up by protestors. Caro met many protesters who were camping there who believed that another world is possible beyond the normative capitalist framework, and she got to spend time with activists from around the world who had participated in other occupations, from the Arab Spring to the Indignados, the anti-austerity movement in Spain. During those weeks of marching and chanting and dancing and protesting, Caro again realized the power and energy of collective action.

It was at this time that she started working with Daniel. She arrived in Hometown as a second-year graduate student who took a side job as Daniel's research assistant to help pay expenses, given the meager pay that doctoral students usually receive. She was not particularly interested in ethnography (though she understood that to finish her Ph.D. she would be expected to master a method for data collection) but she was very interested in learning about immigrants' rights activism in Casa Hometown. Though she had no experience in ethnographic fieldwork, Caro was a quick study and very soon was doing observations and interviews with undocumented day laborers, the jornaleras and jornaleros of Hometown. She was a hit with the men who waited for jobs by the roadside: one of the only women in that setting, her friendliness and warmth ingratiated her quickly to the jornaleros. So, as she worked on the research project with Daniel doing activist work with the Latinx immigrant community in Hometown, she began to develop her own dissertation research on race, history, and immigration in town.

Caro, who originally planned to write her dissertation on the Colombian peace process, decided to focus on Hometown instead. She was inspired by the history of the creation of Casa Hometown, which was started by a coalition mostly comprised of local African Americans and Latinxs (many of them undocumented jornaleros), as recounted in chapter 3. Carolina had been studying U.S. immigration for a while by then, and she had never read anything about the relation between African Americans and the fight for the rights of undocumented immigrants, and this history sparked her interest. So for the next few years Caro read on the topic and did archival research on the history of African Americans in Hometown, going back to the colonial era. She eventually also became interested in the history of the Lenape (the original inhabitants of New Jersey) and wrote her dissertation on how the processes of illegalization that excluded Native Americans and African Americans from access to landownership during the colonial era relate to the present-day production of immigrant illegality in Hometown. Caro's work on the colonial history of Hometown influenced our collective project, as we made it a point to interview African Americans in town as part of our ethnography.

Meanwhile, Caro and Daniel worked as volunteers in Casa Hometown, translating for people in court, helping them to complete official documents, taking them to doctor's appointments, organizing events, going to marches, and so on. Caro organized an alternative healing day at Casa Hometown featuring massage therapy, energy work, and herbal treatments for the sick and hurting members of Casa Hometown, people injured at work who were now looking for some kind of remedy for their pain. With Daniel and two members of another grassroots immigrants' rights organization, she organized a conference at Rutgers called "Undocumented/Unafraid: Stopping Obama's Deportation Machine," in which experts and immigrants spoke publicly about their insights and experiences, educating the broader university community about the problems facing the undocumented. Then for two years she stood side by side with Mirian and Lucy in Casa Hometown and learned from their work as activists and community leaders.

Thanks to all these experiences Caro became not only an ethnographer, but also an activist and community organizer.

An Awakening: Lucy's Story

Carolina and Daniel met Lucia (Lucy, she calls herself) on one of their first visits to Hometown, in September 2011. They had spent the morning sitting in Casa Hometown, people flowing in steadily through the open door, Rita attending to them. She would frequently stop to explain to the ethnographers what was going on. The place seemed chaotic, with children playing on the floor, the TV blaring, women and men talking and crying and laughing. A typical morning at Casa Hometown.

In the midst of it all, Lucy quietly came in and took a seat at Rita's desk. A short woman with a round, dimpled face usually creased in amusement, Lucy looked despondent. Rita explained to Caro and Daniel that Lucy's husband, Lalo, had a Washington driver's license—Washington State being one of the few willing to give a driver's license to applicants without proof of residency—and when it expired he had returned to Washington to get it renewed. Driving back, he was stopped by a cop in North Dakota. Now Lalo was in jail somewhere outside Bismarck, and Lucy came to Casa Hometown seeking help in getting him out and safely returned to Hometown, rather than being deported to Mexico.

Lucy and Lalo met in Santo Tomás Mazaltepec, a farming village in Oaxaca, in southern Mexico, in February 1999. Lucy's family had moved there from Mexico's capital, the Distrito Federal (DF), when Lucy was eight years old. Lucy's mom took care of the land and raised the family while Lucy went to school. Lucy was studying to get her BA in business administration when Lalo came into her life. He had been living in Hometown, in New Jersey, for a couple of years but he was back home on vacation when he asked her to marry him. "Not until I finish my degree," she said. "OK," he replied, "I'll come back in a year and marry you then." He did. She was twenty years old and had just gotten her bachelor's degree. Lucy jokes that they spent their honeymoon crossing the desert.

Before they got married Lalo had promised Lucy he was done with his American dreams. Lucy was very clear that she wanted to live near her mother and never wanted to go north. But almost immediately after the wedding Lalo changed his mind. He explained to Lucy that there were no opportunities for farmers in Mexico and asked her to say goodbye to her family and come with him to the United States. As instructed, Lucy went to her mother's house, but begged her mother to take her back. "Lucy," her mother said, "you are married now and must follow your husband." Besides, she reassured her, Lalo had crossed the border many times now; "he knows the way." So Lucy and Lalo went north, to the border, first to Tijuana by bus before crossing on foot into California. The border wasn't as militarized then as it is now, but the first time they tried to cross they were caught by the Border Patrol and sent back to Mexico. They tried again the very next day, setting off in the dark of night with a group of about ten other migrants. This time they were lucky: The Border Patrol again appeared, detaining everyone in the group except for Lucy and Lalo, who somehow escaped detection. They walked on alone for nine hours, feeling totally lost in the desert and throwing themselves on the ground when they heard the Border Patrol helicopters in the sky above them. They finally made it to a Dunkin Donuts somewhere in southern Arizona, where someone helped them find a *coyote* (smuggler) who drove them to Los Angeles, huddled under a tarp in the flat-bed of his truck. From there they took a flight to Newark (this was pre-9/11, and they were able to board the plane without showing identification), and then a bus to Hometown, where Lalo had family and where he had previously been working. Lucy has not been back to Mexico since.

"Hometown is a tranquil but strict town," Lucy explains. "You don't mix with the American community and they don't mix with you." When Lucy first arrived in town there were not many Latin Americans living there, and most of the Latin Americans were men. On her first day there she planned to look for work as a day laborer (jornalera) with Lalo. *La Vía*, as people call it, is a spot on the side of a main road leading into Hometown, at the foot of the tracks of the freight line that runs between Hometown and the coast. It is where jornaleros wait to be hired by people who need workers for the day. Lucy had heard about it and was excited to go, but Lalo explained that it is a place only for men. "You should stay home," Lalo said. So Lucy stayed home. She had two kids soon after and spent the next ten years caring for them. Occasionally she would care for other people's kids as well, when their moms had to go to work. She would later describe this period in her life as her time of being asleep: "I was sleeping until I found Casa Hometown," she said. "I had my routine as a housewife, taking my kids to kindergarten and taking care of my home. I thought that as long as my husband had a job there would be no need for me to leave the house."

Her wake-up call came the day Lalo was arrested in 2011. She had begun volunteering at Casa Hometown a couple of years earlier—she had time, once her kids started in school—but she did not think too deeply about the problems faced by her community. She would come to Casa Hometown and help with tasks like sorting the clothing donations and cleaning the kitchen. But Lalo's arrest made her realize that she herself, like the rest of the un-documented community, was vulnerable to detention and deportation. She set her mind to getting her husband out of jail and to learning as much as possible in the process so that she could help others thereafter.

Lalo was arrested in North Dakota on suspicion of having a fake driver's license. Driver's licenses are very important for undocumented people in Hometown, as elsewhere, allowing them to get to work and live their lives (Stuesse and Coleman 2014), but the state of New Jersey requires that applicants present valid documents (like a U.S. passport) to get a license. Lalo was originally planning on flying between New Jersey and Washington State to renew his expired license, but he heard of someone who had been detained at the airport as he tried to pass through security. So Lalo instead decided to travel with a friend by car. It was nighttime when the cop pulled them over on the wide-open plains of North Dakota, offering no reason for doing so. When the cop saw the men's driver's licenses he became suspicious, asking them why they had licenses from Washington while driving a car with New Jersey plates? On that basis they were arrested and taken to the local county lockup. Lalo was denied his one phone call, despite his insistence that it was his right to get one. "You have no rights," he was told.

Lucy was in a panic. For two days she had no word from Lalo but was afraid to go to the police to inquire about his disappearance. So she was forced to wait, fearing the worst. When Lucy finally heard from her husband she learned that he had been detained and was at risk of being deported. Lucy immediately went to Casa Hometown to ask for help. They referred her to a lawyer who works with the undocumented community in New Jersey, and with her help she was able to get Lalo released. This required her to go through an elaborate process that included getting money for the bond so that Lalo could leave the jail. To do that, Lucy had to find someone with papers to sign the bond guaranteeing that Lalo would come to court when summoned. Lucy asked a Puerto Rican woman from Hometown whom she barely knew to sign the bond, and to her surprise the woman agreed. "That's one of the most difficult parts about getting out of jail when you are undocumented," Lucy said. "Coming up with a person willing to sign the bond and put themselves on the line is not easy, and many people are deported when they fail to find someone."

At first, Lalo's detention made Lucy even more afraid of the police. It also raised an issue that many undocumented immigrants have to confront: how to talk about these issues with their children. When Lalo was detained, he and Lucy's two citizen children (ages nine and seven at the time) had a hard time understanding the situation. Lucy didn't know how to tell them that their father was in jail and that both of their parents were undocumented and could be deported at any moment. "Our main preoccupation in life is our immigration status, not so much for us but for our kids. Lalo's immigration process is not just his but also ours, the entire family's." Lucy tried to explain to them that she and Lalo came to the United States on foot, so if things go south with their dad's court case they would all have to literally go South. (Lalo disagreed, telling her that if he should be deported, she should stay with the kids in the U.S.) The children had never been to Mexico and had no desire to move there. Misunderstanding, they told Lucy that if she needed a passport she should just go get one.

Lalo now has a work permit, but his detention opened Lucy's eyes: "I was sleeping for ten years. Now I know the law and what to do in case of trouble. I know how the system works and what to do in case someone is detained. All of that has made me useful for my community. I want to keep getting prepared and I want to work with my community towards immigration reform." With the conclusion of our project, Lucy has gotten a job at a fast food restaurant and takes care of her home and family, while volunteering at Casa Hometown in her spare time. She feels safe in her town. As long as she keeps fighting for her community, she believes, nothing can touch her. She knows immigrants have the right to be respected and treated with dignity. That is what she is fighting for.

Conclusion

Prior to our meeting, the four of us had disparate experiences, the products of our having been born in four different countries and being or arriving in the U.S. with different sets of beliefs, privileges, knowledges, and goals. Our paths intersected in an unlikely place, the small suburban borough we call Hometown, in the heart of the "Garden State," the great state of New Jersey. Given our different backgrounds and perspectives, it is not surprising that we each came to this research project with different understandings and expectations. Yet, through our mutual engagement in the course of doing ethnographic research, we discovered new possibilities for what we could do in the world and for what ethnographic practice could be. In the next chapter, we introduce the problem of immigrant worker vulnerability that we studied in Hometown, before turning (in chapter 4) to a more detailed account of our decolonial research process and the ways in which we joined our research to the work of activism in support of the undocumented.

3

REFLECTIONS ON FIELDWORK
IN NEW JERSEY

Research does not come out of nowhere. Every structured, long-term re-search undertaking—what researchers informally refer to as a "project"—has a history of its own, a social, personal, and political-economic framework within which it comes into being, grows, and develops. In this chapter and the next, we describe the project that the four authors of this book devel-oped and implemented in Hometown, NJ, which we present here to illus-trate some of the themes discussed in more abstract terms in the preceding chapters. We offer this account not as a prototype for how to decolonize anthropology, nor as an example of how we think all anthropology must be practiced, now and for all time. Nor do we imagine our work to be without precedent: As chapter 1 showed, we acknowledge a debt to the many creative approaches to ethnography that have preceded our own. Rather, the work on which this book is based represents one possible avenue for decolonizing ethnographic research, informed by the insights gleaned from other similar attempts. In doing so, we point the way for others—always in consultation with local collaborators—to develop their own approaches, to employ new ideas, and to generate new possibilities for doing decolonial ethnographic work. Ultimately, we hope to expand the spaces of experimentation that ear-lier practitioners of decolonial, engaged, and activist research have opened, spaces in which more inclusive, more democratic, and more emancipatory modes of social research can be practiced.

By challenging the norms of ethnographic practice, our project tried to undermine the fundamental inequities and power imbalances that characterize dominant anthropology, from the colonial period to today, which we have identified as key components of anthropology's coloniality. Our project decentered the academic goals typically associated with ethnographic research, subordinating them to the aims of social transformation that constituted the "broader impacts" (see below) of the project. This required the academic researchers on the project—Daniel and Carolina—to make room for the insights, theories, and engaged ethnographic practices of the undocumented community members—Lucy and Mirian—who made up half of the research team. As time went on—and in ways unanticipated in the original research design—Lucy and Mirian became scholars of their own community, gaining a deeper understanding of the vulnerabilities to which they and their friends and neighbors were exposed and mobilizing this knowledge—and ultimately the research process itself—in their efforts to fight back against those conditions. The results of this process illustrate some of the ways in which ethnography can be a tool not only for privileged outsiders to know the lives of cultural others. Indeed, the project demonstrates that those historically cast as "research subjects" can themselves use ethnography for individual self-discovery, community organizing, and political resistance.

In using an activist approach to study work accidents, wage theft, and, later, domestic violence among undocumented workers and their families, we arrived at new understandings of what "rights" might mean to undocumented immigrants in New Jersey. In particular, we came to understand the perspectives that immigrant-rights activists hold on workplace abuses and the ways in which they mobilize these perspectives in their political work—from the mundane scenes that play out in doctors' offices and courtrooms to the more spectacular protests and demonstrations that activists organize to display their grievances to a broader public. Ethnography, we suggest, can be decolonial when it enables research subjects and their communities to organize and struggle more effectively to demand and defend their rights—however these might be understood—in a context of racist, sexist, capitalist exploitation.

This chapter begins with a brief historical and ethnographic description of Hometown and the problems confronting its immigrant residents—a context necessary to understand our decision to develop an activist research project there. We deliberately do not provide the kind of "thick description" that many anthropologists crave, determined to keep the focus on the research process itself by presenting only the minimum of contextualizing ethnographic detail. We then turn to a discussion of Caro and Daniel's experiences in the community and their plans for doing research, followed by an account of how Mirian and Lucy became involved in the project. This is followed, in chapter 4, by a closer examination of the research itself and the ways in which Mirian and Lucy's participation transformed both the activist and the academic dimensions of the project.

The Hole in the Donut: Immigration and Activism in Hometown, NJ

New Jersey is an interesting state in which to study immigration, in part due to its history as a collection of autonomous municipalities, complicating any attempt to generalize about the state as a whole.[1] In terms of immigration law, some New Jersey towns are highly securitized, with restrictive municipal ordinances that limit undocumented immigrants' ability to work, rent property, or own businesses, while others are "sanctuary cities" that exhibit a welcoming stance toward immigrants (Rodriguez 2017). The state is thus a patchwork of contiguous and sometimes overlapping political, legal, and social milieus through which immigrants move in the course of their daily rounds of work, school, socializing, and home. New Jersey ranks among the top destinations for immigrants in the U.S.: in 2015, immigrants constituted 22 percent of the state's population (only California [27 percent] and New York [23 percent] ranked higher) (Zong and Batalova 2017), and New Jersey ranks fourth in the nation (after Nevada, California, and Arizona) in the percentage of its workforce that is undocumented (Fine et al. 2014). As a whole, the state is relatively tolerant as far as immigration law is concerned. But there is substantial variation across municipalities, a fact to which undocumented workers must attend as they travel between jobs or simply shop for groceries in an unfamiliar town.

An island in the middle of a vast suburban sea of what used to be farmland, Hometown Borough is a close-packed cluster of colorful wood-frame houses and stone storefronts surrounding an old town hall. There is a historic Main Street, a stately courthouse with white pillars fronting a trim green lawn, and many beautiful old homes with porch swings and U.S. flags on display. Not far from the Jersey Turnpike and the Garden State Parkway, Hometown is a bucolic place for commuters to reside, an escape from the workday in New York City. More recently, Hometown has also emerged as an ideal place for the settlement of undocumented immigrants who live in the borough and work in the surrounding suburbs. Indeed, a predominantly white town where racial minorities were almost exclusively African American until the mid-1990s, in the past twenty years Hometown has seen a large influx of immigrants and is now about 50 percent Latinx (mostly Mexicans, but also Peruvians, Guatemalans, and others).

Undocumented immigrants began arriving from Latin America in Hometown as early as the mid-1980s.[2] At first only a handful of new immigrants came to Hometown, but after the passage of NAFTA in 1994 more and more workers, mainly from the Mexican states of Puebla and Oaxaca, began to arrive. That early wave of Latin American immigration consisted mostly of men coming to New Jersey from the Mexican countryside to do agricultural and construction work during the warm months, returning to Mexico when the weather turned cold. After 9/11, with the rising securitization of the U.S./Mexico border, these trips back and forth became increasingly difficult, and immigrant workers began settling more permanently in Hometown and bringing their families to live with them. Many of these men found work as jornaleros (day laborers), waiting for jobs at the bus station, at the convenience store called the 6-Twelve (a local riff on the more famous 7-Eleven brand), and at what the jornaleros call the *Vía*, a stretch of road alongside a train track leading into town from the north (see figure 3.1).

In response to the influx of Latin American immigrants, in 2002 the Council of Hometown Borough created a committee they called the "Quality of Life Enforcement Team." The mission of the team (adopted in response to a perceived failure by the federal government to uphold immigration laws) was to enforce borough ordinances, New Jersey statutes, and other rules and regulations, so as to (in the words of one township councilman) "combat the day to day nuisances evident throughout our town that have literally plagued our quality of life."[3] Additional police and code enforcement officers were hired to operate this program, targeting immigrant daily lives in an effort to encourage what in other contexts would come to be called "self-deportation." As part of the Quality of Life Campaign, code enforcement officers would arrive at immigrants' homes in the middle of the night in order to conduct surprise "house inspections," supposedly to fight "overcrowding" while knowing that immigrant workers often share housing to reduce living costs. "They would pull up in front of a house," an immigrant named Rosa remembered; "the code enforcer would go in to check how many people lived in the house. Ask, how many people sleep in this bed? They would count shoes and toothbrushes, count medicines in the medicine cabinet, count glasses, count everything."[4] Meanwhile, a police car would wait outside, and if people were found to be living in an overcrowded house they would be arrested or fined.

FIGURE 3.1. Men wait for work outside a local convenience store, beneath a "No Loitering" sign. Illustration by Peter Quach.

Additionally, the Quality of Life Campaign targeted undocumented workers waiting for jobs at the Via, another public "nuisance" in the eyes of borough officials and many white residents of the town. In 2003, the town council passed an "anti-loitering" ordinance that prohibited waiting on the street for work, effectively closing the muster zone. Various pro-immigrant groups, as well as the day laborers themselves, tried to meet with the council and the mayor to discuss the closure of the muster zone, but, Rosa said, "The people of this town were so used to having the immigrants under their thumbs that they thought they could do whatever they wanted and no one would stop them."[5]

In January 2004, a group of local residents and Latin American immigrants filed a suit in federal court against the borough on behalf of its Latinx day laborers. The suit argued that the anti-loitering ordinance prohibiting workers from congregating in public spaces to wait for work was unconstitutional. From January to April 2004, in what a community leader later called "a magical coalition," members of the Second Baptist Church (its congregation was about 90 percent African American) allowed jornaleros to use their church as a hiring hall and community space where they could meet and organize. In April 2004, jornaleros were able to wait for work on the street again when a federal judge ruled in their favor, stating that the borough was indeed violating Latinx workers' right to seek employment. The muster zone reopened, the Quality of Life Campaign was discontinued, and a relative détente emerged between the borough and its immigrant population. The people—Latinx, African American, and white—who had united to fight the municipality subsequently formed Casa Hometown, an immigrant rights advocacy organization and workers' center that offers various services to immigrant workers and their families in Central New Jersey.

But the problems facing undocumented workers in New Jersey persist, even as Hometown has emerged as a relatively safe place for immigrants to live. Hometown Borough is part of the New Jersey patchwork of municipalities, and the policies and politics of one town have implications for others. Hometown Borough is an island in the sea of Hometown Township, the neighboring town that completely surrounds the borough of the same name. Or, to mix metaphors, Hometown Borough is the hole in the township's donut, and the two places couldn't be more different.[6] Whereas Hometown Borough is now relatively tolerant of immigrants and is less than 40 percent white, Hometown Township is 85 percent white, and immigrants are only welcome if they are there as contracted laborers. Immigrant residents of the borough do not like to enter the township for fear of being stopped by the police on any imaginable pretext. Driving with a broken taillight, for example, or riding with too many people in the car, or riding a bike on the sidewalk, or "loitering" can be enough to get you arrested. And once you are arrested, you are fed into the computer of U.S. Immigration and Customs Enforcement (ICE), and from there it is a short step to detention and deportation.[7]

In addition to the constant fear of this eventuality, immigrant workers face many perils associated with being an undocumented participant in the U.S. labor force.[8] Workers in Hometown, like immigrant workers elsewhere around the country, are involved in some of the country's most dangerous forms of employment. They work with machinery for which they have been provided little training and no safety equipment. They are mangled by chainsaws, burned by dry cleaning presses, crushed by falling warehouse pallets, sickened by toxic chemicals, trampled by livestock. They fall out of trees, off ladders, and off roofs. Immigrant workers clean up in the aftermath of storms, floods, and other disasters, in perilous and often poisonous conditions. They are required to inhale smoke and asbestos and fiberglass or lose their jobs for complaining. Workers who might consider protesting these conditions to an employer or an oversight agency are often cowed by employers who threaten to expose their undocumented status to the authorities.

And when they are injured on the job, more often than not undocumented workers are denied the compensation and health coverage that they are legally entitled to as workers under U.S. labor law. Many employers cut costs by declining to carry the insurance coverage they are required to have under New Jersey law; others who have insurance may discourage injured workers from using it. Instead, employers of the undocumented often refuse to recognize the injured worker as their employee, leaving her entirely unsupported and shirking their legal obligation to provide workers' compensation. Sometimes the employer will offer the injured worker a plane ticket and a small payoff if they agree to return to their home country without filing an insurance claim. In addition, many employers will refuse to pay their undocumented workers at the end of a job, assuming that the worker will be too frightened by threats to expose her to the authorities to demand payment. In Hometown workers have been driven by their employers to a distant jobsite, only to be refused payment and denied a ride back home. Known as wage theft, the practice of hiring a worker and then refusing to pay the agreed-upon salary is a common problem faced by undocumented workers in New Jersey, as it is elsewhere in the United States.

In the work of the advocacy group Casa Hometown, cases of work accidents and wage theft are routine. With nowhere else to turn, immigrant workers who have been injured on the job or have had their wages stolen come to the center for legal help, medical attention, family counseling, and more. It was through our volunteer work with Casa Hometown that the four of us came together and began to collaborate on a research project into the challenges facing immigrant workers. We aimed not only to understand these problems and their effects but to find ways to address them.

Activist Research in Hometown, NJ

In 2011, with the intention of establishing a research project in the local immigrant community, Caro and Daniel began volunteering in Casa Hometown, initiating activities that would continue into 2015. As practitioners of activist anthropology, their research required Daniel and Caro to spend significant amounts of time working with local activists and immigrant people in need. Through 2011 and 2012, they spent many hours, together and separately, working in the office of Casa Hometown and hanging out with undocumented people. Their duties were varied: they did intake of people reporting problems and seeking help from the agency; translated for monolingual speakers of English or Spanish; drove injured workers to doctors' appointments, physical therapy, or the emergency room; coordinated the work of other volunteers, including Rutgers undergraduates whom they recruited and supervised—in short, whatever needed doing. They also joined in the frequent marches, protests, and demonstrations for immigrant rights organized by Casa Hometown and other local and statewide associations (Goldstein 2014). Daniel was eventually appointed to the board of directors of Casa Hometown and became involved in the ongoing political and fundraising activities of the center. He also began working with other immigrant rights groups, in nearby towns and around the state. Caro worked with immigrant women at Casa Hometown, becoming involved in an effort to create a women's handicraft cooperative, helping to organize workshops on natural healing and medicine, and translating at meetings and events. She also spent time brainstorming ideas for her own dissertation project in the community. In addition to their service work, Caro and Daniel began doing exploratory research. They spent a lot of time sitting around with jornaleros waiting for work at the *Vía*, chatting about their lives and work and the families they had left behind. In these early days of the project, Caro and Daniel wrote fieldnotes of their experiences and observations and did some preliminary individual and group interviewing with day laborers and with visitors to and clients of Casa Hometown. On the basis of the insights they developed from this initial research and in consultation with the director, staff, and clients of Casa Hometown, Caro and Daniel began to formulate a more specific research plan.

The research they proposed would focus on deportations, work accidents, and wage theft as three key vulnerabilities to which immigrant workers were exposed, to understand the sources of these threats and the ways in which local people responded to them. As a legal anthropologist with a particular interest in human rights, Daniel was especially keen to understand the ways in which undocumented workers—typically understood as hiding from the law, remaining always in the shadows to avoid detention and deportation—at times may become active users of the law in defense of their rights as workers. Having seen many cases of this in Casa Hometown—Mirian's battle for health care and compensation following her accident at the horse farm was a case in point—Daniel felt that this would provide an interesting and little-studied angle on the immigrant experience in the United States. It would also offer a different perspective on the undocumented who, rather than merely being seen as the passive victims of the law, may emerge as active users of the law and the legal apparatus in defense of their own basic rights. Caro was interested in including people from outside the Latin American community in our research, particularly African Americans, and on learning about the history of race relations in Hometown. That, she felt, would contribute to the decolonial aims of the project, as it would give us a historical background to understand how undocumented immigrants are oppressed and how they resist in New Jersey. Furthermore, we hoped that the project would aid Casa Hometown and its staff in better understanding the challenges their immigrant clients faced on the job and offer some insights into how they could better serve the local community.

From the outset, Daniel wanted this project to be different from his previous work in Bolivia. He hoped to build on what he had learned from these experiences—about the possibility of combining academic work with advocacy and activism, about the role of research assistants in data collection, and about the potential for anthropology to contribute meaningfully to the amelioration of injustice. To do so, he and Caro wanted to design a project that was fully collaborative in its methodology, grounded in an engaged perspective, and intended to produce data that would be useful not only to academics but to the community itself. Of course, a project like that would cost money, most importantly to cover the salaries of the paid assistants they planned to hire. In addition to Carolina herself, these would be two local individuals, themselves undocumented immigrants, whom Daniel and Caro would train in the methods of social research.

To fund the project, Daniel and Caro wrote a grant application to the National Science Foundation. They intended to apply as co-PIs but were informed that the NSF does not allow for professors and students to apply together as principal investigators. So, they agreed that Daniel would be the principal investigator of their project. The research Caro and Daniel proposed to the NSF was explicitly activist in nature, concerned not just with studying the problems facing immigrants but struggling alongside them to address these problems. To their credit, NSF staff and reviewers welcomed this approach. Every proposal to the NSF is evaluated in terms of both its "Intellectual Merit"—that is, its potential contribution to scientific understanding—and its "Broader Impacts"—that is, the contributions it makes to society at large. In the case of the latter, Caro and Daniel proposed training local community members to become researchers themselves, a process that would also contribute to the aims of ethnographic research as a scientific methodology. In their proposal, the methodological justification read as follows:

> From its inception, the proposed research has been envisioned as a collaborative effort, developed and executed in close cooperation with New Jersey–based community organizations active in the localities where the research will be conducted. The ideas and hypotheses presented in this proposal have been developed in conversation and collaboration with leaders and members of Latino [sic] migrant communities and their advocates in New Jersey. These individuals, along with others whom the project will identify and train, will continue to work as collaborators in the research, helping to collect the data needed to answer the questions listed above, and to analyze the data to interpret the final results. The project thus represents a kind of "engaged anthropology." . . . Engaged anthropology is not merely extractive, mining local communities for data without contributing to the resolution of the problems that it studies; rather, it takes seriously the possibility that through research, anthropologists can help to bring new understandings and make material contributions that can positively impact the people with whom they work. . . . From this point of view, anthropological research is a dialogue between researcher and research subjects, who are also stakeholders and participants in the research project itself. This approach conforms well with the NSF's own commitment to research that has "broader impacts" beyond its academic contributions.

The benefits of an engaged approach are numerous and, in the case of the present proposal, accrue to all parties involved. For research subjects, especially the Latino residents of Hometown, NJ, the research promises to shed light on issues of the utmost concern to them and their families, as they struggle to make a life for themselves in the United States. More directly, the training they will gain through this project will prepare them to take on other kinds of employment, both in future research projects and in other jobs that require the kinds of skills that ethnographic research training provides, such as observation, interviewing, computer skills, and the like. For the researchers, working collaboratively with members of the Latino community affords access to people and information that outsiders could never adequately attain, given the inaccessibility and resistance of the undocumented population to standard research approaches. An engaged methodology will enable the collection of data in new ways, leading to new discoveries that other research plans would struggle to achieve.

Engaged anthropology of the type described here, then, is not merely ethically imperative in the contemporary moment. It is also required by science, as it will generate the data needed to answer the research questions proposed. Particularly when studying populations and topics with high degrees of political sensitivity like those described here, a traditional, extractive approach to data collection is simply inadequate. The methodology that guides this project is at once ethically appropriate and scientifically necessary, both for the "broader impacts" it will generate for the study population, and for the "intellectual merit" of the project's organization.

Caro and Daniel received funding from the NSF to support the project in the summer of 2013 and officially began doing research that fall. Their first task was to hire and train what they then thought of as "research assistants" to assist them in their work.

On Research Assistants and Graduate Students

The role of assistants in the work of ethnography is one of the least scrutinized elements in social research. Despite the widespread use of paid helpers— variously described as "research assistants," "key informants," or, more recently, "collaborators"—rarely have anthropologists discussed these individuals' roles in the research process. Native research assistants were critical to the success of such pioneering anthropologists as Franz Boas and Bronislaw Malinowski, who used the work of their assistants as the basis for their own broader generalizations about native "culture" (Briggs and Bauman 1999; Lassiter 2005). With the passage of time, anthropologists began to acknowledge more explicitly the role of local research collaborators in their work, though rarely did that extend to including them as coequals in the research, analysis, and writing of ethnography. As Middleton and Cons have observed, this elision is ironic given the often central role of these individuals in the research itself: "If research assistants are regularly written into grant proposals, budgets, and research designs, their presence tends to be conveniently erased in the all important progressions from fieldwork to published ethnography" (Middleton and Cons 2014, 282). Roger Sanjek has noted that the (often deliberate) decision by (often white male) anthropologists to leave out the contributions of research assistants (often people of color) represents "anthropology's hidden colonialism," an observation that echoes the larger argument of this book (Sanjek 1993).

Similarly obscure is the relationship between professors and graduate students and the roles that each play in the others' work. The mentor/mentee, advisor/student relationship in academia is usually a lopsided one. In some disciplines the advisor is understood to be the one who possesses knowledge and whose role it is to inscribe this knowledge on the blank slate of the student. The student, meanwhile, is meant to absorb knowledge, spongelike, and to apply it to her own empirical research. In some fields the student is understood to be something like a bud off the advisor's stem, the intellectual offspring of the great mind. Even in anthropology, where the student is expected to establish herself as an independent scholar by developing her own research project, the advisor/student relationship remains a largely paternalistic one, the student imagined to be a product of her advisor's guidance and intervention. This model of the teacher/student relationship is another expression of academic coloniality, colored by the deep inequality and power embedded in the academic hierarchy, another element that divides those who know (professors) from those who are striving to know (graduate students) from those who are the objects of knowledge (research subjects).

Like many anthropologists, in each of his Bolivia projects Daniel had employed local individuals to assist him in the research process. And he had worked with many graduate students on various projects, in a variety of capacities. But the relationship between Daniel and Carolina was rather different, mostly because Carolina would not tolerate a strict hierarchy. This became clear right from the start of their work together. In fall 2011, Daniel hired Caro to be an assistant on the preliminary research in Hometown. But it was a busy time for Caro. In addition to her graduate classes and her work as a teaching assistant, she was actively involved in the Occupy Wall Street movement, spending much of her time commuting from school in New Brunswick to her home in Brooklyn and going to Zuccotti Park in lower Manhattan. Plus, she was new to ethnographic research, having never studied or practiced it. Daniel was cautious in assessing Caro's abilities and concerned about the extent of her commitment to the research project.

Their collaboration had a rocky beginning. Caro was slower than Daniel would have liked in writing and sending him her fieldnotes, and Daniel, regarding Caro as a paid research assistant, was annoyed. On October 14, 2011, he sent Caro an email that read, in part:

> I still don't have your notes, Caro, not from this week or, more troubling, last week. I must insist that you send me your notes—without them, all your work is for naught, as there is no record of what you have learned to feed into the project. I will not take you back to Hometown on Tuesday if you have not first sent me the notes from these last four visits. And . . . henceforth I am going to require that you write them up and send them to me within one or two days of fieldwork, whether or not you are camped out on Wall St.

Caro replied later that night. She apologized for her late submissions, but assured Daniel that she was taking notes while in the field and did not lose any detail by writing up later. But she also pushed back against his tone and his expectations, suggesting that she might leave the project if her approach was unacceptable:

> I work hard for this project. I spend all my time in the field talking to people and getting them to talk to me. I not only write fieldnotes, but I reflect on what can be learnt from my work. . . . You telling me you won't take me to Hometown unless I send my fieldnotes denotes a lack of trust in me and the quality of my work that makes me feel I'm a freshman. I really love this project and I would like to keep working on it, this is why I'm telling you now what you can expect from me: I can commit to sending the notes by the end of the week . . . but I am a grad student and (I would like to think) an organizer with a million things to do and I need to manage my own time.

To which Daniel replied:

> I am sorry if my last email connoted a lack of trust. I do trust you, even
> though, as you correctly observe, I barely know you. I certainly don't
> mean to make you feel like a fresh(wo)man. On the other hand, this is
> an employer/employee relationship, and it is my right (my obligation,
> even, to the project, the funder, etc.) to establish certain rules about
> how the project will be run. However, it was wrong of me to do that
> via email and in such a dictatorial manner, and for that I apologize. . . .
> We can talk in person . . . about a reasonable set of expectations re-
> garding time frame of when and how you submit your fieldnotes. I
> value your contributions to this project, and I'm sure we can come up
> with a schedule that fits with your other obligations and still allows
> you to write timely and detailed notes.

Despite Daniel's assertion that the relationship was one of employer and
employee, that frame quickly evolved into one of collaboration and inter-
dependence. Daniel and Carolina came to trust and respect one another,
working as equal partners in the research process. In a kind of turnabout
that is probably more common than is usually acknowledged, Caro became
Daniel's teacher as well: even as Daniel taught Caro how to do ethnographic
fieldwork, Caro taught Daniel how to think from a perspective of decolonial
feminism. By reading Caro's own writings—in course papers and dissertation chapters, as well as in her rich and detailed fieldnotes—and in long
conversations in the car as they drove to Hometown, Daniel became increasingly interested in these perspectives and began to read more widely in the
area of decolonial feminist theory. Caro would recommend things to read—
some of them written by her own professors, Daniel's colleagues in other
departments at Rutgers, whose work he had not previously encountered—and
Daniel in turn would push Caro to think about how these abstract theories
might be brought to bear on what they were learning in Hometown. For
Daniel, using decolonial theory shouldn't empower elite scholars to simply
"make shit up" (his characterization of literary analysis of the sort that
Caro had been doing); it required instead a firm grounding in social reality,
gleaned through ethnographic research. Caro laughed at this depiction of
decolonial scholarship but took the message to heart, ultimately writing her
own doctoral dissertation based on decolonial ethnographic and archival
research. Daniel served as one of Caro's thesis co-advisors, but their relationship was characterized by trust and mutual support, defying the traditional power hierarchy of the professor/student relationship.

At the same time as they struggled to establish a clear, horizontal work-ing relationship, Caro and Daniel also had to find other "research assistants" (as they then thought of them) to help with data collection and analysis. For this, they relied on their contacts and connections at Casa Hometown.

A Different Approach to Ethnography

Mirian was still wearing a neck brace when Caro and Daniel first asked her to work with them, a result of her work accident on the horse farm described in the previous chapter. Mirian had already been in Hometown for a year and a half at that point, and since leaving the horse farm she had been volunteering in Casa Hometown and serving on its board of directors. She was in constant pain and could not work a regular job, but had won her case in court, and her employer's insurance was paying for her treatment and recovery. Despite her personal struggles, Mirian was serving as an organizer in her community, leading the monthly meetings held by the jornaleros in Casa Hometown and working to organize support groups and a women's cooperative. She had also begun writing her own songs about her life as an undocumented woman and performing them at public events. Daniel and Caro were impressed by Mirian's intelligence, her resilience and inner strength, and her status as a leader among the undocumented residents of Hometown, and they invited her to join the project as a paid research collaborator.

Lucy, meanwhile, had been in Hometown for fourteen years, and, like Mirian, she served on Casa Hometown's board of directors. And, like Mir-ian, Lucy was a leader and activist in her community. Caro and Daniel asked her to join the project after seeing how she mobilized her community in the aftermath of Hurricane Sandy, a devastating storm that rocked New Jersey in October of 2012. Six months after the event, a meeting was called between the Red Cross and the members of Casa Hometown to discuss the needs of the community and how the Red Cross might assist in its post-storm recov-ery. In advance of the meeting, Lucy had taken it upon herself to assess these needs, compiling a resource that the Red Cross could use to evaluate areas of possible intervention. On her own initiative and with no training or prepa-ration, Lucy conducted a survey of forty local families. She discovered that people in Hometown were deeply affected by the hurricane, despite the fact that theirs is not a coastal town. Many day laborers worked tirelessly helping with storm cleanup, and the everyday problems that undocumented workers face—including wage theft and work accidents—were intensified after Sandy. Although the meeting led nowhere—the Red Cross, it turned out, was only interested in helping homeowners whose properties were damaged by the hurricane, which excluded the majority of undocumented people—Daniel and Caro were deeply impressed by Lucy's initiative in conducting the survey and the quality of the insights at which she arrived. They asked her to work with them on their research project.

When they joined the research team, Mirian and Lucy had no idea what ethnography was, though they immediately understood the potential of ethnographic research to contribute to their work as advocates for and activists in the undocumented community. Both of them expressed enthusiasm for learning more, and more deeply, about their own community and the problems people faced. At their first official meeting in August 2013, Caro and Daniel explained that after two years of working on their own, they were ready to have local people join their team. Caro told them that her dissertation research focused on the colonial history of New Jersey and its relationship to present-day conceptions of immigrant "illegality." Daniel then explained that he was interested in work accidents and wage theft and the ways in which immigrants use the legal system to defend themselves against exploitation. They asked Mirian and Lucy, what would you be interested in studying as part of this project? Here, the question of rights (part of the original academic framing of the project) emerged as a local concern, particularly of activists involved in immigrant rights advocacy. Lucy immediately said she wanted to help her community to know and understand their rights. Too often, she explained, undocumented people are afraid to defend themselves, falsely believing themselves to be entirely without rights and so unwilling to take action when they are abused or exploited. Lucy thought she could use the research project to help people better understand their rights and to act to secure them. Mirian took a similarly activist approach to the project, saying that she wanted to help the Latin American community in Hometown to be more united. In her work as an organizer, she said, she found people to be too isolated from one another to act cohesively to advance their collective interests. By learning more about the community and communicating that knowledge to her research subjects, Mirian believed she could foster stronger ties between individuals and families in Hometown.

In addition, Lucy and Mirian (like Caro and Daniel) hoped that their work on the project could also benefit Casa Hometown. Casa Hometown performs valuable work for the undocumented community of Hometown, serving as a workers' center and a provider of legal services. Casa's staff are mostly unpaid. The organization has no stable source of external funding but is supported mostly by the dues paid by its members. Membership recruitment is thus a critical component of the work of Casa's staffers and activists. Mirian and Lucy believed in the mission of Casa Hometown, understanding it to be a central node for educating and organizing the undocumented community. The research, they felt, would bring them into more intimate contact with people who could benefit from Casa Hometown's services, and by encouraging these individuals to become members of the organization, they would be serving Casa Hometown in return.

At that first meeting, the team also discussed the idea of writing a play as a way to disseminate some of the information the project learned to the local immigrant community. Caro had been reading about theater and activism for one of her classes in Caribbean Philosophy and was interested in the emancipatory potential of community theater. Surprisingly, Mirian said she had also been thinking about writing a play because one of her jornalero friends had mentioned the idea to her and, together with her songs, playwriting seemed to be an artistic means for accomplishing some of her activist goals.

And so it was decided: The four would work together as ethnographers and would also collaborate in the writing of a play. After discussing the plan with the board of Casa Hometown, it was also determined that the four researchers would continue to work as volunteers in the center. This volunteer work was a way of assisting Casa Hometown, part of the activist dimension of the project. It also provided an opportunity for meeting more people in town and creating new opportunities for ethnographic interviewing.

During the first few months of working together, Caro and Daniel trained Mirian and Lucy in the basics of ethnographic fieldwork. From the grant budget they purchased iPads with keyboards and taught them how to write fieldnotes. They discussed the basics of observation, helping them to use all their senses to note the fabric of everyday life, instructing them to attend closely to everything people did and said in their daily encounters. They explored rapport building and unobtrusive questioning and the importance of confidentiality and anonymity in all their writings and recordings. Much of this was obvious to Mirian and Lucy, who through their activist work already understood the importance of maintaining good relations with the people with whom they worked. Daniel and Caro provided them with human subjects and IRB training, and they earned online certification through Rutgers University and the CITI program. After a time the four of them began doing interviews together, so that Lucy and Mirian could understand the use of an interview guide, the techniques of interviewing such as "letting the informant lead," and how to work the digital voice recorder. All of these methods they adopted quickly, and in time they were able to begin conducting their own interviews. But they soon developed their own approach to ethnography, informed by their roles as organizers and leaders of Casa Hometown.

Conclusion

For all of the goodwill we each brought to the project, as the preceding narrative recounts, our project nevertheless contained complex power dynamics and inequalities, unfolding in a space of sometimes profound contradiction. Daniel—a phenotypically white Rutgers professor and citizen of the United States—was the principal investigator of the NSF grant that allowed us to carry out our project; and as much as we made most decisions collectively, all the team members knew that Daniel had control of the budget and the final say on decisions affecting the work. Caro, too, held a kind of privilege and power that Mirian and Lucy lacked. While neither Lucy nor Mirian is white-passing and both are undocumented, and while Mirian is disabled due to her work accident, Caro came to Hometown with her white skin, her abled body, her proficiency in English, and her F1 visa. At the beginning of the project Carolina was under the illusion that because they had all been friends for a couple of years, Lucy and Mirian regarded her as their peer. But Caro realized that this was not the case when Mirian referred to Caro as her *maestra* or teacher, a title that Mirian and Lucy also used in referring to Daniel. That day Caro became aware that the power asymmetries between them don't only lie in the difference of their skin color, their English proficiency, and their immigration status, but also in their institutional affiliations and the access to resources and prestige that such affiliation conveys.

Thus, as much as we aimed to decolonize our ethnographic practice, our work remained embedded within a colonial and patriarchal framework. The one man of the group, a phenotypically white, heterosexual professor, ultimately held the reins of the project; the woman in the group with the lightest skin enjoyed a status that the other women did not. Daniel and Caro each explicitly recognize the privilege these gendered and racialized configurations bestow and acknowledge that such structural inequalities were part of the context in which our project took place. The contradictions inherent in attempting to do decolonizing work while in many ways operating within coloniality structured Daniel and Caro's very access to Lucy and Mirian's ideas and thoughts, ideas that are the cornerstone of our book. Recognition of these facts is, we believe, critical to our efforts to overcome their effects.

For their part, Mirian and Lucy set out on their work intending to do their absolute best as ethnographers, working to meet Daniel and Caro's expectations about what "data collection" should look like and striving to learn and practice it. But Mirian and Lucy also took seriously their sense of obligation to their community and to the organization, Casa Hometown, with which they worked to defend immigrant rights. They readily incorporated ethnography into their activist toolkits, finding it to be a useful instrument for their work in community organizing and education. Mirian and Lucy did not draw lines between or around "ethnography" and "activism" or feel the need (as activist anthropologists, Daniel included, sometimes did) to justify the validity of activist anthropology to anyone else. In their work on the project, Lucy and Mirian adopted a rich and mutually sustaining blend of ethnography and activism, focused largely on educating their ethnographic subjects about their rights and helping them to find assistance with their problems. They also joined their work as ethnographers to their volunteer work with Casa Hometown, using their research to feed their organizing and to strengthen the organization. At the same time, through their work as ethnographers, Mirian and Lucy grew personally as they gained a better sense of themselves as immigrants, as women, and as organizers and a deeper understanding of the causes and consequences of the problems facing their community. Through their work, they enacted a true synthesis of academics and activism and in the process revealed the potential of ethnography as a decolonial instrument of individual and collective political transformation.

All of this is clearly depicted in the fieldnotes that Mirian and Lucy wrote, two to three entries each per week over a two-year period (2013–15), supplemented by observations in the fieldnotes written by Caro and Daniel during the same time. They wrote their fieldnotes in Spanish (excerpts quoted here were translated by Daniel and Caro). Many of these notes record Lucy and Mirian's reflections on their own personal and professional growth as they worked as ethnographers, as well as the many encounters between Mirian and Lucy and other members of the local immigrant community as they went about their fieldwork. Excerpts from these notes, along with Mirian and Lucy's explicit reflections on their experiences (elicited primarily through informal conversations and more structured interviews that Daniel and Caro conducted with them before, during, and after the fieldwork period) reveal the ways in which they creatively blended activism and ethnography, suggesting the potential of each to sustain and inform the other as part of a decolonizing approach to social research. We explore this in more detail in the next chapter.

UNDOCUMENTED ACTIVIST THEORY
AND A DECOLONIAL METHODOLOGY

Lucy and Mirian initially struggled to adapt to their new identity as anthropologists. They felt uncertain about what the work would entail and doubted their ability to do it. And even though they were residents of Hometown and members of the local immigrant community, they soon discovered that approaching people in the role of ethnographer was different from engaging them in their ordinary roles as community members and activists. But as ethnographers of their own community, Mirian and Lucy had an immediate advantage over outsiders like Carolina and Daniel. People knew them from their work in Casa Hometown, recognized them as undocumented like themselves, and usually showed little hesitation in speaking to them. Some people, however, remained aloof and uncertain, refusing to trust them or to share their stories.

Like other ethnographers, Lucy and Mirian had to draw on their personal resources to establish rapport with their field collaborators. One morning at the start of fieldwork, Lucy was hanging out with the men at the *Vía*, chatting about their experiences crossing the border from Mexico into the U.S. But Lucy detected a certain reserve on the part of the men, who seemed nervous about telling her these stories. So, she wrote:

I took the risk of sharing my own story with those who had spoken of their experiences. I told them about the first time I crossed on foot, how after ten hours of walking Immigration caught us and returned us to

Mexico, and the following day we went back, walking for nine hours, and that time we made it. I think [sharing] these stories helped us to feel identified with one another.[1]

For the most part, Lucy and Mirian had a relatively easy time establishing rapport, as they already had the confidence of many local people. Instead of having to seek out informants, people would often come to them: Knowing them to be advocates for the local community, undocumented people sought them out to tell them about their work accidents or to ask their help in dealing with various immigration-related problems. Mirian and Lucy's fieldnote entries often begin with statements like,

El señor Federico called me last night, asking my help with a case he had, for driving without a license.[2]

Other times, their observations emerged through their volunteer and advocacy work:

This is the story of la señora Adela, who came to Casa Hometown looking for help, because she was referred to us by [another organization].[3]

As it had been for Daniel and Carolina during their preliminary studies, encounters in Casa Hometown became the source of much ethnographic data for Lucy and Mirian, supplementing their efforts to contact people in other social settings.

Lucy and Mirian's dispositions as caring, approachable people also made for excellent fieldwork relations. This is reflected throughout their notes and interviews, which capture their basic orientations to the people around them—not as the objects of research but as full human beings, like themselves, dealing with terrible hardships as a result of their structural positions and sometimes poor life choices. One day as she was walking around town looking for someone to chat with as part of her fieldwork, Lucy ran into a friend

who asked me to accompany her to the county courthouse, where she had a case, her petition for a divorce. She asked me to come with her because, according to her, I know a little more English than her, and I said, amiga, you shouldn't trust appearances, and we both laughed a little. But she asked me to do her this favor, so I said ok, and we headed to the court. On the way I asked her if she had ever been there before and she said yes, and I said: then you already know where to go, and she said, yes, amiga, but I'm so scared you wouldn't believe it! I told her, you have nothing to be afraid of, you are not a criminal, and she replied, that is true, but in these times they'll accuse us of anything, we can't make one false move or we'll be incriminated with something. And I said yes, in that we agree, but we have to be brave.[4]

This note illustrates Lucy's compassion and willingness to put herself at risk in order to help a friend (just entering the courthouse can be a dangerous move for an undocumented person). At the same time, the note is full of rich ethnographic observations that bear directly on one of the project's main research questions: the extent to which undocumented people are willing to use the legal system to defend their rights and advance their interests (in this case, in a divorce proceeding). It also demonstrates the ease with which Lucy was able to get right to the emotional and experiential aspects of being undocumented and engaging with the state—an insight that an outsider to the community might never gain. Lucy's own subject position, including her experience with the U.S. legal system, made her an excellent ethnographer, providing her with a particular standpoint from which to observe. For instance, on entering the courtroom that day, filled with trepidation about exposing herself to the gaze of the state, Lucy noted with surprise that "the security guard, instead of watching the security cameras, was very busy checking his Facebook page, and though I stared right at him, he didn't even notice that we were watching him."

Simply roaming around town to elicit random encounters was a key research/activist strategy for both Lucy and Mirian. When they weren't volunteering at Casa Hometown or engaged in more formal research activities like interviewing, they might go out for a walk and inevitably become involved in some interesting encounter in which they could provide assistance and about which they would later write in their fieldnotes. Again, this was facilitated by their good public reputations and their willingness to help others, as well as a developing eye for detail and a good ethnographic anecdote. It also reveals the ways in which their activist work and ethnographic work were beginning to overlap. Mirian, for example, would sometimes visit Open Door, a food pantry run out of a local church, where both immigrant and nonimmigrant people would go for free produce or a hot meal. One day, after walking around town for a while, Mirian decided to stop by:

I encountered several people there that I know, and they asked me where to find the office of Casa Hometown. I was talking with a mother and daughter, the daughter had had an accident and couldn't work, the mother couldn't work due to her age and because she had diabetes.[5]

The conversation ends with Mirian encouraging these people to come to Casa Hometown to receive help with their problems and an exhortation that they become members of the organization.

On another occasion, Lucy went to the laundromat to wash her family's clothes and encountered an acquaintance named Alejandra, with whom she began a conversation:

> *I asked her how she was doing and she said, not so good. And I said, why not so good? Then I said, if something has happened, if I can help you with something, and so she told me: She was having problems with her tenants, there was a couple who had rented a room in their house, and the husband was hitting the wife, she had bruises on her face and arms. And I said, oh my God, and then what happened?*[6]

At the end of the conversation, Lucy urged Alejandra to come to Casa Hometown for help in dealing with this situation. In both of these instances, Lucy and Mirian used their fieldwork encounters to recruit people to Casa, encouraging them to become members of the organization and to take advantage of the services it provides. These encounters in turn were documented in fieldnotes and sometimes led to more comprehensive ethnographic interviews. Another time, Lucy spoke with a woman who was battling her ex-husband for custody of their daughter:

> *She told me she was doing really badly, and for my part I told her that she was invited to Casa Hometown, there we could help her to investigate and do whatever we could to get her daughter back. She said that she would come by and visit us, because she was desperate. I told her not to worry, that everything would be ok, that the solution would soon appear.*[7]

On another occasion, Lucy described meeting a woman named Lilia in the supermarket. Her husband had been detained on drunk driving charges, and Lilia was struggling to choose between spending money on her husband's legal defense and providing for the basic needs of the couple's three children. Lucy's fieldnotes of this encounter demonstrate all the themes mentioned earlier: Lucy's profound compassion for the woman's situation, drawn from her own experience of her husband's detention; her promise to employ her and her organization's resources to resolve the woman's case; and the rendering of this experience in writing:

> *She told me sadly, "You know that now I am father and mother to my three children, the little that I have been able to save I want to use for my*

children. It is a little selfish of me but I have to support my kids, because my husband's situation is very insecure, we don't know what his fate will be." And I wanted to give her a few comforting words, and I told her that we will try to get her an affordable lawyer, that we have lawyers that work with us who don't charge a cent. She said ok, that she would try, but I could tell that she was more inclined to help her children. But I won't lose hope that we can fight her husband's situation, given that they have a citizen son and the eldest child is a Dreamer and they have a daughter who will turn 15 next year and can qualify [for DACA], so we agreed to make a date with a lawyer who is expert in this subject and tell her the case. [Until then], this note is in suspense.[8]

Interviewing and Educating

The blending of advocacy, activism, and research intensified as Mirian and Lucy gained more confidence in their abilities as researchers and began to conduct interviews unaccompanied by Daniel or Carolina. Mirian and Lucy used their casual or work-related encounters with immigrants to initiate conversations and, if a person had an interesting story, they would invite that person for an interview. Here again, however, they occasionally encountered skepticism and resistance to their ethnographic interventions. Lucy recalled that "people asked me why I wanted to record them; sometimes they didn't trust me not to use their real names. Sometimes they would ask me again and again who I work for and what the data is for."[9] When confronted with these doubts, Lucy and Mirian would explain that the research was part of a project associated with Casa Hometown and that they were trying to understand the different vulnerabilities to which immigrants were exposed so as to better serve undocumented people.

In their interviewing, as in their less-structured encounters with undocumented people around town, Lucy and Mirian followed through on this promise to use the information they gained through research to better serve the community. Their interviews became amazing hybrids of data collection and pedagogical exhortation, in which the interview subjects would narrate their personal histories and the problems they were dealing with as undocumented immigrants (usually focused around work accidents, wage theft, detention, and deportation, though other topics frequently arose), followed by instructions from the interviewer on how to handle these problems successfully. Although they could have (and in the past, indeed had) done education and advocacy work through their involvement with Casa Hometown, the research process created abundant new opportunities that they would otherwise not have had, enabling them to contact people whom they otherwise would not have encountered. Additionally, the knowledge they gained through the research—in particular, about the extent to which people in their community suffered in silence from work accidents and wage theft—provided them with better information to use in their outreach. Mirian and Lucy developed an approach that mobilized the information gathered through ethnography to support their activist work while using the ethnographic process itself to extend their activism.

This was evident from the very beginning of their interviewing. Carolina and Daniel accompanied Mirian on her first solo interview. The interview subject was a woman who had suffered a work accident and was disabled by the terrible pain in her back and neck. They sat in the woman's living room, sipping soft drinks that they had brought with them for the occasion, while Mirian and the woman conversed. Although Mirian had run through the usual protocol, asking the woman for permission to interview her and to record the conversation, the two women spoke with the intimacy of old friends (they had only just met). Mirian spoke from the experience of her own work accident and listened as the woman in turn recounted her story. As Caro and Daniel watched, both Mirian and the interviewee began to cry. As the conversation began to wind down, Mirian advised the woman on her rights as a worker, explaining that she had the right to compensation for her accident, that the employer was legally obligated to carry insurance that would provide medical care, and that she had the right to take him to court for failing to do so. The woman sat listening in astonishment to this news. By the end of the conversation, Mirian had recruited the woman to join Casa Hometown, promising her legal help in pursuing her right to compensation and care.

As they left the woman's home, Daniel asked himself what he had just witnessed. It did not resemble any interview he himself had ever conducted or even read about. In talking it over with Carolina, they began to realize that what Mirian and Lucy were doing was crafting a different kind of research, one that could not be evaluated in terms of the canonical standards. This was activist research in which neither component took priority over the other. It was also deeply grounded in empathy and an insider's sense of the basic humanity of her interlocutor: a woman, undocumented and disabled just like her. From one perspective, this clearly demonstrates the effectiveness of an activist approach for gaining ethnographic knowledge about the topic under study (i.e., work accidents and the rights of the undocumented). But it also demonstrates the utility of ethnography for activists and the community they serve when the academic anthropologist steps back and lets the local activist-ethnographer do her work. In this case, and in many others that would follow, Mirian used the semi-structured interview as an opportunity to advise an individual in trouble while also building her organization, recruiting that individual to become a Casa Hometown member. In doing so, Mirian (and Lucy, in her own interviews with consultants) worked to build a coalition of people who could struggle together to demand their rights and advance a collective agenda. An important point here is that this work could really only be done by someone like Mirian, someone who shared an identity and set of experiences with the person being interviewed. The emotional connection that they so readily established opened a whole new set of insights into the lived experience of the academic questions being studied, in this case work accidents and their effects on those who live them.

Lucy and Mirian continued to use their ethnographic research to learn about problems in the community and then to organize people in response, not just as individuals but collectively. Not everything they did pertained to the themes of the research or was related to immigrants' troubles with the U.S. government. For example, through their interviewing and informal conversations, Lucy and Mirian learned of a man, himself a Latin American immigrant, who ran a small shipping business, sending packages to and from Latin America for his immigrant clients in Hometown. But many people had complaints about this man and felt that he was ripping them off. So Mirian and Lucy organized these people to come out and protest publicly, blocking the entrance to his store until the man relented. Again, this was an issue that fell outside the strict purview of the project; nevertheless, it was something that Lucy and Mirian learned about through ethnography, and they felt compelled to act. In doing so, they again drew on their own personal identities and emotions. Mirian wrote in her fieldnotes:

> *This man has a business sending packages to various countries, and he was behaving badly toward his own clients. I found this very offensive, given that we are from the same country, and how awful to feel that a person from your own country is creating this kind of problem. . . . So I told him that . . . we have had many complaints about him and that we were contacting all the people to whom he owed money and that we would have a protest in front of his store. This cheater felt the pressure, and after eight days he called [his clients] to pay them what he owed them.*[10]

Lucy and Mirian, together with Caro and Daniel, were also active in organizing events and rallying community participation in them. Often these were political events: demonstrations, marches, and protests against U.S. immigration policy, detentions, and deportations. On May 1, International Workers Day, many organizations that work to support undocumented workers and their families in the northeastern U.S. gather in New York City for a march in Union Square. There they cheer and applaud speeches, performances, and public demonstrations. The research team collaborated with the leadership of Casa Hometown to organize community participation in this event, which included transportation from New Jersey to Manhattan and back. Each year, Casa Hometown would march and Mirian would sing one of her songs about immigrant rights and the experience of living undocumented to the people assembled in Union Square. Other notable occasions included marches around Hometown in support of immigrant rights; protests outside the homes of local wage thieves; and a conference at Rutgers University called "Undocumented/Unafraid" (organized with Unidad Latina en Acción, another New Jersey immigrants' rights organization), which brought together academics and activists, including Mirian, for a discussion about undocumentation and New Jersey life. In all of these events, Lucy and Mirian (along with Daniel and Caro) used their fieldwork encounters to build support, recruit participants, and organize the involvement of local people in collective action. The rally described at the end of our play in chapter 5 is a good example of how their activist work included mobilizing the local community, sometimes in support of individuals in crisis (see figure 4.1).

The efforts to combine fieldwork, organizing, and advocacy—and particularly, to serve people's needs while recruiting them to become Casa members and so bolster the organization that provides those services—could be stressful for the activist-researchers. In her fieldnotes Mirian often remarked on the challenges of organizing her community. Her complaints frequently focused on people's failure to take advantage of the services that she and her organization provided. People's lack of understanding of their own rights was critical in this regard, as was their willingness to accept Casa's services without becoming official members and without making an ongoing commitment to the organization. One time, for example, Mirian wrote:

A man came to Casa Hometown with tickets issued by the housing inspector. He told me the police came to his house late at night with the housing inspector. When he found 13 people in the house the inspector said the house was only meant for seven people, so he gave them a $500 fine for every extra person living in the house. I told him that this is what happens when people don't come to our Casa Hometown workshops to

FIGURE 4.1. Marian and Carolina perform a scene from the play *Undocumented, Unafraid* (see chapter 5). Illustration by Peter Quach.

learn about their rights. The housing inspector and the police can't come into your home unless you allow them to. That is the problem with some people. . . . They only come to Casa Hometown when they have a problem and then they disappear.[11]

Lucy and Mirian discovered that most immigrants who are injured on the job or are victims of wage theft do not know that they can sue their employers in court until they visit Casa Hometown. It is a curious feature of U.S. labor law that, although undocumented people are not eligible for employment, if they are injured on the job they are entitled to the same benefits as an authorized worker.[12] This is enforced in New Jersey through the state's Workers' Compensation Act, which prohibits employers from discriminating against employees on the basis of national origin or citizenship status and requires them to provide medical benefits and compensation to workers injured on the job.[13] New Jersey obligates employers to carry private insurance to pay these awards to their employees and maintains a public fund to which injured workers can apply if their employer does not abide by the law.[14] Workers who are denied these basic rights are entitled to sue their employer in court. Mirian said that "people come to [Casa Hometown] to find help, but not legal help. Once they come here we tell them that they have the right to go to court and that is a very profound discovery for many people. Being undocumented doesn't mean having no rights, and people don't know that."[15]

Teaching people about their rights became an important part of their work as organizers, and this mission was further extended through their ethnographic research. For example, Lucy interviewed a woman who had suffered several work accidents and other "humiliations" at the hands of her previous employers, owing, the woman said, to her inability to speak English:

I informed her that in Casa Hometown we offer an English class, and that she could attend and that it would help her to get ahead. She told me that there are many people who humiliate her in horrible ways, because she is undocumented they don't give her any importance. I told her that even though we are undocumented we have rights, as human beings, and therefore it is good to educate ourselves and to attend educational forums [at Casa Hometown] whenever they are offered.[16]

By the second year of our work together, Mirian and Lucy began taking the project in new thematic directions. At the outset, Daniel and Caro had asked Lucy and Mirian to think about topics that they might be especially interested in studying, and in the course of their inquiries the experiences of immigrant women emerged as a central concern. Lucy and Mirian began to make domestic violence a particular focus of their attention, but they soon encountered difficulties. Lucy wrote:

> *I'm looking to write fieldnotes about domestic violence, so I have been asking women from the community who I see every day on my way to my kids' school. I haven't gotten any results by just asking people. I think it is an issue that, when it affects you, you don't want to talk about it for fear of being judged or for fear that people will judge your partner.*[17]

Not to be deterred, Lucy called her *comadres* in the community and asked them for the names of women who suffered from domestic violence. She called these women and asked if she could visit them. Some of them were willing to see her, and though no one agreed to be interviewed, Lucy was able to write fieldnotes about their stories. "With our project I learned a lot about domestic violence," Lucy said. "I know things are difficult for women in Mexico, because many times their partners abuse them and there is no support for them from the state. But I thought things would be different in the United States because there is more protection for women."[18] But for undocumented women that is not the case, as Lucy learned through her research. Because women are afraid of getting their partners deported and being left alone to care for their children and themselves, and because of their own fears about being undocumented, they often decline to report the abuse they endure to the police.[19] "I would talk to women and encourage them to get help, if not from the police at least from Casa Hometown."

Mirian spoke with a woman who had suffered domestic violence at the hands of her intimate partner and had hired a lawyer to help her, but the lawyer had done nothing. The woman claimed to have reported the case to the police, but Mirian sensed that she was not telling the truth. Here was another opportunity not only to provide individual services, but to build her organization. Never one to pull her punches, Mirian said to the woman:

> *Tell me something: you suffered domestic violence, and you called the police when it happened? And she told me no, she never called the police. Ok, I told her the truth, that it is very necessary that you get a police report to serve as evidence that you were the victim of domestic violence. And she told me, yes, but the lawyer said first that I had a case and now that I paid him he tells me I don't have a case, but he kept my money. And I said: that is why we have to stick together in an organization, to be informed, and whatever questions we have, we should ask people that are in the*

organization. I invited her to join Casa Hometown, to learn some En-
glish and to learn about her rights, because many people take advantage
of those who are afraid to confront life's realities.[20]

Similarly, Lucy reported an encounter in which she also (unsuccessfully) encouraged an immigrant crime victim to call the police and employ legal resources to resolve her situation:

Micaela is a young woman barely 20 years old, from Mexico, who says
she is running away from her husband who is an American citizen. I met
her in the local pharmacy, I saw that she looked a little nervous, so I went
up to her and I asked if I could help her with something, and she told me:
no, thank you. I said ok, and went over to the next aisle, but there she
was at my side, and she said, yes, I do need help, and so we chatted a bit
about her history. She told me that her husband abused her physically
and verbally, and that she had endured it for a long time, but she was not
going to take it anymore, Micaela had been married for three years. So
I told her, go to the police and denounce him, but she said, No![21]

In all of the preceding accounts, Mirian and Lucy demonstrated how their activism inverted the priorities typically associated with academic research (as described in chapter 1). Even as they investigated the topic of immigrants' engagements with the legal system—the principal thesis on which the entire project was founded and funded—Lucy and Mirian turned the question of immigrants' use (or refusal to use) the legal system to advance their rights and interests into a priority of their activism, urging their research subjects to use all resources at their disposal to defend themselves. In each of these cases, upon learning that the victim had failed to engage with the law to respond to domestic violence, Lucy and Mirian advised the women they interviewed on what they should have done, exhorting them to denounce those responsible for the wrongs done to them. This requires victims to confront their fears of deportation, to understand that even undocumented people have certain rights when they are the victims of crime, and to call on authorities like the police and lawyers to help them get the justice they deserve.[22] In this work, then, Mirian and Lucy used the context of the interview as a platform for learning about problems and doing activist work to address them. As Lucy put it, "My work day to day is to exhort women to denounce these types of violence."[23] Or, as she said about domestic violence, "It is good to create consciousness in the community and to say: E.N.O.U.G.H."

As they grew as activists and researchers, Lucy and Mirian also developed their own theory of undocumentation, of what it means to be undocumented in the U.S. and wherein lie the principal sources of the problems facing undocumented people. Their theory in some ways conflicted with those typically held by most academics, including Carolina and Daniel. In most critical writing by immigration scholars and journalists, the suffering of undocumented people in the U.S. is a result of structural and systemic forces that produce immigrant "illegality," which disqualifies undocumented people as rights bearers and renders them "deportable" by the state (see, e.g., de Genova 2002, 2007). Nevertheless, scholars contend, most undocumented people are allowed to remain in the U.S. to continue to serve the needs of U.S. capital for cheap labor (Goldstein and Alonso-Bejarano 2017; Gomberg-Muñoz and Nussbaum-Barberena 2011). This arrangement consigns immigrants to "shadow communities" where they live more or less in hiding, their behavior biopolitically regulated and their ability to socially reproduce severely constrained (Chavez 1998, 2008; Coleman and Stuesse 2014). Immigrants in this literature can appear passive, the victims of an unjust and exploitative system, the enormity of which they are powerless to confront.

Mirian and Lucy accepted the basic premise of this theory. In their words and writing they frequently referred to the unjust system of laws and policing that detain and deport members of their community and that take no account of the many contributions that these people make to their adopted country. Like other immigrants, they were well aware of their importance to the U.S. economy and pointed to these contributions as evidence of their right to live unmolested in this country. Through their ethnographic work, Lucy and Mirian became especially aware of the prevalence of work accidents among the undocumented and of how these are the physical expressions of what it means to live in the shadows.

But Mirian and Lucy rejected the implication that immigrants are rightless and powerless to resist the suffering that illegalization imposes on them. In their theory of undocumentation, structural factors are only one part of the story, one cause of immigrant suffering. The other critical factor is what they perceived to be lack of unity on the part of the immigrant community, a result of people's failure to know their rights and to demand them collectively. In this, they articulated what we call *an undocumented activist's theory of undocumentation*, which says, "The system is indeed rigged against us, but we can't just lie down and take it. We can't hide in the shadows, we have to fight back together in defense of ourselves and our loved ones." Theirs is a theory that emphasizes human rights, especially the right of all people to live and work in peace without oppression from the government. It reflects the value of collective self-determination that lies at the heart of other decolonial struggles in the United States such as the Civil Rights and Black Power movements. As Mirian said:

> We must fight for our rights despite our fear. Fear is not a justification for lack of action to me because if we all got together we could achieve many things. And I think that, of course, there will be people arrested and people deported, even killed. But I take the example of Blacks in this country. I have heard that it used to be the case that Blacks couldn't sit at the front of the bus. But one day they made a decision: They said, we need to have respect for one another. We need to have dignity. We need to have equality between Blacks and whites. They won the fight for equal rights because they were united. They sat at the front of the bus together and they reclaimed their humanity.[24]

We call this an undocumented activist's theory because it is a perspective that emerged through Lucy and Mirian's work as activists as they struggled to rally their community to organize and defend themselves against state violence and workplace abuses. It emphasizes activist values, including action in the face of oppression, resistance to injustice, and empowerment against imposed weakness and invisibility. It argues that the conditions under which undocumented immigrants live can only be changed if they are willing to engage in collective action by coming out of the shadows to demand human dignity and respect.[25] Lucy said, "When the community is not organized we cannot achieve anything. If people in the community were organized and we were all standing together in front of the cannon I think that only then would change come, because we have to all be on the same tune to achieve things."[26] This emphasis on unity and solidarity as the only means to achieve social justice for the undocumented was shared by Mirian: "For me our main problem as undocumented people lies in the lack of unity among our community. Take for instance the fight for drivers' licenses in New Jersey. Everybody wants their license, but when the time comes to come together and demand that we are given access to drivers' licenses people don't show up. In 2016 we organized a march in Trenton for the licenses and maybe 800 people showed up. How many of us undocumented folks are there in New Jersey? Many more than that, so for me it's just not enough."[27] Undocumented activist theory is also evident in Mirian's fieldnotes. At times she sounds harsh in criticizing immigrant workers' own failures to take care of themselves in dangerous situations. For example, Daniel once asked Mirian for her perspective on why immigrant workers suffer from so many accidents on the job, expecting her to point to the exploitative nature of the U.S. labor system or the failure of employers to provide adequate safety equipment and training to their workers. To Daniel's surprise, however, Mirian answered that not enough immigrants bother to learn about safety equipment and how to use it, and when they are injured they don't seek the support to which they are entitled. Another time, describing the aims of a workshop she organized at Casa Hometown to educate workers on workplace dangers and how to avoid them, Mirian wrote:

> What we want is that they can identify the dangers and that we do it for ourselves, that we don't get all defensive and put all the blame on our patrones, but that we take prudent measures in the first place, for ourselves and for our own safety. Because if we are working in the sun, and we don't bring water, and we don't ask the patrón for any, I believe that we, too, have to be aware and concerned for our own wellbeing everywhere we go, and not think like a child that makes excuses for everything, and say: I didn't drink [water] because my patrón didn't give me any! Making ourselves into the victims. Nor can we risk our lives to earn a few more pennies, we should realize that our health is the most important thing.[28]

Lucy shared Mirian's perspective on these matters. In her written accounts, Lucy's increasingly strident exhortations of immigrants to demand their rights seemed to emerge from a belief in the need for the undocumented to unite and assert themselves more forcefully in the face of challenges. One day while she was walking around Hometown distributing flyers for an upcoming event at Casa Hometown, a *charla* (chat) for mothers of children with special needs, Lucy ran into a group of women whom she knew to have special-needs children. One woman was the mother of a boy named Efraín:

> I asked them why they hadn't asked for help [from the school], and they responded that because they don't speak English, they didn't want to be insistent about it. I told them that that was not a sufficient reason and that when you want to accomplish something you have to put your mind to it, and we've got to move heaven and earth to get help for our kids. Efraín's mother said to me, but sometimes, señora, people give you nasty looks, and I told her, that doesn't matter, sometimes we have to deal with that, but we should never allow it to defeat us.[29]

Lucy was not merely demonstrating bravado in this instance, but acting in accordance with her theory of undocumentation. Judging from the apathy that she and Mirian encountered among immigrants in their activist fieldwork, this theory was not a widely held one; nevertheless, for Lucy and Mirian, it guided their actions and shaped their perspectives on what they observed. In their fieldnotes, one observes a mounting frustration with these circumstances, in which immigrants don't show unity in confronting their abuse and exploitation. Writing about a Casa Hometown workshop on resisting deportation, Lucy said:

> *Well, this afternoon Casa Hometown held an immigration forum with a very prestigious and well-known lawyer. The whole community had been invited about a week and a half ago, it had been announced in Casa Hometown, and I personally made phone calls. And it's a shame that only eight people showed up, nine counting the director of Casa Hometown. . . . It's a pity because people keep coming to Casa Hometown with their problems, above all because of relatives detained by ICE, and sadly day after day the deportations and separations of families continue. But my question is . . . why when there are forums like this, don't people attend? Really, I don't think I understand my people all that well. . . . I hope that for the next meeting we can get more people together, because difficult times for us are coming and we really have to educate ourselves, day after day.*[30]

The final line of this note warns of "difficult times" ahead for undocumented immigrants, a prediction that unfortunately came true with the election of Donald Trump as president in 2016. Lucy's writing was realistic about the circumstances facing immigrants, and she was often critical of those who prefer to live in ignorance, hiding in the relative safety of Hometown and hoping to avoid the many dangers that surround them. For Lucy the only option is to come out of the shadows: "If we don't confront our fears we will always be afraid. We must face our fears and come out of the shadows. Besides, hiding makes no sense because if the government wants to find you, they will find you."[31] Mirian's thoughts echo Lucy's in this regard. In her understanding of the world, fear of the state should not be a reason for undocumented people to feel that they can't engage in collective organized action, since the all-seeing eyes of the state are everywhere and can't be avoided: "That is what I tell immigrants who tell me they want to hide from the state. This country has already found us through our phones, through Facebook and Whatsapp, not to mention the cameras everywhere. I believe that there is no hiding from the government, and that coming out into the light to demand our rights is the only way forward."[32] This perspective emphasizes a discourse on rights and individual behavior that some might critique as neoliberal, a way to "blame the victim" and accord responsibility to the individual for her own oppression.[33] For Mirian and Lucy, however, "blame" is not the right lens through which to interpret their theory. As Mirian put it:

> It is not about assigning blame. This is about feeling that we have the right to exist. To say, I exist and I am here. To me being afraid to take action is not justified because the day when we have a multitude of people fighting for the rights of the undocumented will be the day when we get respect. I would like to see a march like the [2018 March for Our Lives], where thousands of people across the nation take the streets in solidarity with immigrants and with one another. This is about people gaining consciousness of their worth and of their power, and I don't just mean us undocumented people.[34]

It is important to note here that for Mirian the lack of action in support of the rights of the undocumented on the part of documented people is also part of the problem. Lucy agreed that the issue at hand is not to assign blame, but rather to raise consciousness among the community about their rights and the importance of collective action: "This is not about blaming people for their illegal status, but rather about raising the consciousness of our people. Many choose not to participate in our actions for fear of losing their job, for example, or for fear of the police. But think, for instance, about the big 2006 marches when hundreds of people went to New York City from Hometown. That year thousands of immigrants took to the streets everywhere in the country. If we had continued marching in a massive way our reality today would be very different."[35] Lucy and Mirian's theory of undocumentation states that direct organized action on the part of undocumented immigrants themselves is the only way to change their situation of so-called illegality, and it makes immigrants themselves accountable for stepping out of the shadows and demanding the recognition of their humanity.

It is important to recognize this perspective *as a theory*. Even if one disagrees with it, this set of ideas cannot be dismissed as a form of false consciousness, a misrecognition of the "reality" of illegalization that immigrants face in the U.S. It is, rather, a coherent framework for interpreting the daily experiences that Lucy and Mirian have lived as undocumented people and for making sense out of the data they collected through their work as ethnographers. To call their perspective on undocumentation a theory is to acknowledge that theorizing is not the sole preserve of academics and scholars. It is a decolonial move, recognizing that all kinds of people—including ethnographers' collaborators—are theorists, often developing their own explanatory frames that make sense given their own knowledge and experience. This is not unprecedented in anthropology: Anthropologists have long advocated for the use of indigenous terms and concepts in understanding local cultural realities,[36] and more recently scholars have called for anthropological attention to indigenous or "native" theory (Simpson and Smith 2014) and "theory from the South" (Comaroff and Comaroff 2012a). Recognizing this kind of theory *as* theory is an important part of decolonizing anthropology.

As with other nonacademic theories—that is, sets of ideas produced by those outside the academy and often regarded as insufficiently theoretical—undocumented activist theory emerges inductively. It is based on and comes out of experience and observation, rather than being an a priori set of assumptions about the meaning of social life. To that extent it might be considered a variety of what some sociologists call "grounded theory" (Glaser and Strauss 1967), or what some anthropologists call "lateralist" theory (Boyer and Howe 2015)—theory that emerges through research or the experience of being a full participant in the world about which one theorizes. Whatever the case, to identify an undocumented activist's theory of undocumentation as a theory is to bring theory down from its lofty pedestal, to challenge the coloniality of a view of theory as something beyond the grasp of ordinary folks, something that can only be applied by experts to interpret the lives of others. It is instead to find theory produced by people who lack a theoretical passport, so to speak; it questions "the existence of higher levels of truth claims beyond the particularities of fieldwork experiences and ethnographic narratives" (Boyer and Marcus 2015, 9). Undocumented activist theory suggests one possible set of ideas by which undocumented people—in this case, undocumented activists—interpret their own experience.

To consider undocumented activist theory *as* theory also opens new insights into the worlds of undocumented immigrants. It enables us to say something beyond the familiar academic concepts ordinarily applied to their lives and experiences. Undocumented activist theory restores agency to people for whom self-determination is denied, both by the state that craves their labor but not their public presence within the nation and by those academics who would subscribe to an overly structural perspective on the immigrant condition. Because undocumented activist theory comes from members of the community being studied, it can say things about that community that well-meaning outsiders are not positioned to say. Mirian and

Lucy can be critical of their friends and neighbors for their lack of solidarity and their passivity in the face of oppression; Daniel and Carolina would have more difficulty making such an assertion. Whether or not one thinks it is correct, the theory opens new spaces for talking about undocumentation, from the perspective of activists hoping to challenge the situations they view as unjust. Undocumented activist theory brings new voices to the conversation beyond those of academics, journalists, politicians, and white liberal activists, most of them external to the undocumented community. In its focus on the full humanization of the undocumented, undocumented activist theory brings new questions to the debate—questions about the rights of the undocumented, which may be overlooked by those whose main concern is a critique of the prevailing conditions that oppress and exploit them. And undocumented activist theory, unlike most academic theory, is inherently activist: It identifies problems and proposes solutions, all in the same breath.

Lucy and Mirian's undocumented activist theory of undocumentation also recognizes the lies that immigrants have told themselves—that the United States is a land of opportunity, where everyone can get rich and be happy. The reality of the "American Dream," Lucy says, is much different; and in laying bare this reality in her fieldnotes, she reclaims it, offering an immigrants' take on the meaning of the American Dream. In a note titled *Sin Alivio* [No Relief], Lucy wrote:

> *In this fieldnote I want to share with you the life story of immigrant José, who came to this country in search of an American Dream and left his family behind. José has been here for 10 years and has missed a lot of his kids' lives. I asked him if the sacrifice was worth it and he said it isn't. That's why he's planning on returning to his country, because he has been waiting for too long for an immigration reform that allows him to fix his papers. I was saddened when he told me how much he has given to this country since he arrived. He said he only came to find a better future but now it's time to go back. I said I'm glad he will see his family again. Then I asked, "What about the American Dream? Did you get it?" He replied that his dream was to have a work permit and be here legally, but it has already been 10 years. But he accomplished part of the dream, which was to build a house in Mexico.*[37]

"For many people building a house in their home country is part of the American Dream," Lucy wrote in another fieldnote entry. "For many it's about dreaming for their kids. For me it's also about getting my papers one day."[38] In her work, Lucy reclaims the American Dream as something that is accessible to undocumented immigrants, even those who end up getting deported or going home. This, too, is part of her undocumented activist theory of undocumentation. The dream, whatever it might be, is the goal to be achieved through organized, ongoing resistance.

Conclusion

The benefits of the project's approach to ethnography are clear. On the one hand, the research produced fascinating new insights into the lived reality of immigrants in a securitized environment. Of course, having two undocumented women on the research team made access to a potentially closed community much easier. But more important than access was the quality of the work they did. Mirian and Lucy were excellent ethnographers, with a keen eye for detail, a passion for inquiry and investigation, and a willingness to take risks and confront the unknown. Though they began the project with no knowledge of or experience with ethnographic research, they quickly became highly adept at observing, interviewing, and writing fieldnotes. Not everyone could do this: On several occasions the team hired other individuals as research assistants—usually undocumented men, in an effort to incorporate their perspectives—but these arrangements were unsuccessful. One of the men, whom we call MGF, was himself an amateur ethnographer prior to joining the project who, for his own amusement, would interview people on the street about being undocumented and write up his observations in a pocket notebook. But he never quite understood the goals of the project, nor did he produce the kinds of data that Lucy and Mirian did. (One excerpt from MGF's fieldnotes, rendered in the form of a poem, appears as the epigraph of this book.)

Mirian and Lucy, in contrast, engaged their subjects through their own experiences as undocumented women, a status they embodied legally, physically, and emotionally. As the victim of a work accident who carried that burden throughout the fieldwork period, Mirian could feel the pain of undocumentation with every turn of her head, every movement of her leg. Lucy knew the numbing fear of having a loved one detained and threatened with deportation. All of this led to an ethnography that was deeply emotional, at times even spiritual, grounded in their felt, lived experiences with work accidents, illegalization, and detention. This perspective contributed to the quality of their fieldwork and writing. Indeed, some of their most poignant fieldnotes reveal the depth to which violence penetrates immigrant lives. Lucy wrote of her interview with Dolores, a single mother with a young son who had previously experienced domestic violence at the hands of her intimate partner and later a devastating accident in the factory where she worked. She said:

> It seems to me that señora Dolores has lived through a very bad experience owing to this accident and not only has it affected her but her whole family, especially her oldest son, who has been affected psychologically. Years ago, Doña Dolores suffered domestic violence, and the boy lived through it all, and as a result Dolores said that her son had come to believe that the police were bad and now he was directing his fear toward them. But now that Dolores mentioned it I noted that something else was going on with her oldest boy, that as a consequence of her accident her son had become filled with rage, and crying she told me that her son had said, that he would like to get a gun and kill whoever was responsible for the accident. His words were very strong. I think that at the first chance I have to speak to with Dolores, we have to find help for her son.[39]

In addition, Lucy and Mirian's participation opened up new avenues of inquiry that had not previously been part of the research design. The question of domestic violence, discussed previously, was a significant example of this, but there were others, and these, too, involved a blend of ethnography and activism. Again, these interests emerged from their own experiences and observations as undocumented women and their goals of raising individual consciousness while trying to build and mobilize collective organizations. For example, as organizers, Mirian and Lucy were interested in the ways in which women come together socially and politically. One time Mirian noted, "Organizing women is much more difficult than organizing men in Hometown. Women have so many domestic duties that it is hard to get them to attend a meeting."[40] In their research, Lucy and Mirian came to understand that, while men congregate in places like the *Vía* owing to their work as day laborers, undocumented women have no central meeting place. Lucy said, "We are in the shadows and we have no place to congregate and talk about our work like jornaleros do. We tried to create a women's collective but women have to tend to their houses and their jobs and they have no time to organize."[41] However, Mirian believes that being an undocumented woman gives her a better vantage point to talk about rights in the United States, part of what we have identified as undocumented activist theory: "Undocumented women know what we are talking about when we demand our rights. We are the most vulnerable, so we know what we mean when we say we are human and we deserve dignity."[42]

Had Carolina and Daniel chosen different collaborators, the results of this project would likely have been different as well. As dedicated activists, Mirian and Lucy's approach to ethnography was crosscut by their work as organizers in the undocumented community of Hometown. Whereas Daniel and Carolina came to the project with a mix of academic and activist concerns, Mirian and Lucy came to it as activists whose principal concern regarded how this work could contribute to and extend their activism. The ontological status of anthropology as a social science was never among their interests. For Lucy and Mirian, the ethnographic methodology was useful only insofar as it could function as an instrument for community organizing and education. Yet, through this approach to ethnography, the research team gathered huge quantities of data. Among the four of us, we wrote thousands of pages of fieldnotes, recorded over 100 interviews, and collected reams of secondary documents and information. Lucy and Mirian demonstrated something that activist anthropologists know well: that ethnography as activism can be powerfully productive for both social action and academic data collection.

But more than that, Lucy and Mirian were explicit in their awareness that ethnographic interviewing provided them a unique opportunity to identify and advise people in trouble, and in this, too, we find the decolonial thrust of their work. In chapter 3, we suggested that ethnography can be decolonial when it enables research subjects and their communities to organize and struggle more effectively to demand and defend their rights, however these might be understood, and that is what Mirian and Lucy achieved in their work. By integrating ethnography and activism, they found an approach that could accomplish more than either of these on their own. Mirian noted that activist outreach, far from conflicting with the goals of their research, underwrote and supported it: "For me an interview is a mix of talking to people and doing activism. I tell people about their rights as I conduct my questions so they know this is a two way street and they can benefit from my interviews. It's the same for me when I am observing things to write in my fieldnotes. I don't just observe people, I interact with them, ask about their problems and give them advice based on my experience."[43] Lucy, too, was very frank about combining research and activism. At the completion of the two years of collaborative work, Lucy observed that "when people told me about wage theft or work accidents I would tell them to go to another lawyer, or go to this lawyer, or go to the hospital."[44] She also used the interviews to build community and connection, putting people in touch with others who shared their experiences: "I would tell them, go talk to such and such, they had your same problem."[45] Interviewing, Lucy noted, was always about much more than data collection: "The objective that we want to achieve," she said, "is to educate our community."[46]

Mirian and Lucy modeled a decolonial approach to social research by taking the goals and methods of the project into their own hands and applying them toward their own ends. They used the tools and techniques of ethnographic research to teach other undocumented people to challenge exploitation, mobilizing them to step out of the shadows and to collectively demand their basic human rights. They created bonds and organized collective responses through their ongoing recruitment to Casa Hometown and their coordination of public protests and other events by the undocumented community and their allies in Hometown. By providing Lucy and Mirian with the skills, the equipment, and the financing to do this kind of research,[47] the project became something much greater than an academic inquiry. It became an exercise in decolonization, in which the subaltern became the researchers, the researchers became the students, and the research became an instrument of social resistance, transformation, and liberation.

UNDOCUMENTED
THEATER

Writing and Resistance

As the previous chapter emphasized, to us decolonial fieldwork is about empowering, educating, and communicating. For Lucy and Mirian, participant observation and interviewing were always opportunities to inform undocumented people of their rights and to help them to defend those rights when they were violated, at home and in the workplace. In doing so, they felt themselves to be working not only as researchers collecting data or as activists trying to empower and inform members of their community. Like many critical ethnographers, Lucy and Mirian also understood themselves to be storytellers, recording and recounting the often-invisible sufferings and struggles of people like themselves, forced by U.S. immigration law and policing to inhabit the shadows of U.S. society. And in doing so, they were stepping out of those shadows and working to enable others of their community to do the same. In a variety of ways, all the members of our research team employed different forms of writing to publicize the struggles of undocumented people and, at the same time, to extend the project of decolonial engagement.

Fieldnotes became one mechanism for doing this, and Lucy and Mirian modeled this for the rest of the team. Though neither of them had done much writing prior to working as ethnographers, their work provoked them to become more fluent and more prolific with the written word. They became comfortable writing on the iPad keyboards, and the practice of writing almost daily became engrained in them. For each of them, the writing assumed a special form and function. Lucy clearly understood her fieldnotes as a forum to tell stories about the immigrant community, and she wrote them with her readers in mind. She began many of her notes by inviting the reader into her ongoing narrative of local life, with statements like, "Hello once more. We continue to work hard compiling the histories of our immigrant community."[1] This style of writing was facilitated by the team's collaborative approach, in which we all wrote notes to and for each other and shared and commented on what each other wrote. But Lucy seemed to have a larger audience in mind, often giving her notes titles that made them into stories or morality tales for readers beyond her research colleagues. These stories—with titles like "American Dream?," "False Promises," and "A Hard Lesson"—denounce different situations of exploitation that Lucy learned about in her research, and in her notes she explained that she used these situations to educate people about their rights and the importance of organizing. On one occasion, for example, she wrote, "Today I will tell you about Camilo, who threw his back out carrying heavy objects for his job. He told me he needed some days off to recover but his patrón said no. So I told him to go back to his patrón and demand the days off with pay."[2]

Mirian, too, developed her own mode of expressive communication and pedagogy in her writing, in her case through song. She began singing with her father when she was very young and was always praised for her voice, but she truly found her calling after becoming active with Casa Hometown. It was May 1, 2012—May Day, also known as International Workers' Day—and Casa Hometown had been invited to participate in the celebration at Union Square in New York City. Mirian decided she would sing a song for the occasion, but she could not find a song that expressed what she wanted to convey about immigrant workers' rights and the spirit of belonging she felt in Hometown. So, Mirian wrote her first song. Before the thousands gathered in the square that day, she sang about the Casa Hometown "family" and the basic humanity of the undocumented. Since then, Mirian has written thirty-five songs, which she performs at local and national events. Like Lucy with her fieldnotes, Mirian's songs have an activist, outreach aim: "What I want with my songs is for people to realize that we are all human. Singing for me is a release of all the things I have inside, and, because everybody has a relationship with music, it is a form of reaching out to people maybe more powerful than organizing is."[3] When she is singing, Mirian is the decolonial theorist calling attention to the dehumanizing qualities of the U.S. immigration system and inviting her fellow humans to act in solidarity to resist it. For example, in her favorite song, titled "Sin Fronteras" [No Borders], Mirian advances what in the previous chapter we called an "undocumented activist theory of undocumentation":

Oiga, amigo y hermano
Uniendo las manos no te sueltes más
Todos países unidos no somos vencidos
Unámonos más
Todo es posible haciéndolo así
No pensemos en fronteras
Que mucho daño ha pasado ya
Mira todo el racismo que en este mundo se mira no más
Cómo poder instruirnos rompiendo fronteras
Uniéndonos más
Que los países hermanos y Afro-Americanos han sufrido ya
Cómo poder detenernos mirando a los niños llorar y llorar
Porque a muchos padres los han detenido para deportar
Mira, amigo y hermano
Extiende tu mano y no permitas más
Que los derechos humanos sean violados
Como Martin Luther King
Quien fue un hombre fuerte y digno de honor
Hombre que murió en la lucha para defender su comunidad

Listen, friend and brother
Let's join hands and not let go
Together our peoples cannot be defeated
We must be more united
Everything is possible if we all believe
Let's stop thinking of borders
Because they have hurt so many
Look at all the racism in this world
Let's teach ourselves to break borders together
Because our fellow countries and African American brothers
Have suffered enough
How can we hold back when we see the children crying
Because everywhere their parents are detained and deported
Listen, friend and brother
Extend your hand and don't allow
The violation of human rights
Like Martin Luther King
A strong man with honor
Who died in the fight to defend his community

Here again, the lines between fieldwork and activism, fieldnotes and other forms of writing, begin to blur. Just as Lucy's notes are stories of immigrant suffering and resistance, Mirian's fieldnotes are songs: Not only do her notes recount instances in which she sang at events, they are songs in themselves, as in these notes from April 18, 2015:

Yo soy la que canto al viento
Y lo digo muy de adentro
Me gusta la buena vida
Sin alborotarme tanto
Pues la vida es muy valiosa
Hay que disfrutarla bien
Nomás cantando canciones
Y andarme paseando en tren
Los caminos de este mundo
Yo los quiero recorrer
Cantándoles mis canciones
Y disfrutarlas muy bien
No les doy la despedida
Porque siempre volveré
Y les cantare cancines
Escúchenlas donde estén
Sólo quiero ser su amiga
Y pasarla muy alegres
No necesitamos nada
Ni vino ni borracheras.

I am she who sings to the wind
And I speak from deep within
I love the good life
Without too many disturbances
Because life is very precious
We must enjoy it every day
I just want to sing my songs
And travel around by train
I want to amble along
The paths of this world
Singing you my songs
And enjoying them in full

I do not say goodbye
Because I will always be back
Singing you my songs
You can hear them wherever you are
I just want to be your friend
And pass this joyful time together
We need nothing more,
Not booze nor drunkenness

One of the most thrilling and remarkable days in Mirian's life was the day she received the official copyright for her song "Sin Fronteras" from the U.S. government. Her and Lucy's decision to allow their real names to be used in this book is a similar expression of the pride they take in their writing and their desire to be recognized for their achievements.

The idea to write a play occurred simultaneously to Carolina and Mirian at the very beginning of our project, and they brought their idea to the rest of the team (Figure 5.1). All quickly agreed. In doing so, our team became part of a long history—from the ancient Greeks to Shakespeare to the Theater of the Oppressed—in which theater is understood as a means of social transformation. In our work we contributed to the tradition of creating "theater in the service of social change" (Prentki and Preston 2009, 12), which in the twentieth century can be traced back to the political theaters of the 1930s, the happenings and alternative theaters of the 1960s, the popular and community theaters of the 1970s, and the radical theaters of Bertolt Brecht and Augusto Boal (Prentki and Preston 2009, 12). In particular, our work was influenced by *Teatro Campesino* (Farmworkers' Theater), a theatrical group founded in California in 1965 on the picket lines of Cesar Chavez's United Farmworkers Union. Rooted in a radical Latin American theater tradition, all of the original actors of the group were farmworkers, and they performed *actos*, or short skits, on flatbed trucks and in union halls enacting events inspired by their lives (Broyles-González 1994).

In our case, the central idea—inspired also in part by the work of the Sistren Theater Collective, a Jamaican women's organization that creates plays and performances drawn from the members' life experiences (Sistren, with Ford-Smith 2005), and by theories of "community theater" (Rodd 1988; Taylor 2003)—was to use the dramatic form as an instrument of public political engagement, to translate some of our research findings about immigrant workers' rights into a message that ordinary people could process. This approach would go well beyond the academic framework—well beyond the writing that any of us had previously attempted—in an effort to decolonize ethnographic knowledge, extending it beyond written ethnography.

Over the course of two years, the four of us met regularly to write and practice the play. Many other collaborators came and went during that time, contributing to the project in various and lasting ways. In consultation with other undocumented workers who participated, we decided to base the play on Mirian's work accident, recounted in chapter 2, which we developed (á la the Sistren methodology) (Sistren, with Ford-Smith 2005) from testimony to scripted performance. We also identified other themes that we wanted to touch upon in the play, including fear of deportation and separation from family. The pedagogical message of the play emerged out of our ethnographic fieldwork: that under U.S. law everyone has rights as workers regardless of their immigration status. We wanted to show that an undocumented worker has the right to bring her employer to court if her rights are violated and that an undocumented woman can in fact win back her rights if she stays strong and united with her community.

Mirian wrote the initial draft of her story, which others subsequently edited into scenes. Many of the characters in the play were based on real people from Mirian's experience, while others were created for dramatic purposes. "Manuela," for example, is a fictional character whom Mirian ("Roberta" in the play) meets in the hospital. Like many undocumented workers who are injured on the job, Manuela decides to return to Mexico, accepting her boss's hush money to disappear. Manuela's experience embodies the situation that many immigrants face after their accidents, in which they feel hopeless and alone, with no money and no job, and have to choose between returning home and staying in the United States. The ending of the play is meant to communicate the dangers that people face by not fighting for their rights.

We performed the play for the first time in August of 2015, as part of the *clausura*, the formal conclusion of our research project in Hometown. The stage was a bare floor at the front of Casa Hometown's main meeting hall, with some chairs and a few simple props. A capacity crowd had filled the rows of folding chairs, eager to view this extraordinary event. The lights dimmed.

FIGURE 5.1. The cast of the play. Illustration by Peter Quach.

SIN PAPELES, SIN MIEDO

Una obra de teatro de un acto
Escrito y producido por
Teatro Sin Papeles
Un proyecto de
Casa Hometown
Hometown, NJ

Reparto (en orden de aparición)

CABALLO	WILLIAM	MANUELA	DAISY
JULIA	HECTOR	DOCTORA	ADRIANA
ROBERTA	LUCINDA	JOSEFINA	

Escena 1

Hay un letrero en el escenario que dice "ESTABLO" y hay dos sillas. La cortina está cerrada y escuchamos un CABALLO relinchar (SFX). Luego JULIA grita en la oscuridad.

JULIA: ¡Suelte al caballo! ¡Suéeeeeltelo!

ROBERTA: ¡Ayyyyyyy!

Se abre la cortina y vemos a ROBERTA en el piso y oímos a un CABALLO salir corriendo (SFX). JULIA corre hacia ROBERTA.

ROBERTA: ¡Aaaaayyyyyyyyy! Me duele mucho, ¡no me puedo parar!

JULIA: ¡Doña Roberta! ¿Se encuentra bien? ¡Vi cómo la pisó el caballo! Déjeme ayudarla. Siéntese en este banco.

Caminan juntas hacia el banco.

ROBERTA: ¡Mira Julia cómo tengo mi pierna! Alguien llame a un médico por favor.

Entra WILLIAM con HECTOR.

WILLIAM: ¡Todos a trabajar! Esto no es nada. ¡Eso es lo que te pasa por no tener cuidado! ¿Cuántas veces te he dicho que tengas bien al caballo? ¡Es que ustedes no sirven para nada!

Examina la pierna de ROBERTA.

WILLIAM: No se fracturó. Peores cosas me han pasado a mí trabajando con los caballos. No es necesario ir al hospital.

UNDOCUMENTED, UNAFRAID

A play in one act
Written and produced by
Teatro Sin Papeles
A project of
Casa Hometown
Hometown, NJ

Cast (in order of appearance)

HORSE	WILLIAM	MANUELA	DAISY
JULIA	HECTOR	DOCTOR	ADRIANA
ROBERTA	LUCINDA	JOSEFINA	

Scene 1

On stage is a sign that reads "STABLE" and two chairs. The curtain is closed and we hear a HORSE whinny (SFX). Then, JULIA screams in the dark.

JULIA: Let go of the horse! Let it go!
ROBERTA: Ayyyyyyy!

The curtain opens and we see ROBERTA *on the floor and hear a* HORSE *galloping away (SFX).* JULIA *runs to* ROBERTA.

ROBERTA: Aaaaayyyyyyyy! It hurts so much, I can't get up!
JULIA: Doña Roberta! Are you okay? I saw the horse step on you! Let me help you. Sit on this bench.

They walk together to the bench.

ROBERTA: Julia, look at my leg! Somebody please call a doctor.

WILLIAM *enters with* HECTOR.

WILLIAM: Everyone back to work! This is nothing. This is what happens when you're careless! How many times have I told you to hold the horse tight? All of you are completely useless!

WILLIAM *examines* ROBERTA's *leg.*

WILLIAM: There's no fracture. Worse things have happened to me working with horses. No need to go to the hospital.

WILLIAM mira alrededor a JULIA y a HECTOR

WILLIAM: Y mucho menos llamar una ambulancia, ¿me oyen? Ustedes saben que si viene la ambulancia les van a mandar a la migra. Y nadie acá quiere que venga la migra.

WILLIAM sale con JULIA. ROBERTA se queda en el banco con HECTOR.

HECTOR: Tranquila Doña Roberta, acá pasan accidentes así todo el tiempo. Todo va a estar bien.

ROBERTA: ¿Y si no? Estamos totalmente aislados en esta finca y usted escuchó a Don William decir que está prohibido pedir una ambulancia.

Entra JULIA.

JULIA: Aquí le manda Don William, que se ponga este hielo y se tome estas pastillas, con esto se le va a quitar el dolor.

Le da unas pastillas y una bolsa de hielo a ROBERTA.

ROBERTA: ¿Qué clase de medicina es esa?

JULIA: Es medicina para caballo. Se llama Biú. Tómese dos. Esto le va a quitar el dolor.

ROBERTA no quiere tomarlas.

HECTOR: Yo he tomado Biú a veces. No se preocupe, la va a ayudar.

ROBERTA *(tomándose el Biú)*: A mí me gustaría ir al hospital . . .

WILLIAM *(desde lejos)*: ¡Julia! ¡Hector! Vuelvan a trabajar ahora mismo. ¡No estamos en hora de descanso!

JULIA *(mirando a Roberta)*: Todo va a estar bien Doña Roberta. Sólo quédese acá sentadita hasta que yo vuelva por usted.

ROBERTA: ¿A dónde voy a ir? No me puedo mover.

JULIA y HECTOR salen del escenario. Se cierra la cortina.

INFORME DE DERECHOS DE LXS TRABAJADORXS[4] 1 se proyecta en una pantalla mientras LUCINDA (desde lejos) lo lee.

LUCINDA: Cada trabajadora, sin importar su estatus migratorio, tiene derecho a recibir el salario mínimo federal. Quien trabaje horas extra tiene que recibir tiempo y medio del salario normal.

WILLIAM looks significantly at JULIA and HECTOR.

WILLIAM: And we certainly don't need to call an ambulance, you hear me? You know that if the ambulance comes, they will send you to *la migra*. And no one wants *la migra* to come.

WILLIAM exits with JULIA. ROBERTA stays on the bench with HECTOR.

HECTOR: Stay calm Doña Roberta, accidents like this happen here all the time. Everything's going to be fine.

ROBERTA: And if not? We are totally isolated on this farm, and you heard Don William say that it's forbidden to call for an ambulance.

JULIA enters.

JULIA: Don William says that you should put this ice on it and swallow these pills to take away the pain.

JULIA gives some pills and a bag of ice to ROBERTA.

ROBERTA: What kind of medicine is that?

JULIA: It's for horses. It's called Biu. Take two. This will kill the pain.

ROBERTA refuses to take the pills.

HECTOR: I've taken Biu sometimes. Don't worry, it will help.

ROBERTA *(taking the Biu)*: I would like to go to the hospital . . .

WILLIAM *(from offstage)*: Julia! Hector! Get back to work right now. This isn't break time!

JULIA *(to ROBERTA)*: Everything's going to be fine Doña Roberta. Just sit here until I come back for you.

ROBERTA: Where can I go? I can't move.

JULIA and HECTOR leave the stage. The curtain falls.

WORKERS' RIGHTS MESSAGE 1 is projected on a screen, while LUCINDA (off stage) reads it aloud.

LUCINDA: Every worker, regardless of immigration status, must be paid at least the federal minimum wage. Anyone who works overtime must be paid at least one and one-half times the regular rate of pay.

Escena 2

Otro día. Escuchamos un CABALLO relinchar (SFX). Se abre la cotina y vemos a WILLIAM. ROBERTA entra cojeando con JULIA.

WILLIAM: ¡Está tarde Roberta! Tú tienes que estar acá a las 5:00 de la mañana y ya son casi las 6:00.

ROBERTA: Esta medicina para caballo me da mucho sueño Don William. Además sólo me dura el efecto un momento. No puedo permanecer parada mucho tiempo. Llevo días tratando de trabajar, ¡pero no puedo!

WILLIAM: Tienes que hacer más ejercicio. Eso es lo que te hace falta. Ya han pasado cinco días desde que te caíste y tú sólo te andas quejando. Ya sabes que si no puedes trabajar pues hay muchos otros que querrían tu lugar.

JULIA: ¿Pero no ve su pierna toda hinchada e inflamada? ¡Apenas se puede parar!

WILLIAM: Es así cuando uno trabaja con caballos . . . Roberta, ha venido gente a visitarte. Yo ya te dije que *nadie* puede venir. ¿Me entiendes? *Nadie*. Acá dejamos que los trabajadores vivan en la finca, pero no somos un hotel.

Sale WILLIAM del establo. JULIA toca la frente de ROBERTA.

JULIA: Doña Roberta, ¡tiene fiebre! ¡Y mire! Le tiembla todo el cuerpo. Déjeme mirar su pierna.

ROBERTA se sube el pantalón y JULIA mira la pierna de ROBERTA.

JULIA: Doña Roberta, ¡usted tiene un hueco en esa pierna! ¡Qué infección que tiene! Creo que su vida corre peligro. No me importa lo que diga Don William, la voy a llevar ya al hospital.

Se cierra la cortina.

INFORME DE DERECHOS DE LXS TRABAJADORXS 2 se proyecta en una pantalla mientras LUCINDA (desde lejos) lo lee.

LUCINDA: Todas las patronas tienen que cumplir con la ley de OSHA (el Acta de Seguridad y Salud del Trabajo) que requiere que provean para sus empleadas un lugar de trabajo libre de peligros o riesgos para su salud y seguridad física. Cada empleada tiene derecho de trabajar en un lugar seguro, sin importar su estatus migratorio.

Scene 2

Another day. We hear a HORSE whinny (SFX). The curtain opens and we see WILLIAM. ROBERTA enters limping with JULIA.

WILLIAM: Roberta, you're late! You have to be here at 5:00 am and it's almost 6:00.

ROBERTA: This horse medicine makes me sleepy, Don William. Besides, the effect only lasts for a moment. I can't remain standing for long. I've been trying to work for days, but I can't do it!

WILLIAM: You need more exercise. That's what your problem is. It's been five days since you fell and you only go around complaining. You know that if you can't work there are many others who would want your place.

JULIA: But don't you see her leg all swollen and inflamed? She can barely keep up!

WILLIAM: This happens when you work with horses . . . Roberta, people have come to visit you. I already told you that *no one* can come. You understand me? *No one.* We let the workers live on the farm here, but this is not a hotel.

WILLIAM exits the stable. JULIA puts her hand to ROBERTA's forehead.

JULIA: Doña Roberta, you have a fever! And look! You're trembling all over. Let me look at your leg.

ROBERTA rolls up her pants and JULIA looks at ROBERTA's leg.

JULIA: Doña Roberta, you have an open wound! It looks like a bad infection! I think your life is in danger. I don't care what Don William says, I'm taking you to the hospital.

The curtain closes.

WORKERS' RIGHTS MESSAGE 2 is projected on a screen, while LUCINDA (off stage) reads it aloud.

LUCINDA: All employers must comply with OSHA, the Occupational Safety and Health Act, which requires employers to provide their employees with work free from health and safety hazards. Employers must ensure a safe workplace for all of their employees, regardless of immigration status.

Escena 3

Se abre la cortina. MANUELA Y ROBERTA *están sentadas lado a lado. Hay un letrero con una* CRUZ ROJA *que significa hospital.*

ROBERTA: Qué dolor que tengo, Dios mío. No sé qué voy a hacer. ¡Y tengo miedo de que venga la migra por mí!

MANUELA: ¡Por favor no hable tan duro! Vi a la policía afuera hace rato y yo no quiero problemas con Migración.

ROBERTA *(a ella misma)*: ¿Qué voy a hacer?

MANUELA: Cuénteme de su vida. ¿Cuál es su nombre? ¿Usted tiene familia?

ROBERTA: Sí. Me llamo Roberta. Tengo tres hijas, que ahora se quedan solas en Guatemala. Yo trabajaba allá haciendo medicinas naturales, sin embargo la plata no me alcanzó para pagar los gastos de la casa y del colegio, además del costo de la universidad. Mi hija mayor, Josefina, quiere ser ingeniera. ¿Y usted? ¿Cómo se llama?

MANUELA: Me llamo Manuela. Soy de México. Dejé a mis cinco hijos allá. Como usted, vine para ganar más, para que ellos tengan una vida mejor.

ROBERTA: ¿Hace cuánto tiempo esta aquí?

MANUELA: Diez años. ¿Y usted?

ROBERTA: Llegué hace cuatro años, la mayor parte aquí en Nueva Jersey. Trabajé seis meses en la finca de los caballos, antes de mi accidente.

MANUELA: Qué horror. ¿Dónde le duele?

ROBERTA: Me duele todo el lado izquierdo del cuerpo. Desde el cuello hasta la pierna. Ésta es la segunda vez que vengo al hospital. La primera vez me trajo una compañera y me pusieron una inyección. También me recetaron medicina para el dolor. Pero no me ha servido. ¡No puedo trabajar!

MANUELA: ¿Y su patrón qué le dice?

ROBERTA: ¡Ja! Es terrible el patrón. ¡Si fuera por el patrón yo no podría venir al hospital! Si le contara . . .

MANUELA: Puedo imaginármelo.

ROBERTA: Estoy esperando a mi compañera que me lleve de vuelta al trabajo. ¿Usted por qué está acá?

MANUELA: Mire, yo tuve un accidente también. Estaba trabajando en una fábrica y me cayeron unos estantes en la espalda. Creo que me rompí la pierna. Me duele mucho. El patrón me trajo al hospital esta tarde y se fue para su casa. Me dijo que diera un nombre falso y dijera que me caí en mi casa. Le hice caso, porque tengo miedo de que me pidan mis papeles.

ROBERTA: ¿Qué va a hacer?

Scene 3

The curtain opens. MANUELA and ROBERTA are sitting side by side. There is a sign with a RED CROSS.

ROBERTA: This pain, my god. I don't know what to do. And I'm afraid *la migra* may come for me!

MANUELA: Please keep your voice down! I saw the police outside a while ago and I don't want problems with Immigration.

ROBERTA *(to herself)*: What am I going to do?

MANUELA: Tell me about your life. What is your name? Do you have a family?

ROBERTA: Yes. My name is Roberta. I have three daughters, now living alone in Guatemala. I worked there making natural medicines, but the money wasn't enough to afford the home, school, plus the cost of college. My oldest daughter Josefina wants to be an engineer. And yourself? What's your name?

MANUELA: I'm Manuela. I'm from Mexico. I left my five children there. Like you, I came here to earn more, so they'd have a better life.

ROBERTA: How long have you been here?

MANUELA: Ten years. You?

ROBERTA: I arrived here in New Jersey four years ago. I worked for six months on the horse farm before my accident.

MANUELA: So terrible. Where does it hurt?

ROBERTA: The whole left side of my body hurts, from my neck to my leg. This is the second time I've been to the hospital. The first time a friend brought me and I got an injection. They also prescribed pain medication. But it hasn't helped me. I can't work!

MANUELA: And your boss, what does he say?

ROBERTA: Ha! He's a terrible boss. He wasn't even going to let me go to the hospital! If I were to tell you . . .

MANUELA: I can imagine.

ROBERTA: I'm waiting for my friend to take me back to work. Why are you here?

MANUELA: I had an accident, too. I was working in a factory and some shelves fell on my back. I think I broke my leg. It hurts a lot. My employer brought me to the hospital this afternoon and went home. He told me to give a false name and to say that I fell in my house. So I did, because I'm afraid that they'll ask for my papers otherwise.

ROBERTA: What are you going to do?

MANUELA: Creo que voy a ir a la Casa Hometown. Es un sitio que queda cerca de acá en donde ayudan a las personas como nosotras.

ROBERTA *(pensando)*: Casa Hometown? Hm, me suena familiar . . .

Entra una DOCTORA con JULIA.

DOCTORA: Señora Roberta, tenemos un problema. Llamamos al número de teléfono que nos diste del lugar donde trabajas y allá nos dicen que ellos no saben quién eres tú. Dicen que ninguna mujer trabaja allá. Necesitamos que alguien pague tu cuenta en el hospital. Como tu accidente fue en el trabajo, el seguro de tu patrón debe cubrir tus gastos. Pero si no tienes patrón, tú misma tienes que cubrir los gastos.

ROBERTA: ¿Cómo es que yo no trabajo allá? ¡Yo claro que trabajo allá! ¿Cómo más me iba a pisar un caballo? Déjeme ir a hablar con mi patrón. Ojalá que sea un malentendido.

DOCTORA: Está bien. Pero necesitas un tratamiento y no podemos darte el tratamiento hasta que se aclare el malentendido.

La DOCTORA sale. MANUELA pone su mano en la mano de ROBERTA.

MANUELA: Buena suerte Doña Roberta.

ROBERTA: Buena suerte a usted Doña Manuela.

Se cierra la cortina.

INFORME DE DERECHOS DE LXS TRABAJADORXS 3 se proyecta en una pantalla mientras LUCINDA (desde lejos) lo lee.

LUCINDA: Todas las patronas tienen que dar a sus empleadas el equipo necesario para protegerse contra los peligros que enfrentan en su trabajo. Las patronas pueden recibir multas en caso de no proveer el equipo necesario, sin importar del estatus migratorio de sus empleadas.

Escena 4

Escuchamos relinchar un CABALLO (SFX). Se abre la cortina. Está el letrero "ESTABLO" y los dos sillones. ROBERTA está entrando con muletas. En el establo está WILLIAM.

WILLIAM: ¡Roberta! ¿Qué estás pensando? ¿Cómo es posible que dieras mi nombre y el número de aquí en el hospital? ¿Sabes el problema que me has causado? Yo te dije claramente que no dieras mi nombre en el hospital.

MANUELA: I think I'll go to the Casa Hometown. It's a place near here where they help people like us.

ROBERTA *(thoughtful)*: Casa Hometown? Hm, that sounds familiar . . .

A DOCTOR enters with JULIA.

DOCTOR: Ms. Roberta, we have a problem. We called the phone number you gave us for where you work, and they say they don't know who you are. They say that no women work there. We need someone to pay your bill at the hospital. As your accident was at work, your employer's insurance should cover your expenses. But if you have no employer, you yourself have to cover the costs.

ROBERTA: How could I not work there? Of course I work there! How else would a horse step on me? Let me talk to my boss. Hopefully it's a misunderstanding.

DOCTOR: That's fine. But you need treatment and we cannot treat you until this misunderstanding is resolved.

The DOCTOR exits. Manuela puts her hand in ROBERTA's.

MANUELA: Good luck, Doña Roberta.

ROBERTA: Good luck to you, Doña Manuela.

The curtain closes.

WORKERS' RIGHTS MESSAGE 3 is projected on a screen, while LUCINDA (off stage) reads it aloud.

LUCINDA: All employers must provide workers with safety equipment for hazards faced in their jobs. Employers can be fined for not providing proper equipment to all workers, regardless of immigration status.

Scene 4

A HORSE whinnies (SFX). The curtain opens. There is the "STABLE" sign and the two chairs. ROBERTA enters on crutches. WILLIAM is in the barn.

WILLIAM: Roberta! What were you thinking? How could you give my name and this phone number at the hospital? Do you know the trouble you've caused me? I told you clearly not to give my name at the hospital.

ROBERTA: Me perdona patrón, pero cuando me preguntaron cómo me accidenté les tenía que decir. Y luego me pidieron su nombre para que su seguro cubra mis gastos.

WILLIAM: ¡Muéstrame tu Green Card y yo cubro tus gastos! ¿O es que quieres que te eche a la migra? Mira Roberta, yo no voy a permitir que tú me perjudiques. Te prohíbo absolutamente que hables con nadie, que recibas visitas o que salgas de esta finca. Tú no eres nadie. Te podría matar como si fueras un mosquito, ¿me entiendes? Tú no eres nadie.

Sale WILLIAM furioso. Entra JULIA.

JULIA: ¡Don William está furioso! Yo escuché lo que le dijo ahorita. Roberta, creo que su vida está en riesgo. El patrón la quiere matar. ¡Se tiene que escapar!

ROBERTA: Dios mío, ¿qué voy a hacer? Ni siquiera puedo caminar.

JULIA: Escóndase en el establo de atrás. Yo voy a distraer a Don William. Dentro de unos pocos minutos la saco a escondidas de acá.

ROBERTA se sienta al lado de los banquitos. JULIA sale del establo.

ROBERTA: Dice el patrón que no soy nadie, que no valgo nada. Pero, tengo mis sueños. Tengo mi música . . .

ROBERTA canta "Le Doy Gracias a Mi Dios que Está en el Cielo."

Le doy gracias al Señor que está en el cielo
Que me dio otra oportunidad
De estar siempre en esta tierra linda
Aunque soy discriminada de verdad
De estar siempre en esta tierra linda
Aunque soy discriminada de verdad
Inmigrante, así soy y así he sido
Pero siempre así he de luchar
Y aunque sufra, yo un día triunfaré
Con mi Dios al frente yo voy a ganar
Sí yo soy inmigrante, pero tengo mi valor
Sí yo soy inmigrante, pero tengo mi valor
Caminé yo por el desierto
Diez días yo no comí
Atravesé las fronteras y me escapé de morir
Atravesé las fronteras y me escapé de morir
Sólo Dios que está en el cielo un ángel mandó por mí

ROBERTA: *Patrón*, forgive me, but when they asked how the accident happened I had to answer them. And then they asked your name so your insurance could cover my expenses.

WILLIAM: Show me your green card and I will cover your expenses! Or do you want me to give you to *la migra?* Look Roberta: I will not allow you to slander me. I absolutely forbid you from talking to anyone, receiving visits, or leaving this farm. You are nobody. I could kill you like you were a mosquito, you understand me? You're nobody.

WILLIAM storms out. JULIA enters.

JULIA: Don William is furious! I heard what he told you just now. Roberta, I think your life is in danger. The *patrón* wants to kill you. You have to escape!

ROBERTA: My God, what am I going to do? I can't even walk.

JULIA: Hide in the back of the barn. I'll distract Don William. In a few minutes, I'll smuggle you out of here.

ROBERTA sits next to the benches. JULIA leaves the barn.

ROBERTA: The patrón says I'm nobody, that I'm worthless. But I have my dreams. I have my music . . .

ROBERTA sings "I Give Thanks to My God in Heaven."

I thank the Lord who is in heaven
Who gave me the opportunity
To be in this beautiful land
Though it's true I'm discriminated against
To be in this beautiful land
Though it's true I'm discriminated against
An immigrant, who I am and always will be
That's how I'll always fight
Though I suffer one day I'll triumph
With God leading the way, I will win
Yes, I'm an immigrant but I have value
Yes, I'm an immigrant but I am brave
I walked across the desert
For ten days and didn't eat
I crossed borders and escaped death
I crossed borders and escaped death
But God who is in heaven sent an angel for me

Sólo Dios que está en el cielo un ángel mandó por mí
Sólo Dios que está en el cielo un ángel mandó por mí
Sólo Dios que está en el cielo un ángel mandó por mí

Entra JULIA en silencio.

JULIA *(llevándose un dedo a los labios)*: Shhhhh.

JULIA ayuda a levantar a ROBERTA y salen los dos en silencio del establo. INFORME DE DERECHOS DE LXS TRABAJADORXS 4 se proyecta en una pantalla mientras LUCINDA (desde lejos) lo lee.

LUCINDA: Todas las patronas tienen que dar a sus empleadas la capacitación necesaria para realizar todas las tareas en sus trabajos en un idioma que la trabajadora entienda. Las patronas pueden recibir multas en caso de que no capaciten a sus empleadas, sin importar su estatus migratorio.

Escena 5

Se abre la cortina a una casa en Ciudad de Guatemala. ADRIANA y DAISY se sientan en el comedor de su casa en una mesa. Hay un letrero que dice "CIUDAD DE GUATEMALA." JOSEFINA entra a la casa cargando una caja de cartón mediana.

JOSEFINA *(entrando a la casa)*: Finalmente pude hablar con nuestra mami hoy.

DAISY *(preocupada)*: ¿Qué le pasó?

JOSEFINA: Tuvo un accidente en el trabajo. Me dijo que no les cuente a ustedes para que no se preocupen. Pero nosotras tenemos que apoyarnos entre nosotras y apoyar a nuestra mamá.

DAISY: ¿Y qué dijo? ¿Pero está bien?

JOSEFINA: Tiene mucho dolor en su espalda y su pierna, por ahora necesita encontrar un sitio en donde vivir. Ya no se puede quedar más en la finca en donde estaba trabajando.

DAISY: ¿Qué va a hacer?

JOSEFINA: Después hablamos de eso. ¡Hoy nos llegó esto! ¡Regalos de Navidad de mamá! *(señala la caja)*.

ADRIANA: ¡Síiii! ¡Regalos! Pero Navidad fue hace meses ya.

DAISY: ¡Yo le había dicho a mami que no nos mande regalos y se compre cosas para ella!

JOSEFINA: Tú sabes cómo es ella, Daisy. Si está en Estados Unidos es para podernos dar una mejor vida.

But God who is in heaven sent an angel for me
But God who is in heaven sent an angel for me
But God who is in heaven sent an angel for me

JULIA enters silently.

JULIA *(putting her finger to her lips)*: Shhhhh.

JULIA helps ROBERTA get up and they both leave the stable silently. WORKERS' RIGHTS MESSAGE 4 is projected on a screen, while LUCINDA (off stage) reads it aloud.

LUCINDA: All employers must provide workers with proper training for any job they are asked to perform. Training must be provided in a language the worker understands. Employers can be fined for not providing proper training to all workers, regardless of immigration status.

Scene 5

The curtain opens on a house in Guatemala City. ADRIANA and DAISY are sitting at the dining room table. A sign reads "GUATEMALA CITY." JOSE-FINA enters the house carrying a medium-size cardboard box.

JOSEFINA *(entering the house)*: I was finally able to talk to our mom today.
DAISY *(worried)*: What happened to her?
JOSEFINA: She had an accident at work. She told me not to say anything so you wouldn't worry. But we've got to stick together and support our mom.
DAISY: And what did she say? Is she okay?
JOSEFINA: She has a lot of pain in her back and leg, and now she needs to find a place to live. She can't stay on the farm where she was working.
DAISY: What is she going to do?
JOSEFINA: We'll talk about that later. Today we got this. Christmas gifts from mom! *(she indicates box)*.
ADRIANA: Yes! Presents! But Christmas was months ago.
DAISY: I'd told mommy not to send gifts for us and to buy things for herself!
JOSEFINA: You know how she is, Daisy. She's in the United States to give us a better life.

Ponen la caja sobre la mesa y la abren.

ADRIANA *(sacando un celular)*: ¡Un celular!

JOSEFINA: Sí. Tiene una pantalla para que podamos hablar con ella y verla. ¿Te gusta Adriana?

ADRIANA: ¡Sí!

ADRIANA *(sacando una chamarra de la caja y tratándosela de poner)*: Parece que es muy pequeña para mí.

JOSEFINA *(ayudándole a quitar la chamarra)*: Sí, es muy pequeña. Es que ya eres una niña muy grande. Has crecido muchísimo desde que mami se fue. Dame la chamarra, se la podemos dar a la hija de doña Aurelia.

ADRIANA *(sacando una muñeca de la caja)*: ¿Es que mami no sabe que ahora soy grande?

DAISY: Claro que sabe. Pero cuando se fue eras muy pequeña y los niños crecen muy rápido. Cuando hablemos con ella le pedimos una chamarra más grande para que sepa cuánto has crecido.

ADRIANA *(mirando la muñeca)*: No, no le digamos nada de la chamarra. No quiero que se ponga triste. ¿Puedo ir a jugar con mi muñeca?

JOSEFINA: ¡Ve a jugar, pues!

ADRIANA sale por una puerta hacia otro espacio de la casa. Se quedan JOSE-FINA y DAISY hablando en la mesa.

DAISY: ¿Qué le pasó entonces a mamá?

JOSEFINA: La verdad no entendí bien. Estaba mala la comunicación. Sé que no puede trabajar Daisy. Dice que tal vez se devuelva para acá.

DAISY: ¿Pero quién la va a curar acá? Tienen que curarla en el trabajo.

JOSEFINA: Eso le dije yo. Pero está muy preocupada. No por ella, por nosotras. Daisy, mami no nos va a poder seguir mandando plata. No en mucho tiempo. Hasta que pueda trabajar otra vez.

DAISY: ¿Qué vamos a hacer?

JOSEFINA: Bueno, mañana voy a ir a la universidad a retirar mi matrícula. Voy a hablar con Doña Aurelia y le voy a pedir que me dé trabajo.

DAISY: ¿Te vas a salir de la universidad y te vas a poner de costurera?

JOSEFINA: No hay nada más que pueda hacer. Tenemos que pagar los gastos de la casa, de tu colegio y el colegio de Adriana. Tú sabes que tenemos que mantener la casa estable para ella. He estado pensando. Si esto tarda mucho tiempo y mamá no puede trabajar, tal vez pueda irme yo también para los Estados Unidos. Así podría tener un trabajo que me paga en dólares y mandarles suficiente plata para la casa y la escuela de ustedes dos.

They put the box on the table and open it.

ADRIANA *(taking out a cell phone)*: A cell phone!

JOSEFINA: Yes. It has a screen so we can talk to her and see her. Do you like it Adriana?

ADRIANA: Yes!

ADRIANA *(taking out a jacket from the box and trying it on)*: This is very small for me.

JOSEFINA *(helping her take off the jacket)*: Yes, it is small. That's because you're a big girl now. You've grown a lot since mom left. Give me your jacket, we can give it to Doña Aurelia for her daughter.

ADRIANA *(taking a doll from the box)*: Mommy doesn't know how big I am now?

DAISY: Of course she does. But when she left you were very small, and children grow fast. When we talk to her we'll ask for a bigger jacket so she'll know how much you've grown.

ADRIANA *(looking at the doll)*: No, don't say anything about the jacket. I don't want her to be sad. Can I go play with my doll?

JOSEFINA: Go play!

ADRIANA exits through a door into another room of the house. JOSEFINA and DAISY continue talking at the table.

DAISY: So what happened to mom?

JOSEFINA: Actually, I didn't quite understand. The connection was bad. I know she can't work, Daisy. She says maybe she'll come back here.

DAISY: But who's going to help her here? They have to help her at her work.

JOSEFINA: So I told her. But she's very worried. Not for herself, for us. Daisy, mommy is not going to be able to keep sending us money. Not for a long time. Not until she can work again.

DAISY: What are we going to do?

JOSEFINA: Well, tomorrow I will go to the university and cancel my registration. I'll talk with Doña Aurelia and I'll ask her to give me work.

DAISY: You're going to leave college and go work as a seamstress?

JOSEFINA: There's nothing else to be done. We have to pay for the house, for your and Adriana's school. You know we have to maintain a stable home for her. I've been thinking. If it takes a long time and mom can't work, maybe I can go to the United States. That way I could have a job that pays me in dollars and send you enough money for the house and school for you both.

DAISY: Y yo me quedo sola con Adriana?

JOSEFINA: Hay veces en que lo único que queda es irnos pal Norte.

ADRIANA entra al comedor con la muñeca.

ADRIANA: ¡Me encanta mi muñeca! ¡Vengan a jugar!

JOSEFINA abraza a ADRIANA.

JOSEFINA: ¡Vamos entonces a jugar!

Salen las tres del comedor. Queda encima de una silla la chamarra demasiado pequeña. Se cierra la cortina.

INFORME DE DERECHOS DE LXS TRABAJADORXS 5 se proyecta en una pantalla mientras LUCINDA (desde lejos) lo lee.

LUCINDA: Todas las trabajadoras, sin importar su estatus migratorio, tienen derecho a recibir compensación en caso de lesión o muerte en el trabajo. En el estado de Nueva Jersey, la patrona o su empresa de seguros tiene que pagar los gastos médicos de sus empleadas, así como sus salarios perdidos por discapacidad temporal o permanente.

Escena 6

Hay un escritorio con una silla al frente a un letrero que dice "CASA HOME-TOWN." LUCINDA está sentada en un escritorio. ROBERTA está sentada al frente del escritorio.

ROBERTA: Muchas gracias por recibirme Doña Lucinda. Yo conocí a Doña Manuela en el hospital y ella me mandó para acá. Me dijo que ustedes depronto me puedan ayudar.

LUCINDA: Sí, para eso estamos acá. Para ayudarnos entre la comunidad inmigrante. Yo recuerdo cuando llegué a este país, no tenía nada. Fue gracias a la comunidad que yo me pude superar. Unidos logramos más.

LUCINDA saca una carpeta del escritorio y la abre.

LUCINDA: Cuando hablamos por teléfono usted me contó que tuvo un accidente de trabajo hace unas semanas y tuvo que salir huyendo. Ha hablado con un abogado ya?

ROBERTA: Fíjese que un amigo me llevó a consultar con un abogado, pero él quiere cobrarme $500 antes de hacer nada. No tengo plata. Pero todavía a mí me duele mucho la espalda. Al principio era mi pierna, pero ahora sobre todo me duele acá (se toca el hombro izquierdo).

DAISY: And I'd stay alone with Adriana?

JOSEFINA: There are times when the only thing left to do is to go to the North.

ADRIANA enters the dining room with the doll.

ADRIANA: I love my doll! Come play!

JOSEFINA hugs ADRIANA.

JOSEFINA: Let's play then!

The three leave the dining room. On a chair, the too-small jacket remains.
The curtain closes.
WORKERS' RIGHTS MESSAGE 5 is projected on a screen, while LUCINDA
(off stage) reads it aloud.

LUCINDA: All workers, regardless of immigration status, are entitled to receive workers' compensation benefits in case of an injury or death on the
job. In the state of New Jersey, the employer or its insurance company
must pay for the worker's medical treatment, temporary disability benefits in place of wages lost, and benefits for permanent disability.

Scene 6

There is a desk with a chair in front of it, and a sign that says "CASA
HOMETOWN." LUCINDA sits at the desk. ROBERTA sits on the chair in front.

ROBERTA: Thank you very much for seeing me, Doña Lucinda. I met Doña
Manuela in the hospital and she sent me here. She said that maybe you
can help me.

LUCINDA: Yes, that's what we're here for. To help each other in the immigrant community. I remember when I came to this country, I had nothing. It was thanks to the community that I could overcome my struggles.
United we achieve more.

LUCINDA takes out a desktop folder and opens it.

LUCINDA: When we talked on the phone you told me you had a work accident a few weeks ago and had to flee. Have you spoken to a lawyer yet?

ROBERTA: My friend took me to see a lawyer, but he wants to charge me $500
before doing anything. I don't have any money. But my back still hurts a
lot. At first it was my leg, but now it especially hurts here (she touches her
left shoulder).

LUCINDA: En este caso la vamos a llevar otra vez a la doctora. También puede consultar con una buena abogada, la que colabora con nosotros. Usted tiene derechos en este país, aunque no tenga papeles. ¿Dónde está viviendo actualmente?

ROBERTA: Tuve que salir de la finca corriendo. No tengo casa. Me estoy quedando en donde una amiga en Lakewood. Pero ella comparte su casa con otras dos familias, entonces no sé por cuánto tiempo me pueda quedar allá.

LUCINDA: Todo va a estar mejor ahora. Se puede quedar en mi casa hasta que encuentre algo.

Se cierra la cortina.

INFORME DE DERECHOS DE LXS TRABAJADORXS 6 se proyecta en una pantalla mientras LUCINDA (desde lejos) lo lee.

LUCINDA: Ningúna empleada puede ser despedida por pedir compensación después de un accidente de trabajo. Es ilegal que una patrona despida a una empleadoa por exigir su derecho de compensación y de trato médico después de sufrir una lesión.

Escena 7

Se abre la cortina. Están las dos sillas y el letrero del hospital. En una silla está ROBERTA. La DOCTORA está a su lado.

ROBERTA: Doctora, dígame por favor qué tengo. Han pasado unos meses desde mi accidente, pero me duele tanto la espalda que todavía no puedo caminar.

DOCTOR: Sabemos finalmente lo que te pasa, Roberta. Estás herida en tu columna vertebral donde te pisó el caballo. Necesitas un trasplante del cuarto disco vertebral.

ROBERTA: ¿Me van a operar? ¿Cuándo podré trabajar? No puedo mandarles plata a mis hijas y la mayor quiere venirse para acá a trabajar.

DOCTORA: Sí, te vamos a operar. Tardarás varios meses en poder caminar bien. Pero tu patrón todavía niega que tú hayas trabajado anteriormente en su finca. No quiere pagar nada de los gastos. Además, tienes una deuda pendiente con el hospital de la primera vez que viniste, cuando te pasó el accidente. No podemos seguir adelante hasta que no pagues tu deuda. Puedes ir a tu casa mientras tanto.

ROBERTA: ¡Pero ni siquiera tengo suficiente para vivir! Vivo hace meses de la caridad de Doña Lucinda y sólo he podido hacer unos ahorritos de lo que me pagan por ahí por cantar canciones en la calle.

LUCINDA: We're going to take you back to the doctor then. You can also consult a good lawyer who works with us. You have rights in this country, even if you don't have papers. Where are you living now?

ROBERTA: I had to run away from the farm. I don't have a place to live. I'm staying at a friend's place in Lakewood. But she shares her home with two other families, so I don't know how long I can stay there.

LUCINDA: Everything will be okay now. You can stay at my house until you find something.

Curtain closes.

WORKERS' RIGHTS MESSAGE 6 is projected on a screen, while LUCINDA (off stage) reads it aloud.

LUCINDA: A worker cannot be fired for seeking compensation following an injury. It is illegal for an employer to fire a worker who seeks her right to compensation and medical care following an injury.

Scene 7

Curtain opens on the two chairs and the RED CROSS hospital sign. ROBERTA is seated in one chair. The DOCTOR is at her side.

ROBERTA: Doctor, please tell me what I have. It's been months since my accident, but my back hurts so much that I still can't walk.

DOCTOR: We now know what happened to you, Roberta. You injured your spine when the horse stepped on you. You need a transplant of the fourth vertebral disc.

ROBERTA: You're going to operate on me? When can I work? I can't send money to my daughters, and my eldest wants to come over here to work.

DOCTOR: Yes, we will perform surgery. It will take you several months to be able to walk properly. But your employer still denies that you previously worked on his farm. He refuses to pay any of your expenses. You also have a debt to the hospital from the first time you came, when you had your accident. We can't go forward with the surgery until you pay your debt. You can go home until then.

ROBERTA: But I don't even have enough to live! I've survived on Doña Lucinda's charity for months now, and I've only been able to save a small amount of the money I get singing my songs on the street.

DOCTOR: Hay Charity Care para los que no pueden pagar, pero no cubre todo. No sé que más decirte.

Se cierra la cortina.

Escena 8

Se abre la cortina al letrero de "CASA HOMETOWN."

ROBERTA está sentada en el escritorio con un cuello ortopédico. Apenas se puede mover. MANUELA está sentada frente a ella, también le cuesta moverse, su pierna está inmovilizada al lado de muletas. LUCINDA está hablando por teléfono atrás.

ROBERTA: ¿Pero qué se va a ir a hacer a México Doña Manuela? Su pierna todavía no está bien.

MANUELA: Estoy cansada Doña Roberta. Cansada de luchar. La abogada dice que no me puede seguir ayudando porque di un nombre falso cuando llegué al hospital y el juez ahora no me cree nada de lo que digo de mi accidente. El patrón me ha ofrecido pagarme el tiquete de vuelta a México además de 1,000 dólares en efectivo.

ROBERTA: ¡Pero precisamente por eso! Él le ofrece el tiquete y la plata porque sabe que le va a tocar pagarle mucho más al final por el accidente.

MANUELA: Pero es que mi patrón no tenía seguro a diferencia del suyo.

ROBERTA: ¿Qué importa que no tenga seguro? Eso es problema de él. La ley dice que cualquier empresa o empleador tiene que tener seguro y si no lo tiene pues él personalmente le tiene que pagar a usted. Sea paciente Doña Manuela. ¿Quién la va a curar en México? ¿El Estado? ¡Ja! ¿Qué va a hacer si su pierna no lo deja trabajar? Si se va cierran su caso y todo estará perdido.

MANUELA: No aguanto más esta situación. Llevo casi un año sin trabajar y mi familia necesita que envíe dinero. Hoy por la tarde salgo para México. Vine a despedirme de usted y a desearle suerte en su recuperación.

ROBERTA se para con mucho esfuerzo y MANUELA también se para con esfuerzo. ROBERTA camina hacia ella y la abraza. LUCINDA se acerca y las abraza también.

ROBERTA: Vaya con Dios, Doña Manuela.

MANUELA sale.

LUCINDA: Roberta, hablé una vez más con su abogada. Por fin la corte ha aceptado su caso y va a haber un juicio contra su ex patrón.

DOCTOR: There is Charity Care for those who cannot pay, but it doesn't cover everything. I don't know what else to tell you.

Curtain closes.

Scene 8

Curtain opens on the sign for "CASA HOMETOWN."
ROBERTA is sitting at the desk with a neck brace. She can barely move. MANUELA is sitting across from her next to a pair of crutches. She also has trouble moving and her leg is immobilized. LUCINDA is behind them on the phone.

ROBERTA: But what are you going to do in Mexico, Doña Manuela? Your leg is still not right.

MANUELA: Doña Roberta, I'm tired. Tired of fighting. The lawyer says he can't keep helping me because I gave a false name when I arrived at the hospital, and now the judge doesn't believe anything I say about my accident. My employer has offered to buy me a return ticket to Mexico plus $1,000 in cash.

ROBERTA: But that's just why you should stay! He's offering the ticket and cash because he knows that in the end he'll pay you a lot more for the accident.

MANUELA: But unlike yours, my employer was uninsured.

ROBERTA: It doesn't matter that he has no insurance! That's his problem. The law says that any employer must have insurance and if he does not then he will personally have to pay you. Be patient Doña Manuela. Who will heal you in Mexico? The state? Ha! What will you do if you can't work because of your leg? If you leave, your case will be closed and all will be lost.

MANUELA: I can't bear this situation any longer. I have spent almost a year without work and my family needs me to send money. This afternoon I am leaving for Mexico. I came to say goodbye to you and wish you luck in your recovery.

ROBERTA gets up with great effort and MANUELA also stands with effort. ROBERTA walks over to her and hugs her. LUCINDA approaches and hugs them, too.

ROBERTA: Go with God, Doña Manuela.

MANUELA exits.

LUCINDA: Roberta, I spoke with your lawyer again. The court has finally accepted your case, and there will be a trial against your former employer.

ROBERTA: ¿Es posible que una corte de los Estados Unidos me va a apoyar? No tengo papeles ni visa. ¿Cómo me va a apoyar en contra de un ciudadano, hombre blanco y rico que habla bien el inglés?

LUCINDA: No debe importar Roberta. Toda persona tiene derechos en este país. Sin embargo, para presionar al juez vamos a organizar una protesta frente a la corte antes del juicio.

ROBERTA: ¡Ojalá que el juez sea justo!

Se cierra la cortina.

INFORME DE DERECHOS DE LXS TRABAJADORXS 7 se proyecta en una pantalla mientras LUCINDA (desde lejos) lo lee.

LUCINDA: Ningúna empleada puede ser despedida por denunciar ante OSHA la existencia de una violación de su seguridad en el lugar de trabajo. Cada trabajadora, sin importar su estatus migratorio, tiene el derecho de pedir una inspección de OSHA cuando corre peligro en su lugar de trabajo.

Escena 9

Se abre la cortina. Varias personas están marchando frente a la corte. Cargan pancartas con mensajes exigiendo el apoyo de la corte para los inmigrantes y para ROBERTA. LUCINDA pide a la gente que escuche.

LUCINDA: Señoras y señores, gracias por venir para apoyar a nuestra compañera Roberta, quien sufrió una lesión grave hace varios meses. Su patrón no quería pagar sus gastos médicos y Roberta no ha podido tener una operación que necesita para curarse. Ahora, con la ayuda de Casa Hometown y nuestra amiga la abogada, esperamos los resultados del juicio para decidir el caso.

La GENTE gritando, apoyando, aplaudiendo.

LUCINDA: Ahora quisiera presentarles a la persona que ha sufrido tanto por ser trabajadora indocumentada en este país. Roberta, por favor.

La GENTE aplaude. ROBERTA se aproxima.

ROBERTA: Gracias a todas las compañeras y compañeros que me han apoyado hoy en día. Quisiera cantarles algo, si me permiten. Esta canción trata de una amiga que se llamaba Manuela. Nos conocimos en el hospital, las dos heridas de accidentes de trabajo. Yo me quedé para exigir mis derechos, mientras Doña Manuela volvió a México para estar con su familia. Ayer, recibimos noticias de que Manuela falleció en México

ROBERTA: Is it even possible that a court in the United States will support me? I have no papers or visa. Would they support me against a citizen, a rich, white man who speaks good English?

LUCINDA: It shouldn't matter, Roberta. Everyone has rights in this country. However, to pressure the judge, before the trial we will organize a demonstration outside the courthouse.

ROBERTA: Hopefully the judge will be fair!

Curtain closes.

WORKERS' RIGHTS MESSAGE 7 is projected on a screen, while LUCINDA (off stage) reads it aloud.

LUCINDA: A worker cannot be fired for reporting a safety violation or workplace hazard to OSHA. All workers, regardless of immigration status, have the right to request an OSHA inspection when facing a danger at work.

Scene 9

The curtain rises. A crowd of people is demonstrating in front of the court. They carry banners with messages demanding that the court support migrants and support ROBERTA. LUCINDA asks them to listen.

LUCINDA: Ladies and gentlemen, thank you for coming to support our *compañera* Roberta, who suffered a serious injury several months ago. Her employer refuses to pay her medical expenses, and Roberta has not been able to get the surgery she needs to get better. Today, with the help of Casa Hometown and our friend the lawyer, we await the results of the trial to decide the case.

PEOPLE shouting, supporting, applauding.

LUCINDA: Now, let me introduce you to the person who has suffered so much for being an undocumented worker in this country. Roberta, please.

PEOPLE applaud. ROBERTA approaches.

ROBERTA: Thank you to all of you who have supported me today. I'd like to sing you a song, if I may. This song is about a friend of mine named Manuela. We met at the hospital, both of us injured in work accidents. I stayed here to demand my rights, but Doña Manuela returned to Mexico to be with her family. Yesterday, we received news that Manuela died in por complicaciones médicas relacionadas a su accidente. Esta canción la dedico a su memoria.

ROBERTA canta "Las Accidentadas."

Voy a contarles la historia
De una mujer especial
Que se llamaba Manuela
La encontre en el hospital
Éramos accidentadas
Y nos fuimos a curar
Manuela no dio su nombre
Tampoco sus apellidos
Ni dirección de su casa
Su patrón le habia prohibido
Perdió todos sus derechos
Por aceptar la mentira
Su patrón también le dijo
Acepta este dinero
Te compraré tu boleto
Y te vas para tu pueblo
Te compraré tu boleto
Y te vas para tu pueblo
No duró ya mucho tiempo
Y hoy Manuela está muerta
Adiós Manuela querida
Hoy te estamos despidiendo
Adiós Manuela querida
Hoy te estamos despidiendo
Y su patrón ni en cuenta
De lo que hoy está pasando
Patrón, que Diós tome en cuenta
La injusticia que has dado
Patrón, que Diós tome en cuenta
La injusticia que has dado

LUCINDA está hablando por su celular. La GENTE aplaude. Una vez que termina ROBERTA, LUCINDA se aproxima una vez más muy animada.

LUCINDA: Roberta, acabé de hablar con su abogada. ¡Usted ganó! ¡Ganó su caso!

Mexico from medical complications related to her accident. This song is dedicated to her memory.

ROBERTA sings "The Injured."

I will tell you the story
Of a special lady
Whose name was Manuela
We met at the hospital
We were both injured
And wanted to get well
Manuela didn't give the hospital
Her real name
Nor her home address
Her boss had forbidden it
She lost all her rights
For agreeing to lie
Her boss also told her
Accept this money
I'll buy you a ticket
To go back home
I'll buy you a ticket
To go back home.
It wasn't that long ago
And now Manuela is dead
Farewell dear Manuela
Today we tell you goodbye
Farewell dear Manuela
Today we tell you goodbye
And her *patrón* has no idea
Of what's happened to her
Patrón, may God take account of
The injustice you have done
Patrón, may God take account of
The injustice you have done

LUCINDA is talking on her cell phone. PEOPLE applaud. Once she finishes, LUCINDA approaches again, excited.

LUCINDA: Roberta, I just talked to your lawyer. You won! You won your case!

ROBERTA: Dios mío, ¿cómo es posible?

LUCINDA: Según la ley, cualquier obrera u obrero tiene derecho de atención médica en caso de un accidente sufrido en el transcurso de su trabajo. No importa si es ciudadana o no.

JULIA: ¿Entonces el patrón tiene que pagar los gastos médicos?

LUCINDA: Sí Julia. El patrón tiene que pagar todos los gastos médicos, incluso la deuda de la primera visita. En otras palabras, usted puede tener su operación.

Muchos aplausos.

ROBERTA: ¡Qué maravilla!

LUCINDA: Además el patrón tiene que pagar un monto por todo el salario perdido mientras usted está incapacitada.

ROBERTA: ¡Tengo que llamar a mis hijas! Josefina no tiene que migrar y puede volver a la universidad. Muchas gracias Doña Lucinda. Nada de esto hubiera pasado sin la ayuda de Casa Hometown.

LUCINDA (*hablando al público*): Pero así debe ser la justicia Roberta. No sale así todas las veces. Muchos sufren por sus accidentes y después son victimizados por segunda vez por la policía, la migra, y la corte que no les ayudan, sino más bien los perjudican por no tener papeles. Todos los que están aquí corren riesgos siempre. Sin embargo, la ley dice que todos los que trabajan en este país tienen ciertos derechos en común.

INFORME DE DERECHOS DE LXS TRABAJADORXS RESUMEN se proyecta en una pantalla mientras LUCINDA lo lee.

LUCINDA (*a la audiencia*): Todas los trabajadoras, sin importar su estatus migratorio, tienen estos derechos:

- El derecho a un salario mínimo, con tiempo y medio para las horas extras
- El derecho a un lugar de trabajo seguro y saludable
- El derecho a recibir equipo y capacitación
- El derecho a recibir trato médico y compensación en caso de lesión o muerte en el trabajo
- El derecho a reportar violaciones de sus derechos a OSHA, sin miedo de ser despedida

ROBERTA: Es esencial que tengamos el coraje para exigir nuestros derechos. No nos los van a dar sin que luchemos.

TODOS: ¡Sin papeles, sin miedo! ¡Sin papeles, sin miedo!

ROBERTA, JULIA y LUCINDA se abrazan. Se apaga la luz, las voces siguen gritando hasta que se desvanecen lentamente.

ROBERTA: My God, is it possible?

LUCINDA: Under the law, any worker is entitled to healthcare in case of an accident in the course of their work. No matter if you are a citizen or not.

JULIA: Then, the employer has to pay her medical expenses?

LUCINDA: Yes Julia. The employer must pay all medical expenses, including debts from the first hospital visit. In other words, you can have your surgery.

Much applause.

ROBERTA: How wonderful!

LUCINDA: In addition, the employer must pay the full amount of lost wages while you are disabled.

ROBERTA: I have to call my daughters! Josefina doesn't have to come and she can go back to college. Thank you so much, Doña Lucinda. None of this would have happened without the help of Casa Hometown.

LUCINDA (to the audience): But this is how the justice system should work, Roberta. It doesn't always work this way. Many people suffer from their accidents, and then are victimized a second time by the police, the immigration office, and the court. Instead of helping, they harm them further for being undocumented. Everyone here is always at risk. However, the law says that everyone who works in this country has certain rights in common.

WORKERS' RIGHTS MESSAGE SUMMARY is projected on a screen, while LUCINDA reads it aloud.

LUCINDA (to the audience): All workers, regardless of immigration status, have these rights:

- The right to be paid minimum wage and overtime
- The right to a safe and healthy workplace
- The right to safety equipment and training
- The right to medical care and compensation in case of an injury or death on the job
- The right to report violations of their rights to OSHA, without fear of employer retaliation

ROBERTA: It is vital that we have the courage to demand our rights. We will never get them without a fight.

ALL: Undocumented, unafraid! Undocumented, unafraid!

ROBERTA, JULIA, and LUCINDA embrace. The lights go out, the chanting continues and fades out.

Conclusion

The panorama we face as scholars and intellectuals concerned and critical of the formation, transformations, and current persistence of the colonial matrix of power is not
so much the "study of colonialism" or "postcolonial studies" around the world but the
need to "decolonize knowledge." And decolonization of knowledge can hardly be at-
tained from within Western categories of thought—neither Spinoza nor Nietzsche will
do. We need to move in different directions.

—MADINA TLOSTANOVA AND WALTER MIGNOLO,
Learning to Unlearn: Decolonial Reflections from Eurasia and the Americas

The principal contention of this book has been that anthropology and, more
generally, social science as a set of ideas and practices—despite decades of
introspection, deconstruction, and auto-critique—remain deeply colonial,
embodying, benefiting from, and contributing to the maintenance of
Western imperial power. Aside from its institutional hierarchies and gate-
keeping strategies, anthropology's coloniality is expressed in its characteristic
method of ethnography and reproduced through its forms of theorizing and
writing. We have suggested that the best and only way to counter colonial
anthropology and its principal method, ethnography, is to rethink research
at every level, from conception to practice to write-up and dissemination.
Perhaps most critically, an anti-colonial social science decenters the scien-
tist as the principal actor in designing and enacting research. It recognizes
the historical "subjects" of anthropological research—themselves often the
subjects of (neo)colonial aggression and exploitation—as more than merely
the objects of ethnographic investigation. Rather, it acknowledges them as
capable producers of knowledge and theorists of their own experience. A

decolonial anthropology decenters academic knowledge as the exclusive goal of social research and decenters academic writing as its exclusive result. Instead, it locates a project of engaged political action—what earlier decolonial anthropologists termed *liberation* or, more recently, *activism*—at the heart of its practice (Allen and Jobson 2016; Gordon 1991; Harrison 1991a). This, we believe, is not only a productive way to do research, but an ethical imperative facing contemporary social science. As Andre Gunder Frank put it in 1969, it is the responsibility of the researcher "to use anthropology only as far is it is sufficient, while doing whatever is necessary to replace the nearly worldwide violent, exploitative, racist, alienative capitalist class system, which embraces most anthropologists and the people they study" (Frank 1969, 137). We would offer the same assertion today.

As we have discussed throughout, this approach did not originate with us, the authors of this book. Our intervention stands on the shoulders of the many individuals, schools, and perspectives variously labeled feminist, native, Black, collaborative, World, applied, engaged, practicing, and activist, to name but a few. What we have tried to do in this book is to draw upon the innovations and insights of these various anthropological approaches and to recenter them within a broader, synthesized twenty-first-century ethnographic methodology that can supplant that of dominant colonial anthropology. In the course of our discussion, we have explored one way of enacting a decolonial, anti-imperial approach, in our case by providing the basic instruments and perspectives of ethnography to nonprofessional researchers involved in our project and offering them the opportunity to join their ethnographic practice to their work as activists for social justice. We do not mean for this methodological suggestion to be prescriptive, but rather to stand as one example of how ethnography can be combined effectively with liberation work. In our case, this approach emerged as a creative expression not from the imaginations of the social scientists but from the lives, experiences, and goals of two inspiring women who participated in the research.

In undertaking ethnographic work of the kind described in the preceding chapters, it was critical to attend to the various labels and social positions that mark the research participants. This project focused on undocumented immigrants in the United States, who may be counted among the most oppressed and harassed people living within the national space of North American society. This political and subject position oriented the perspectives of the various research collaborators, particularly those of Lucy and Mirian, who became integral members of the research team. We also tried to call attention to the positionalities of the other team members, Daniel and Carolina, recognizing the need to mark what typically passes as the un-marked subjectivities of outsider ethnographers, and in doing so acknowl-edged our projects' embeddedness in the nearly inescapable coloniality of modern life. Thus, the racialized and gendered subjectivities of the research-ers were of central relevance to the project's outcomes, another point we raised throughout the book.

Chela Sandoval and other feminist decolonial scholars argue that the subjectivities of women of color are especially impacted by what we have identified here as coloniality.[1] As a result, these scholars contend, in their everyday lives and the strategies they adopt women of color can especially embody the techniques and actions needed to disrupt overlapping systems of oppression. Through their embodied existence as undocumented women—and particularly as undocumented women of color—Lucy and Mirian dis-rupt the liberal rights discourse that excludes them in this country by mo-bilizing a theory of undocumentation that emphasizes a need for solidarity and collective action. When they pulled together to organize the work-ers and immigrant residents of Hometown—their activism fueled by the knowledge and interpersonal connections developed through their ethno-graphic work—Lucy and Mirian created the pathways necessary to unsettle the racist, capitalist, patriarchal discourse on citizen rights in the United States. Their assertion that immigrants do have rights—against the state and capitalist employers seeking to deny them those rights—represents a stance, embodied in the physical form of the injured worker, against the limits that citizenship supposedly places on who can be a legitimate rights bearer. In other words, by claiming rights for injured undocumented work-ers, Lucy and Mirian are challenging the claim that only citizens are en-titled to rights in the United States. They are instead proposing a counter-claim that grounds those rights in the contributions made by those workers while referencing their basic humanity as entitling them to fair treatment under the law.

Personal Transformations

The project described in this book had powerful impacts for all four of us who participated in it as ethnographer activists. As the outsider ethnogra-phers on the research team, Carolina and Daniel came to Hometown with certain expectations and goals in mind. These were both academic and ac-tivist in nature—Caro hoped to conduct her dissertation research as part of the larger project, Daniel to collect data for a book on immigration and workers' rights, both of them concerned to make this information somehow productive for the local community and its advocates.

In their years working in Hometown, however, these priorities shifted. After studying for her dissertation on the coalition between African Americans and jornaleros that resulted in the creation of Casa Hometown (narrated in chapter 3), Caro became very interested in the relation between African Americans and the immigrants' rights movement, a topic that is at the center of her research today. Also, after working with Mirian, Lucy, and Daniel in writing a play and inspired by Mirian's songs, Caro became interested in the use of different forms of "artivism" in the U.S. immigrants' rights movement (see Nossel 2016), another focus of her current research. Today, having finished her degree, she is a professor in the Department of Latino and Caribbean Studies at Rutgers University, teaching about feminism, artivism, and community organizing. As an activist-scholar, she organizes with a community center that offers services to the Latinx community in New Brunswick, where Rutgers is located, and she is imagining and implementing ways to use her class as a means to go beyond the division that exists between Rutgers students and the broader New Brunswick community. She now sees herself as an ethnographer, too, and ethnography as inseparable from activism, but Caro ultimately remains skeptical about anthropology as a discipline, and disciplinary boundaries in general. Although she believes in the potential for social transformation and decolonization of an activist ethnographic practice, Carolina remains uncertain about the possibility of decolonizing anthropology, as she believes that the decolonization of disciplinary knowledge requires a turn toward inter- and transdisciplinarity.[2]

For his part, Daniel believes ethnography to be a powerful tool for social change, a vision reinforced by his experiences with this project and this group of researchers. He has faith that disciplinary anthropology can transform itself in ways imagined in this book, through close scrutiny of its own coloniality and a willingness by its practitioners to change their ways of doing research and writing. However, despite four years of intensive study, Daniel has become cautious about writing academically about immigrant suffering, unwilling to pursue scholarship that would profit from the unacceptable conditions immigrants experience in U.S. society. Although he recognizes the many important contributions made by anthropologists and other scholars of immigration, he no longer feels comfortable doing that work himself. During the life of the project, Daniel's main objective shifted away from academic research and toward collaboration, working with local advocacy organizations in support of immigrant rights while providing mentorship for the less-experienced researchers on the team. He now hopes to explore other genres of writing, including fiction and (inspired by this project) drama, to discuss the situation facing undocumented immigrants in the United States, with the hope of reaching audiences outside academia.

As previous chapters illustrated, Lucy and Mirian made extensive and invaluable contributions to the research project. Perhaps more remarkable, though, were the impacts that Lucy and Mirian's work as ethnographers had on them individually. As mentioned, at the outset of the project Mirian was in constant pain as a result of her work accident and had lost the ability to send money home to her children in Guatemala. Lucy, meanwhile, had been deeply disturbed by her husband's arrest and had only recently begun to awaken (as she put it) to the problems facing the undocumented community. While they were both happy to have the well-paying jobs that the project offered them, at the outset they were very uncertain about their ability to do the work that it required. But through patient mentoring and their dedication to the project, Mirian and Lucy discovered that they were capable of doing research and doing it well. Both Lucy and Mirian reported feelings of anxiety about doing ethnographic work, but they felt sustained by the other members of the research team. The four of us had weekly meetings and conversations, shared our findings and emerging interpretations, and helped navigate tricky situations that arose. We also socialized, getting to know each other's families and personal lives. The result was a spirit of camaraderie, with a shared commitment to the research project and to the defense of immigrants' rights. As Mirian wrote in her fieldnotes toward the end of the project, "When we did the first interview I felt extremely nervous, but I took comfort that I had my beautiful teachers and my great *compañera de batalla* [fellow combatant; sister-in-arms—i.e., Lucy] and when I forgot something, she would help me with it. Each month that passed was a great experience and a blessing for me, and my knowledge kept improving all the time."[3]

Following her accident, Mirian said, she felt badly about herself and unhappy with life. But through this project, she said, "I came to alleviate the conflicts in my life, including to improve my self-esteem. It helped me to write much better, as well as to read and to communicate with other people."[4] Part of this improvement came from doing what Mirian called "mental" as opposed to physical labor, and the way this freed her to express herself musically:

The personal advancements I made were many, like the free expression of thought. If you don't use it, it will get slower each time, so I thank God and you [Caro and Daniel] for the ability to write some of the songs that are now being requested at different sociocultural events or that are related to some human need. And with the passage of time I keep learning and it makes me really happy to be able to learn to use my mind better. After a year I still felt like [I didn't know how to use] my mind, but with the passing of time I got better and better so that today I feel like my mind is working really well.[5]

Mirian and Lucy both described their increased confidence and believe they learned new skills through our project. Mirian said, "Now I have the confidence required to walk up to a person, introduce myself and ask them to come to Casa Hometown. For example the other day I saw a person being stopped by the police. I simply walked up to him and gave him the Casa Hometown card. In the old days I would have run away." When reflecting upon the two years we worked together, Lucy said that doing ethnography empowered her to better help her community and herself: "[Ethnographic work] gave me the opportunity to think about what I wanted to do and what I wanted to learn about. I learned about my own people and other communities, and I learned how to identify the needs of my community. I also learned about myself." Mirian said, "I learned to be observant and to write down my observations, which has helped me in writing my songs. Thinking about other people's work accidents helped me realize how many people suffer accidents here in Hometown and helped me overcome my own accident, and writing a play about my fear of the police and of my old boss also helped me overcome that fear, and I am not afraid" (see figure 6.1).

Lucy and Mirian's personal transformations are evident in their fieldnotes. For one, they discovered new things about their own community and the town in which they reside. Some of this had to do with racial diversity, a particular concern in Caro's dissertation research that merged with the work on our collaborative project. Lucy, for example, learned to see how different communities live in Hometown, including the African American and Puerto Rican communities: "Each community has different traditions and now I am more able to see those traditions without passing judgment." Furthermore, the project brought her closer to different people around town, especially African Americans: "Relations between Latin Americans and African Americans have always been very tense here in Hometown, but after interviewing a few of them and observing them for my fieldnotes

FIGURE 6.1. Mirian performs an original song as part of the play at Casa Hometown. Illustration by Peter Quach.

I now wave to people and they wave back." Mirian shared this experience: "Ever since we took interest in African Americans for this project I started inviting them to Casa Hometown and some of them have actually accepted my invitation and come to visit us."

As time went on, Lucy's and Mirian's voices became more confident and composed, their observations more infused with critical interpretations. In addition, as they learned more about the topics under investigation, their descriptions of their activities showed them to be taking a greater role in the activism, advocacy, and educational work of Casa Hometown. For example, after conducting many interviews with people who had suffered work accidents, Mirian became active in organizing workplace safety demonstrations for immigrant workers, including collaborations with OSHA (the U.S. government's Occupational Safety and Health Administration) to train workers in proper use of safety equipment and to inform them of their rights as workers in the United States. Mirian wrote with the authority of one who has herself suffered a work-related injury when she described the lessons these trainings imparted to workers:

> I explained to them that really, to earn $100 a day, if the patrón doesn't give us protection, we are putting our lives in danger, and it isn't worth it, not even for $500 a day, to enter a basement contaminated with mold . . . which can in turn contaminate our lungs and reproduce inside of them; and that for all the people that, after working in this beautiful country without any protection for their health, and then go back to their country sick and sometimes just to die, and it isn't worth all the effort we have made in the long run. If we don't protect ourselves we won't be able to enjoy the fruits of our effort. . . . It is incredible that all these jornaleros come here to risk their lives, so that their families will have a better life.[6]

Mirian's militancy also grew considerably during the course of our project. In the two years that we worked together she rose as a public figure and community leader, not only in Hometown but also nationally. In September 2013 she answered an invitation by the National Alliance of Domestic Workers to go to Washington, DC, and take a course on self-sufficient cooperatives. In Washington she joined other women and they fasted for nine days in support of immigration reform. She became a member of the National Alliance and in 2015 she walked 100 miles to Washington, along with ninety-nine other women, as part of the Alliance's 100 Miles 100 Women campaign to ask Pope Francis to support immigration reform in the United States. She spent twelve hours in jail after the group blocked an intersection near

Capitol Hill in an act of civil disobedience. But Mirian is no longer afraid of being deported: "I am good for this country," she says. In September 2015 she went to Dallas, invited by the National Day Laborer Organizing Network (NDLON) to attend a course on training organizers. She then spent a month in Texas and learned about the struggles of undocumented women there, writing songs about the experience. She has since then been to many NDLON workshops in New Jersey and New York, learning how to organize day laborers and how to inform people about work accidents.

Lucy also showed remarkable personal growth in the course of the research project. Quieter than Mirian by nature, Lucy also emerged as a leader in her community (even though she dislikes the word *leader* and prefers the term *organizer*). Through the years we worked together she helped organize many of Casa Hometown's events, including the popular *polladas,* where members cook chicken and sell it to raise funds for the organization. Today she continues to participate in marches and immigration workshops. She is a volunteer at a local church which helps newly arrived immigrants, and is still a member of the board of directors of Casa Hometown.

Lucy's sense of outrage and her willingness to stand up for her own rights and the rights of others emerged in part from her work as an ethnographer studying work accidents. At one point during the project Lucy took on a second job, working as a seamstress in a local garment factory. In her field-notes, she described in detail one experience in which she displayed her newfound sense of personal empowerment:

> I had an accident, to the middle finger on my left hand, changing the bobbin on the sewing machine. The bobbin needs to be changed when the thread runs out, but because it is located on the underside of the machine you can't see it. I pricked my finger on that sharp piece of metal. I told the boss of my area, and he yelled at me, "Go to the kitchen!" There are Band-Aids there. So I went to the kitchen. . . . The personnel director heard me, and asked me what had happened. I explained and he offered to help me, he washed my hand and put some cream and a Band-Aid on it, and then he said: "Now get back to work." So I did that, but once I was back at work, my finger was afraid to touch the fabric that I was sewing, my finger trembled and hovered over it, and I thought, "Don't be afraid, finger!" With my right hand I pushed on my left, to try to maintain contact with the machine, but I think that was a bad idea because it started to bleed from the force and pressure that I was putting on it. And I told my friend sitting behind me what had happened to my finger,

and she said, "Does it hurt?" And I answered yes. . . . I kept working but because of the accident I was kind of slow. After about 20 or 30 minutes I felt a presence behind me, but I kept working, and soon I realized it was the manager, because he began to shout at me, "Why are you so slow!" He asked me twice. I kept sewing, and he said, "Go faster! Go faster!" Shouting at me!

When he said that, I stopped my machine, I turned and looked him in the face, and I said, "Forgive me, but I can't go any faster, I had an accident and my finger hurts." Then he said: "Do it faster now. This isn't the first time you've worked with this material. Go faster!" . . . I immediately got up and shut off my machine and unplugged my phone that I was charging, and I just said, "Ok." The whole time he was shouting at me. . . . I gathered up my things and got ready to leave, but then I thought to myself, "Lucia, you can't just leave without saying something." Near the exit door are some stairs leading to the patrón's office, and without a second thought I went up, and I thought to myself, it doesn't matter if they run me off, but the patrón has to know about this. When I first started working there my friends told me that the patrón doesn't get involved in things, that the manager never tells him anything. . . . [The door opened] and it was the patrón himself, and he said to me very kindly, "Can I help you with something?" And I said yes, but first I asked him, "Do you speak Spanish?" He answered, "No!" "Ok," I said, "I only speak a little English, but you are going to understand me." So I told him all that had happened, about how the manager had spoken to me and how he was pressuring me. He asked me for some details, and I asked him to speak to [the manager]. . . . He said he would, and told me to take the rest of the day off and get better. I thanked him for his time and I left.

The most curious thing is that my English is not good, but in that moment it just came right out of me, and I left feeling satisfied that I had told the patrón about how the manager had behaved.[7]

In another note, she recounted how, following her accident, she decided to leave the job in the sewing factory, where she continued to experience physical and psychological abuse:

I felt confident [about the decision to quit] and I told Inés [a coworker] that we have to demand that the manager is dismissed, and she said to me, I don't think he will go. And I said: of course he will, we just have to speak up. And she told me, no, leave things as they are. Then I said to her, I can't work any longer in an environment that is emotionally harmful to me, and I told her, I am going to quit. But when you and the other workers are ready to collaborate, give me a call and we will take action. In my opinion, better times will come. . . . I wanted to take this decision [to quit] because, out of necessity we shouldn't have to permit psychological abuse. Obviously not! We should value our rights, and one of them is to be respected![8]

When we first began our research, Mirian and Lucy knew almost nothing about anthropology or the practice of ethnography. After two years, however, they believe they should receive a degree in anthropology. Anthropology, Lucy says, is "putting yourself in the shoes of someone else." But more than that, ethnography enables her to do something about the problems she encounters: "It's a beautiful experience, knowing you can help people through your fieldwork."[9]

The Future of Anthropology?

Given the many and varied critiques of qualitative social science detailed in this book, one might ask: Is there any hope for anthropology? We believe that anthropology, for all its coloniality, remains a disciplinary space within which new possibilities can arise and take root. Projects of the kind that we describe in this book offer a new generation of researchers the space to think creatively about what research is, how it is conducted, and what its purposes are. As Restrepo and Escobar have suggested in arguing for "other anthropologies and anthropologies otherwise" (Restrepo and Escobar 2005, 102), a pluralizing of what counts as anthropology and an expansion of who can serve as knowledge producers can transform the discipline while also making it into a more powerful tool for action and critique: "Anthropology could indeed be in the avant-garde of the transformation of modern intellectual division of labor . . . if such a project were ever to be entertained seriously" (Restrepo and Escobar 2005, 118).

In terms of theory, a decolonial anthropology can look to other sources of ideas beyond the oft-cited, elite theorists of European philosophy—for a decolonial anthropology, as Tlostanova and Mignolo observe at the opening of this chapter, "neither Spinoza nor Nietzsche will do" (Tlostanova and Mignolo 2012, 57; see also Visweswaran 1988, 1994). Nor Foucault nor Deleuze nor Agamben, for that matter. Alternative theorists would include some of anthropology's own forgotten ancestors and critics, especially indigenous intellectuals and scholars of color (Allen and Jobson [2016] cite Anténor

Firmin, W. E. B. Du Bois, and Frederick Douglass; we also mention work on indigenous methodologies and theories by Linda Tuhiwai Smith, Margaret Kovach, Audra Simpson, Kim TallBear, and others); earlier anthropologists, also scholars of color, who inspired what Allen and Jobson call the *original decolonizing generation* (Harrison [1991b] mentions Allison Davis, St. Clair Drake, Zora Neale Hurston, and Katherine Dunham as important early influences); and the non-Western theorists and writers who have been fundamental to the formulation of decolonial theory, those academics, critics, novelists, and historians writing from the space of the "colonial wound" (including scholars we reference in chapter 1, such as Gloria Anzaldúa, María Lugones, Sylvia Wynter, Enrique Dussel, Nelson Maldonado-Torres, Aníbal Quijano, and Boaventura de Sousa Santos; others frequently mentioned include Emma Pérez, Chela Sandoval, Aimé Césaire, Frantz Fanon, Édouard Glissant, and Lewis Gordon) (Tlostanova and Mignolo 2012, 35–36). Turning to theorists outside the usual Western canon is a way to challenge the authority of colonial anthropology, which tries to limit who can be considered worthy of citation, and in doing so sets the terms of the debate over anthropological theory and practice (see Gupta and Ferguson 1997; Kant de Lima 1992; Krotz 1997).

In addition to alternative scholarly and literary sources of ideas, decolonial ethnographers can also turn to the traditional "subjects" of anthropological research, not only as sources of unprocessed data but as producers of theory. To consider the ideas of the subaltern as theory poses another challenge to dominant anthropologies, helping us to avoid the problems that emerge when we try to process colonized realities through colonial concepts. As Restrepo and Escobar put it, theorizations of the dominant kind "more often than not [operate] as technologies for the domestication of alterity— translating subaltern worlds into Eurocentric terms" (Restrepo and Escobar 2005, 118). Instead, the subalterns become "knowledge-producers in their own right" (Restrepo and Escobar 2005, 118), valued interpreters of their own realities. Calling on theories like what we have termed *undocumented activist theory* can further enhance our border thinking, provoking contemplation and analysis from outside, from the margins, from below. It is a critical element of the decolonial turn, for even if we disagree with the content of the theory itself, recognizing it as theory is a move toward recognizing historical subalterns as fully human and equal. Decoloniality, as Maldonado-Torres says, "is about making visible the invisible and about analyzing the mechanisms that produce such invisibility or distorted visibility in light of a large stock of ideas that must necessarily include the critical reflections of the 'invisible' people themselves. Indeed, one must recognize their intellectual production as thinking—not only as culture or ideology."[10] Our discussion of undocumented activist theory in chapter 4 is an attempt to do just that.

In terms of method, as we have argued throughout, a decolonial approach requires us to move away from the traditional extractive model of social research, in which non-Western others are mined for data by colonial outsiders who export their riches for consumption abroad. This does not mean dispensing with ethnographic fieldwork, as we have shown in the preceding chapters, or limiting ourselves to the resources found in the archives. Rather than, or in addition to, studying texts, anthropologists can study the situations in which those texts are constructed and the processes by which they become meaningful.[11] Many excellent decolonizing strategies already exist and are in use by anthropologists and other researchers. The perspectives of a decolonial ethnography enable us to translate ideas into practices, to make our research work for the benefit of our fifeld collaborators, bridging the divide that separates academic work from the struggles of subaltern populations. In doing so, the techniques of collaborative and participatory research can dissolve some of the historical barriers that centuries of colonialism and coloniality have constructed between researchers and researched. Above all, decolonial ethnography is about enabling local people—historically the objects of research—to become subjects in the research process and to use the knowledge they produce to advance their own decolonizing struggles.

Notes

INTRODUCTION

1. See the contributors to Harrison 1991a.

2. The critiques of an earlier generation of anthropologists analyzing the discipline's colonial roots were inspirational to the decolonizing anthropologists; see, e.g., Asad 1973; Gough 1968, 1990; Huizer and Mannheim 1979; Hymes 1972; Lewis 1973.

3. The scholars associated with the "writing culture" movement in anthropology were influential here; see, e.g., Clifford and Marcus 1986.

4. The bibliography on applied anthropology is much too large to summarize in a endnote. For a history, see Singer 2008. For a discussion of applied and more recent forms of engaged anthropology, see Rylko-Bauer, Singer, and van Willigen 2006.

5. Academic and applied anthropology present themselves as fundamentally antagonistic. Applied anthropology can appear anti-intellectual or atheoretical, disdainful of the work of scholars who don't attempt to apply their findings to the real world. For its part, academic anthropology often dismisses the value of its applied variant, contemptuous of its desire to take ideas out of the ivory tower. Such conflicts suggest that the goals of academic and applied anthropologists are irreconcilable. But neither approach examines their shared coloniality or the privilege that enables them to conduct their research as they do. See Escobar 1991, 1995; Fluehr-Lobban 2003; Stilltoe 2007; Willis 1974.

6. Our depiction of academic anthropology as "colonial," though polemical, should not be understood as ironic. For one thing, some would point out, anthropology cannot be described as a particularly powerful discipline, either in the academy or outside it. Within the social sciences—perhaps the most marginalized of the major academic subdivisions—anthropology is among the most marginalized of disciplines. Compared with other disciplinary scholars, anthropologists have relatively little voice in the larger world of politics and policy making, a fact that anthropologists lament (e.g., Okongwu and Menchner 2000). And anthropologists have been among colonialism's most articulate critics, denouncing imperialism and its impacts on the world's history and its many societies and cultures. But (we would counter) anthropology as a whole

has yet to confront the colonial dimensions of its own practice and privilege and continues to profit implicitly from what many of its practitioners explicitly renounce.

7. Particularly influential for us have been Charles Hale (2008); Jeffrey Juris (2008, 2012); Jeffrey Juris and Alex Khasnabish (2013); Stuart Kirsch (2002, 2010, 2014); Shannon Speed (2006, 2007, 2008); and Angela Stuesse (2016). For a history of "activist anthropology," see Stuesse (2015). Useful sources include both writing about activists and activism as well as writing from an activist perspective, sometimes in the same text. Examples of some of these approaches include Goldstein 2016; Graeber 2009; Howe 2013; Juris and Khasnabish 2013; Lyon-Callo 2008; Razsa 2015; Sanford and Angel-Ajani 2006; Scheper-Hughes 1995.

8. For just a few examples from a broad set of fields, see Allen and Jobson 2016; Cox 2015; Craven and Davis 2013; Dave 2012; Harrison 1991b; Hunt and Holmes 2015; Morgensen 2011; Perry 2013; Pierre 2012; Smith 2012. On indigenous and critical methodologies, see Brown and Strega 2005; Chilisa 2011; Denzin, Lincoln, and Smith 2008; Kovach 2009. Indigenous writing on settler colonialism and its impacts represents another important field of scholarship that has had limited uptake by anthropologists; see, e.g., Coulthard (2014) and the articles in Simpson and Smith (2014).

9. "Public anthropology" is a particularly slippery term, referring to a wide range of ethnographic work. The series in Public Anthropology at the University of California Press and the recurring column in *American Anthropologist* exemplify the breadth of this field and what it can encompass. For more direct inquiries into the nature, prospects, and consequences of public scholarship, see Beck and Maida 2015; Borofsky 2011; Burawoy 2005; Fassin 2013; Gans 2010; Lamphere 2003; Osterweil 2013; Scheper-Hughes 2009.

10. Joel Robbins (2013) calls this the construction of anthropology's "suffering subject." For a native perspective, see Tuck and Yang (2014).

11. The ethnographic method has been widely employed beyond the discipline of anthropology. Scholars from a range of fields—including sociology, geography, political science, public health, and so on—incorporate ethnography into their research design and wrestle with problems of interpretation and representation in their writing. This discussion, then, has relevance for many researchers outside anthropology.

12. We use the term *Latinx* to refer to people of all genders who live in the United States and are from, or descended from those, Latin America. On the term *Latinx*, see Scharrón-Del Río and Aja 2015.

13. "Cultural critique" can be part of a broader "engaged anthropology," as Low and Merry (2010), among others, have made clear; for a critique of critique, see Hale (2006). And for those who "study up," focusing their ethnographic attention on the socially and economically privileged, critique can be a productive form of engagement (Nader 1972). The scenario we describe here is intended for the many anthropologists who work with the disadvantaged and marginalized—the historical objects of anthropological inquiry.

14. Maldonado-Torres 2006. Theory in the decolonial turn shares much with postcolonial theory, even as it diverges from that work in significant ways. This is explored in more detail in chapter 1.

15. Having learned something from the postmodernists, this dominant anthropology might reflect on its own positionality to comment on the role of the anthropological self in the data-collection process. But that is as far as it goes. See Clifford and Marcus 1986; Marcus and Fischer 1986.

16. For an exploration of the many complexities of reciprocity and "giving back" in field research, see TallBear (2014) and the other essays in a special issue of the *Journal of Research Practice* (10 [2]).

17. The diversity of what counts as "engagement" can be seen in the list of books in "engaged ethnography," on a website maintained by Angela Stuesse and her students: *Engaged Ethnography*, http://engagedethnography.weebly.com/ethnography-list.html, accessed January 16, 2018.

18. Scholars in the field of education have been especially generative in developing activist methods for decolonizing what they call "qualitative inquiry" (e.g., Paris and Winn 2014).

19. Although they may not discuss their individual activism in their published writings, many if not most anthropologists of immigration take on some kind of activist or engaged work in the course of their research. For explicit discussion of this, see Gomberg-Muñoz 2016; Holmes 2013; Stuesse 2010, 2015.

20. As we write, undocumented student activists are engaged in a range of projects and protests for immigrant rights, again demonstrating the potential of research and activism to create social change for and by noncitizens.

21. Thanks to an anonymous reviewer for raising this point.

1. COLONIAL ANTHROPOLOGY AND ITS ALTERNATIVES

1. The influence of Michel Foucault was fundamental to this move; see Foucault 1977, 1978.

2. Abu-Lughod 1991; Behar and Gordon 1996; Visweswaran 1994.

3. Maldonado-Torres 2008, 2011. For some of the greatest hits in postcolonial studies, see Ashcroft, Griffiths, and Tiffin (2006). A useful introduction to the study of colonialism and postcolonialism is Loomba (2015). For a synthesis of work in decolonial studies, see Moraña, Dussel, and Jáuregui (2008).

4. Said 1978.

5. Bhambra 2014.

6. Said 1978, 1993.

7. Bhabha 1994, 199. Members of the "subaltern studies group" made significant contributions to this project in their attempts to excavate and examine what Ranajit Guha called "the politics of the people" or the "subaltern classes" (Guha 1982, 4, 8; see also Chakrabarty 2000; Chatterjee 1993). Guha himself, for example, authored historical accounts of peasant uprisings against British colonial rule in India, specifying the peasants' own perspectives on and explanations of their political activity—at the time a radical break from the norms of conventional historiography (Guha 1999).

8. Spivak 1988; see also Spivak 1999.

9. Wynter (2003, 262) describes the continued problem of Western hegemony as one of "over-representation," mistaking a specific set of ideas and values (those of the West, or "Man") as universal: it enables "the interests, reality, and well-being of the empirical human world to continue to be imperatively subordinated to those of the now globally hegemonic ethnoclass world of 'Man.'" See also Wynter 2006; Gordon 2013.

10. E.g., Fanon 1967, 1991; Césaire 1972. Decolonial theory differs from postcolonial theory in other ways as well. Decolonial scholars tend to focus on Latin America instead of South Asia and take as their historical frame the entire period of colonization, beginning with the conquest of the Americas (in contrast to postcolonial studies, which tend to focus on the eighteenth to early twentieth centuries). See Coronil 2004, 2008. Most anthropological studies of colonialism, incidentally, also tend to privilege these later centuries; Gough (1968, 12), e.g., in an early critique, identified the period of colonialism most relevant to anthropology as the nineteenth and early twentieth centuries. See also Bhambra 2014, 115; Mignolo 2007a.

11. Epistemologies of the colonized were targeted for destruction under "modernity/coloniality," which Mignolo (2011a) describes as fully intertwined, two sides of the same historical coin. Modernity is unthinkable without coloniality, from a decolonial perspective, just as coloniality is unthinkable without modernity.

12. Maldonado-Torres (2008) cites W. E. B. Du Bois as the pioneer of decolonial studies; see Du Bois (1903 [1997]).

13. Ann Stoler (2016) writes of "imperial durabilities" and "imperial entailments," ideas that do similar work to "coloniality."

14. On heteropatriarchy and its relation to white supremacy, see Smith 2006.

15. Quijano 1993; see also Mignolo 2007b, 156. Holding this matrix together is what Quijano calls the "coloniality of power," described by Grosfoguel (2007, 217) as the intersection of "multiple and heterogeneous global hierarchies ('heterarchies') of sexual, political, epistemic, economic, spiritual, linguistic and racial forms of domination and exploitation where the racial/ethnic hierarchy of the European/non-European divide transversally reconfigures all of the other global power structures."

16. Santos, Nunes, and Meneses 2007, xxxv. González Casanova (1969) has discussed the phenomenon of *colonialismo interno*, which might also be interpretable in terms of this matrix of power. Castro-Gomez and Grosfoguel (2007, 13) describe the current global system as the *sistema-mundo europeo/euro-norteamericano capitalista/patriarcal moderno/colonial*, to emphasize its multistranded complexity and integration; see also Grosfoguel (2005).

17. Maldonado-Torres argues that the entire formation of Western rationality—the basis, ultimately, of Western science—is predicated on the racist distinction between those capable of rational thought and those for whom such thinking is impossible. The Cartesian *cogito ergo sum*—I think, therefore I am—contains two unacknowledged qualifiers: "'I think (others do not think, or do not think properly) therefore I am (others are-not, lack being, should not exist or are dispensable)'" (Maldonado-Torres 2007, 252). The first part of this statement refers to the "coloniality of knowledge": only the European is capable of rational (i.e., proper) thought; the second part

refers to what Maldonado-Torres identifies as the "coloniality of being": only the European is worthy of recognition as fully human. What Maldonado-Torres calls the "non-ethics of war" (the dehumanization of the enemy as a killable object, lacking in true subjectivity and worthiness) is translated to ordinary life through the idea of race, which naturalizes the objectification and abuse of those it classifies as inferior (Maldonado-Torres 2008; see also Arias 2015; Gordon 2004).

18. On queer de- and postcolonial theory, see Anzaldúa 1987; Mignolo 2000; Perez 1999, 2003; Spurlin 2001.

19. As another mechanism for subordinating the colonized as a nonhuman or subhuman form of life, the gender system is fundamental to the organization of the coloniality of power and so key to understanding broader political, economic, and sociocultural practices and systems. These understandings give gender and sexuality a central place in the analysis of coloniality past and present, a corrective to other decolonial scholarship that either ignores their primacy or reduces gender to the colonizers' "sexual access" to colonized women. Lugones (2007) in particular critiques Quijano's (2000) original formulation; see also Maese-Cohen 2010; Rivera Cusicanqui 2010; Schiwy 2007.

20. Legal anthropologist Sally Engle Merry (2000) illustrates how all of these dimensions of colonialism operated in tandem—Quijano's "colonial matrix of power"— in the U.S. colonization of Hawaii. Prior to the arrival of Euroamericans, Hawaii had a rich and complex political and legal system under which local cultural standards of morality were legislated and enforced. Hawaiians viewed nudity and sexual play as harmless (while also indicating rank and social status, e.g., who could touch whose body revealed one's place in the political hierarchy), and marriage as a loose and flexible union; native Hawaiian women had a great deal of autonomy compared with Western women. Property was often communally owned, and people's work lives were not terribly strenuous. For Europeans and U.S. Americans, these differences from Western norms meant that native Hawaiians were savage and uncivilized, like children not yet fully formed. But this view also implied that Hawaiians, like children, were capable of improvement, if certain changes were implemented: "Hawai'ian natives needed to be clothed, their work habits disciplined, their land privatized, their children schooled, their religion churched, and their family lives readjusted so that marriage was held sacred and women and children were properly subordinated to men" (Lazarus-Black 2000, 141). This was accomplished through changes in the Hawaiian legal system. At first, Hawaiian law shifted to follow principles introduced by the Christian missionaries; later, the legal system became modeled on that of the United States. During this later era, Hawaii became an important production site for the sugar industry, and the islands adopted a plantation system run by wealthy, mostly white elites, with native Hawaiians and Asian immigrants employed as farm labor. The law changed in response, allowing colonizers to enforce labor contracts, defend private property rights, and prosecute disturbances of the public order. New laws also emphasized monogamous marriage and severely restricted women's liberties, including the right to divorce.

The overlap of gendered and racialized forms of discrimination and control—what Merry calls "paternalistic racism," or "power that is gendered as well as raced" (Merry

2000, 139)—is clear in the changing laws of colonized Hawaii. But what is perhaps most interesting in Merry's account is her demonstration that the colonial process was not a straightforward, linear transformation from non-Western to Western ways of life. Faced with the threat of complete domination—that is, of being absorbed into the United States, their own forms of self-government destroyed—Hawaiian lawmakers and politicians willingly adopted Western social and legal norms, hoping that by doing so they might demonstrate themselves to be "civilized" to Western eyes. In the end, of course, this effort failed, as the traditional monarchy fell and Hawaii became the fiftieth U.S. state. But Hawaiians were not merely the passive victims of colonialism: As Merry shows, they were actively engaged in negotiating the terms of their subjugation, surrendering traditional modes of living in exchange for, they hoped, a measure of political autonomy. And indeed, even as the new legal system undermined women's freedoms and emphasized protections for elite landowners at the expense of commoners, it also introduced a language of individual rights, which workers could use to challenge their exploitation in court.

21. Mignolo (2011b, 54) contends that these writings were somehow foundational to the decolonization of the Bolivian state by that country's Constitutional Assembly. Daniel, whose work focused on Bolivia for many years, considers this to be a highly debatable assertion.

22. Spivak 1988; Mohanty 1988, 2004. For an excellent critique of decolonial theorists' refusal to engage the work of postcolonial scholars, and of Spivak in particular, see Asher (2013).

23. When considering modern science and its relationship with Europe, it is important to remember that we are referring to the project of the European Enlightenment and the scientific model that emerged in that context. This does not mean that science originated in Europe. On the myth of science as a European invention, see Dussel, Krauel, and Tuma 2000.

24. Seth 2009, 377. The performance of Western technological prowess sat uneasily alongside the colonizers' desire for the secret knowledges they believed "exotic" conquered peoples to control; see, e.g., Taussig 1991.

25. See Castro-Gómez (2005) on the "hubris of the zero point" (*hybris del punto cero*).

26. To some extent this is beyond the individual researcher's control, as it is embedded within the coloniality of the Western academy. The research process itself is governed by academic institutions, whose decisions determine whether or not to approve and fund the research, and whose rules regulate it to ensure its conformity with scientific convention. At each stage of the process, a coterie of scientific gatekeepers far removed from ethnography's objects shape how ethnographic knowledge is collected, interpreted, and distributed. For example, before an ethnographic research project can begin, the anthropologist must describe her research in a proposal, presented to a review panel for vetting and, hopefully, funding. In anthropology, the research proposal is a deeply conservative document, requiring researchers to render their ideas and plans in terms of established categories of knowledge production—questions, theory, methods, budget, and so on—that must be approved before research may proceed.

Approval is contingent on the ability of the evaluators to recognize the research plans as legitimate (and perhaps even fundable) according to disciplinary norms. Numerous revisions are often demanded. Institutions within academia further regulate the process, most notably the IRB (Institutional Review Board), which ostensibly exists to protect the safety of the researched but more importantly protects the university against legal action should something go wrong with the research; and the ORSP (Office of Research and Sponsored Programs, or some variation thereof), which requires research plans, proposals, and applications to be presented according to precise yet arbitrary guidelines. Failure to comply with the many rules and regulations can delay the start of the project and jeopardize funding. By the time the researcher has run this gauntlet of approvals and permissions, she has a fully realized vision of the research to be transacted; funders, IRBs, and ORSPs resist deviations from what has been approved. First-time researchers are inculcated in the norms of institutional science through the proposal process.

The dominant research paradigm thus requires the researcher to determine the aims and goals of the project, to ask the questions, and record the answers. Variations from this norm can render the process moot: Data collected outside the bounds of prior IRB approval, for example, may be disallowed, the researchers barred from including them in their analyses. Another form of regulation occurs at the end of the research process, when the researcher writes up her results. Here again, deviation from the norm can render the written product unrecognizable to another set of reviewers, those who vet the research for publication. Not citing the right people—including the famous theorists and the less well-known but equally important regional or topical experts—can disqualify a publication, requiring revision and resubmission until the author gets it right. A successful academic career depends on approval from these institutions and gatekeepers; researchers who fail to present themselves in a form recognizable to reviewers and administrators will not advance to the next level of their profession.

27. On humanitarianism, see, e.g., Fassin 2007; Malkki 1996; Redfield 2012.

28. For Santos et al., "the self-constitution of science as a universal form of knowledge that claims the right to legislate over all other forms of knowledge leads to it being frequently regarded in the non-Western world as a Western particularism whose specificity consists of holding the power to define as particular, local, contextual, and situational all knowledges that are its rivals" (Santos, Nunes, and Meneses 2007, xxxv).

29. Internal critiques of anthropology's coloniality are not new, either. As we mentioned in this book's introduction, similar criticisms, in different language, were brought by scholars beginning in the 1960s, when anthropologists became increasingly critical of how the discipline's colonial past continued to color its present and began to imagine steps to a "liberation anthropology" (see Diamond 1979; Gordon 1991; Huizer and Mannheim 1979; Nzimiro 1988); other critiques have come out of Latin America (see Jimeno 2005; Krotz 1993, 1997; Restrepo 2007; Restrepo and Escobar 2005). And those scholars were themselves part of a longer chain of auto-critique that went back even further and that included some of anthropology's greatest minds, including Margaret Mead, Ruth Benedict, Franz Boas, and Claude Lévi-Strauss. See

the discussion in Stocking (1992). Castro-Gomez (1998) suggests that the scholarly anticolonial discourses of the 1960s and 1970s failed to consider the epistemological status of their own thought and so failed to recognize the extent to which their own critiques harbored a colonial logic.

30. Deloria 1969; King 1977; Trask 1991. Indigenous anthropologists have also been active in reorienting the discipline toward decolonial practice; for an early example from Latin America, see the discussion of the Declaration of Barbados in Dostal (1972) and Hale (2006).

31. Haraway (1988) famously wrote of "situated knowledges" against the supposedly neutral and objective stance of modern science; see also Harding (1991, 2008); Mascia-Lees, Sharpe, and Cohen 1989.

32. Briggs and Bauman 1999. Lassiter calls attention to the work of the anthropologist and biographer Paul Radin (1933), an early proponent of collaboration in ethnographic work and a writer who emphasized the significance of individual knowledge and experience in the production of cultural knowledge.

33. Restrepo and Escobar 2005, 118. Escobar (2007, 185) describes this as "the need to take seriously the epistemic force of local histories and to think theory through from the political praxis of subaltern groups."

34. Mignolo (2002, 71, 91) describes "border thinking" as "an epistemology from a subaltern perspective," "an other logic" that is part of a broader assessment of the "geopolitics of knowledge." See Anzaldúa 1987.

35. Escobar 2007, 187. See also Dussel 1996. On the Modernity/Coloniality Research Program, see Escobar 2004.

2. JOURNEYS TOWARD DECOLONIZING

1. This story was originally recounted in Goldstein 2012.

2. Tenure and review processes vary across institutions. At some, faculty are reviewed every two to three years, both pre- and post-tenure, meaning that even scholars with tenure may feel the constraints of the academic track.

3. The Support Our Law Enforcement and Safe Neighborhoods Act (SB 1070) was an anti-immigration law passed by the Arizona Senate that, among other things, made it a federal misdemeanor for immigrants in Arizona to fail to carry their immigration documents with them at all times. For a discussion of Arizona SB 1070, see Chin et al. 2010.

3. REFLECTIONS ON FIELDWORK IN NEW JERSEY

1. For a comprehensive history of New Jersey, see Lurie and Veit (2012).

2. Prior to this wave of Latin Americans a Puerto Rican community had existed in town since World War II.

3. Town Hall Council Meeting, January 5, 2003.

4. Interview with Rosa D., conducted by Carolina, February 25, 2015.

5. Interview with Rosa D., conducted by Carolina, February 25, 2015.

6. Compare with Coleman's (2012) work in North Carolina communities.

7. Federal policy under PEP (which came into effect in July 2015) was originally intended to target only the most dangerous or criminal immigrants. However, this changed under the Trump administration with the issuing of a DHS memo in February 2017, "Enforcement of the Immigration Laws to Serve the National Interest" (http://www.mcclatchydc.com/news/politics-government/white-house /article133607784.ece/BINARY/DHS%20enforcement%20of%20immigration%20 laws). It states that "the Department no longer will exempt classes or categories of removable aliens from potential enforcement. . . . Unless otherwise directed, De-partment personnel should initiate enforcement actions against removable aliens encountered during the performance of their official duties. This includes the arrest or apprehension of an alien whom an immigration officer has probable cause to believe is in violation of the immigration laws."

8. The writing on undocumented immigration and labor is extensive, and we can-not mention it all here. Particularly influential works for us in the anthropology of immigration, activism, and immigrant workers' rights include Chavez (2008); Coutin (2000, 2003, 2016); Gomberg-Muñoz (2010); Heyman (1998, 2016); Horton (2016); Inda (2006); and Stuesse (2016).

4. UNDOCUMENTED ACTIVIST THEORY
AND A DECOLONIAL METHODOLOGY

1. Fieldnotes, January 3, 2014, written by Lucy. All notes were originally written in Spanish; translations were done by Daniel and Carolina.

2. Fieldnotes, March 5, 2014, written by Lucy.

3. Fieldnotes, February 13, 2014, written by Lucy.

4. Fieldnotes, January 14, 2014, written by Lucy.

5. Fieldnotes, February 28, 2014, written by Mirian.

6. Fieldnotes, May 31, 2014, written by Lucy.

7. Fieldnotes, January 2, 2014, written by Lucy.

8. Fieldnotes, September 12, 2014, written by Lucy.

9. Interview with Lucy, May 11, 2015, conducted by Carolina.

10. Fieldnotes, January 8, 2014, written by Mirian.

11. Fieldnotes, April 29, 2015, written by Mirian.

12. An undocumented immigrant's right to benefits under federal law is guaranteed through the National Labor Relations Act (NLRA) of 1935, the Fair Labor Standards Act (FLSA) of 1938, and the Migrant and Seasonal Agricultural Worker Protection Act (MSPA) of 1983, among others. The Wage and Hours Division of the U.S. Depart-ment of Labor continues to enforce the FLSA and MSPA "without regard to whether an employee is documented or undocumented"; "Wage and Hour Division," United States Department of Labor, https://www.dol.gov/whd/regs/compliance/whdfs48.htm; accessed January 5, 2018.

13. *State of New Jersey Department of Labor and Workforce Development*, http://www .nj.gov/labor/; accessed January 5, 2018.

14. "New Jersey courts have held that the effect of one's immigration status has no bearing on the injury suffered or the need, or right, to medical treatment for an injury derived during employment. It is worth noting that benefits paid under the New Jersey Worker's Compensation Act are not government funded but rather paid for through an insurance policy maintained by the employer. Requiring the employer to bear the financial responsibility of worker's compensation further encourages the employer to ensure workplace safety for all workers. Injured workers in New Jersey should seek lawyers experienced in workers compensation law who can help any injured employee obtain the benefits they are entitled to, even permanency benefits, regardless of immigration status"; http://callagylaw.com/employment-rights-undocumented-workers-federal-new-jersey-law/; accessed January 5, 2018.

15. Interview with Mirian, May 21, 2015, conducted by Carolina and Daniel.

16. Fieldnotes, September 8, 2014, written by Lucy.

17. Fieldnotes, October 11, 2013, written by Lucy.

18. Interview with Lucy, May 11, 2015, conducted by Carolina.

19. Undocumented women's reluctance to take domestic disputes to court has intensified under the Trump administration, as the courthouse has become a place for ICE agents to target undocumented petitioners; see, e.g., Katz 2017.

20. Fieldnotes, April 23, 2014, written by Mirian. It should be recalled that this work was done prior to Donald Trump's election as U.S. president, which initiated a period of intensified policing, detention, and deportation of undocumented immigrants. It is unclear whether some of these recommendations would still be advisable under the new administration. For further discussion on this, see the preface.

21. Fieldnotes, August 2, 2014, written by Lucy.

22. Again, it is important to remember that this research was being conducted during the Barack Obama administration, which, despite a record number of deportations, introduced measures like DACA (Deferred Action for Childhood Arrivals) and other policies that seemed to be moving the country toward a greater tolerance of the undocumented immigrant presence. That quickly changed with the election of Trump and the introduction of a much harsher approach to immigrant policing. But at the time, recommending people to pursue their grievances through the police and the courts was not out of line, as the risks of doing so were much less than they were later to become.

23. Interview with Elena, August 6, 2014, conducted by Lucy. In addition to recording the interview, Lucy and Mirian wrote commentaries and reflections about the interview they had just recorded. This quote, for example, is drawn from Lucy's written commentary on the interview of August 6, 2014.

24. Interview with Mirian, April 10, 2018, conducted by Carolina.

25. This program has been followed by undocumented youth across the country organized around the Development, Relief, and Education for Alien Minors (DREAM) Act (see Corrunker 2012).

26. Interview with Lucy, April 10, 2018, conducted by Carolina.

27. Interview with Mirian, April 10, 2018, conducted by Carolina.

28. Fieldnotes, May 28, 2014, written by Mirian.

29. Fieldnotes, December 9, 2014, written by Lucy.

30. Fieldnotes, March 2, 2014, written by Lucy.

31. Interview with Lucy, April 10, 2018, conducted by Carolina.

32. Interview with Mirian, April 10, 2018, conducted by Carolina.

33. We thank Angela Stuesse for raising this point.

34. Interview with Mirian, April 10, 2018, conducted by Carolina.

35. Interview with Lucy, April 10, 2018, conducted by Carolina.

36. For example, in a famous debate with Max Gluckman, Paul Bohannon argued for the use of indigenous legal principles and terms instead of their English equivalents in the anthropology of law; see Mertz and Goodale 2012.

37. Fieldnotes, January 27, 2015, written by Lucy.

38. Interview with Lucy, May 11, 2015, conducted by Carolina.

39. Interview with Dolores, June 5, 2014, conducted by Lucy. Interview commentary written by Lucy.

40. Interview with Mirian, May 25, 2015, conducted by Carolina.

41. Interview with Lucy, May 11, 2015, conducted by Carolina.

42. Interview with Mirian, May 21, 2015, conducted by Carolina and Daniel.

43. Interview with Mirian, May 21, 2015, conducted by Carolina and Daniel.

44. Interview with Lucy, May 11, 2015, conducted by Carolina.

45. Interview with Lucy, May 11, 2015, conducted by Carolina. Upon learning of this, we went back and identified the data produced by these interviews and excluded them from analytical consideration, in deference to IRB requirements and guarantees to our research subjects of confidentiality.

46. Interview with Marcelo, June 12, 2014, conducted by Lucy. Interview commentary written by Lucy.

47. Mirian and Lucy were salaried employees during this entire period.

5. UNDOCUMENTED THEATER

1. Fieldnotes, January 23, 2015, written by Lucy.

2. Fieldnotes, January 30, 2015, written by Lucy.

3. Interview with Mirian, May 21, 2015, conducted by Carolina and Daniel.

4. We use the word *trabajadorxs* to go beyond the binary construction of the Spanish language and be inclusive of people of all genders (see Scharrón-Del Río and Aja 2015).

CONCLUSION

1. Chela Sandoval (2000) engages with Frederic Jameson's (1991) analysis of postmodernism, as he argues that contemporary forms of resistance, oppositional consciousness, and social movements are no longer effective under the imperatives of neocolonial globalization. In Jameson, the previously centered (First World) modern citizen-subject is now absolutely disoriented and in need of a new "cognitive map" capable of pinpointing her within postmodern globalizing cultural conditions. This

decentered postmodern subject, Sandoval argues, finds herself in the position long oc-cupied by the always already historically decentered subaltern citizen subject—"being a woman of color is an everyday battle against the state"—and it is therefore relevant to turn to those historically oppressed peoples and analyze their forms of survival (and resistance) if one wants to grapple with Jameson's "postmodern condition." A "differential" form of consciousness, much like Gloria Anzaldúa's (1987) "mestiza consciousness," emerges among women of color in the passing between and among different oppositional ideologies. This praxis of border crossing and liminality and the recognition of the many ways in which women of color negotiate day-to-day experience provide a threshold for the creation of an alternative mode of being. In this regard, poet Aurora Levins Morales writes, "This tribe called 'Women of Color' is not an ethnicity. It is one of the inventions of solidarity, an alliance, a political necessity that is not the given name of every female with dark skin and a colonized tongue, but rather a choice about how to resist and with whom" (2001, 22; cf. Walia 2013, 14). From this point of view, solidarities among women of color are based on the recognition that their subjectivities are the most impacted by coloniality and that they embody the pathways necessary to concurrently disrupt overlapping systems of oppression. In this context, "facilitating space for other women of color warriors is an intentional politi-cal practice, an offering in the spirit of decolonization" (Walia 2013, 14).

2. On the relation between coloniality and disciplinary/transdisciplinary ap-proaches to knowledge production, see Maldonado-Torres 2012.

3. Fieldnotes, February 6, 2015, written by Mirian.

4. Fieldnotes, February 4, 2015, written by Mirian.

5. Fieldnotes, February 6, 2015, written by Mirian.

6. Fieldnotes, September 30, 2014, written by Mirian.

7. Fieldnotes, June 3, 2014, written by Lucy.

8. Fieldnotes, May 5, 2014, written by Lucy.

9. Interview with Lucy, May 11, 2015, conducted by Carolina.

10. Maldonado-Torres 2007, 262. See also the essays in Grosfoguel and Hernandez (2012); Ndlovu-Gatsheni (2013).

11. Borneman 1995, 669. Taking a swipe at text-based scholars of "culture," Borne-man pointedly adds, "Study of written texts and participant-observation are distinct practices that offer different insights. They should not be collapsed together into trendy cultural studies, where they are often used as an alibi by bourgeois academics to avoid the discomforts and uncertainties inherent in face-to-face interaction with strangers."

References

Abu-Lughod, Lila. 1990. "Can There Be a Feminist Ethnography?" *Women and Performance: A Journal of Feminist Theory* 5:7–27.

Abu-Lughod, Lila. 1991. "Writing against Culture." In *Recapturing Anthropology*, ed. Richard Fox, 191–210. Santa Fe, NM: School of American Research.

Alexander, Jacqui M., and Chandra Talpade Mohanty. 1997. *Feminist Genealogies, Colonial Legacies, Democratic Futures.* New York: Routledge.

Allen, Jafari Sinclaire, and Ryan Cecil Jobson. 2016. "The Decolonizing Generation: (Race and) Theory in Anthropology since the Eighties." *Current Anthropology* 57 (2): 129–40.

Anzaldúa, Gloria. 1987. *Borderlands/La Frontera: The New Mestiza.* San Francisco: Aunt Lute Books.

Appadurai, Arjun. 2006. "The Right to Research." *Globalisation, Societies and Education* 4 (2): 167–77.

Arias, Arturo. 2015. "Violence and Coloniality in Latin America: An Alternative Reading of Subalternization, Racialization and Viscerality." In *Eurocentrism, Racism and Knowledge: Debates on History and Power in Europe and the Americas*, ed. Marta Araújo and Silvia Rodríguez Maeso, 47–64. New York: Palgrave Macmillan.

Asad, Talal. 1973. "Introduction." In *Anthropology and the Colonial Encounter*, ed. Talal Asad, 1–19. Atlantic Highlands, NJ: Humanities Press.

Asad, Talal. 1979. "Anthropology and the Colonial Encounter." In *The Politics of Anthropology: From Colonialism and Sexism toward a View from Below*, ed. Gerrit Huizer and Bruce Mannheim, 85–94. The Hague: Mouton.

Ashcroft, Bill, Gareth Griffiths, and Helen Tiffin. 2006. *The Post-Colonial Studies Reader.* 2nd ed. New York: Routledge.

Asher, Kiran. 2013. "Latin American Decolonial Thought, or Making the Subaltern Speak." *Geography Compass* 7 (12): 832–42.

Beck, Sam, and Carl Maida, eds. 2015. *Public Anthropology in a Borderless World.* New York: Berghahn.

Behar, Ruth. 1996. "Introduction: Out of Exile." In *Women Writing Culture*, ed. Ruth Behar and Deborah A. Gordon, 1–29. Berkeley: University of California Press.

Behar, Ruth, and Deborah A. Gordon. 1996. *Women Writing Culture*. Berkeley: University of California Press.

Berreman, Gerald D. 1968. "Is Anthropology Alive? Social Responsibility in Social Anthropology." *Current Anthropology* 9 (5): 391–96.

Berry, Maya J., Claudia Chávez Argüelles, Shanya Cordis, Sarah Ihmoud, and Elizabeth Velásquez Estrada. 2017. "Toward a Fugitive Anthropology: Gender, Race, and Violence in the Field." *Cultural Anthropology* 32 (4): 537–65.

Bhabha, Homi. 1994. *The Location of Culture*. London: Routledge.

Bhambra, Gurminder K. 2014. "Postcolonial and Decolonial Dialogues." *Postcolonial Studies* 17 (2): 115–21.

Biolsi, Thomas, and Larry J. Zimmerman, eds. 1997. *Indians and Anthropologists: Vine Deloria, Jr., and the Critique of Anthropology*. Tucson: University of Arizona Press.

Borneman, John. 1995. "American Anthropology as Foreign Policy." *American Anthropologist* 97 (4): 663–72.

Borofsky, Robert. 2011. *Why a Public Anthropology?* Honolulu: Center for a Public Anthropology.

Boyer, Dominic, and Cymene Howe. 2015. "Portable Analytics and Lateral Theory." In *Theory Can Be More Than It Used to Be*, ed. Dominic Boyer, James Faubion, and George Marcus, 15–38. Ithaca, NY: Cornell University Press.

Boyer, Dominic, and George E. Marcus. 2015. "Introduction: New Methodologies for a Transformed Discipline." In *Theory Can Be More Than It Used to Be: Learning Anthropology's Method in a Time of Transition*, ed. Dominic Boyer, James D. Faubion, and George E. Marcus, 1–11. Ithaca, NY: Cornell University Press.

Briggs, Charles, and Richard Bauman. 1999. "'The Foundation of All Future Researches': Franz Boas, George Hunt, Native American Texts, and the Construction of Modernity." *American Quarterly* 51 (3): 479–528.

Brodkin, Karen, Sandra Morgen, and Janice Hutchinson. 2011. "Anthropology as White Public Space." *American Anthropologist* 113 (4): 545–56.

Brown, Leslie, and Susan Strega, eds. 2005. *Research as Resistance: Critical, Indigenous, and Anti-Oppressive Approaches*. Toronto: Canadian Scholars' Press and Women's Press.

Broyles-González, Yolanda. 1994. *El Teatro Campesino: Theater in the Chicano Movement*. Austin: University of Texas Press.

Bryant, Susan L. 2013. "The Beauty Ideal: The Effects of European Standards of Beauty on Black Women." *Columbia Social Work Review* 4:80–91.

Burawoy, Michael. 2005. "For Public Sociology." *American Sociological Review* 70 (1): 4–28.

Cannella, Gaile S., and Kathryn D. Manuelito. 2008. "Feminisms from Unthought Locations: Indigenous Worldviews, Marginalized Feminisms, and Revisioning an Anticolonial Social Science." In *Handbook of Critical and Indigenous Methodologies*, ed. Norman K. Denzin, Yvonna S. Lincoln, and Linda Tuhiwai Smith, 45–59. Thousand Oaks, CA: SAGE.

Castro-Gómez, Santiago. 1998. "Latinoamericanismo, modernidad, globalización: Prolegómenos a una crítica poscolonial de la razón." In *Teorías sin disciplina:*

Latinoamericanismo, poscolonialidad y globalización en debate, ed. Santiago Castro-Gómez and Eduardo Mendieta, 169–205. Mexico City: Miguel Ángel Porrúa.

Castro-Gómez, Santiago. 2005. *La hybris del punto cero: Ciencia, raza e ilustración en la Nueva Granada (1750–1816)*. Bogotá: Instituto Pensar, Pontificia Universidad Javeriana.

Castro-Gómez, Santiago, and Ramón Grosfoguel. 2007. "Prólogo: Giro decolonial, teoría crítica y pensamiento heterárquico." In *El giro decolonial: Reflexiones para una diversidad epistémica, más allá del capitalismo global*, ed. Santiago Castro-Gómez and Ramón Grosfoguel, 9–24. Bogotá: Siglo del Hombre Editores.

Césaire, Aimé. 1972. *Discourse on Colonialism*. Translated by Joan Pinkham. New York: Monthly Review Press.

Chakrabarty, Dipesh. 2000. *Provincializing Europe: Postcolonial Thought and Historical Difference*. Princeton, NJ: Princeton University Press.

Chatterjee, Partha. 1993. *The Nation and Its Fragments: Colonial and Postcolonial Histories*. Princeton, NJ: Princeton University Press.

Chavez, Leo. 1998. *Shadowed Lives: Undocumented Immigrants in American Society*. 2nd ed. Fort Worth, TX: Harcourt Brace College Publishers.

Chavez, Leo. 2008. *The Latino Threat: Constructing Immigrants, Citizens and the Nation*. Stanford, CA: Stanford University Press.

Chilisa, Bagele. 2011. *Indigenous Research Methodologies*. London: SAGE.

Chin, Gabriel "Jack," Carissa Byrne Hessick, Toni M. Massaro, and Marc L. Miller. 2010. "A Legal Labyrinth: Issues Raised by Arizona State Bill 1070." *Georgetown Immigrant Law Journal* 25:47–65.

Clifford, James, and George Marcus, eds. 1986. *Writing Culture: The Poetics and Politics of Ethnography*. Berkeley: University of California Press.

Cohen, Colleen Ballerino, Richard Wilk, and Beverly Stoeltje, eds. 1995. *Beauty Queens on the Global Stage*. London: Routledge.

Coleman, Mathew. 2012. "The 'Local' Migration State: The Site-Specific Devolution of Immigration Enforcement in the U.S. South." *Law and Policy* 34 (2): 159–90.

Coleman, Mathew, and Angela Stuesse. 2014. "Policing Borders, Policing Bodies: The Territorial and Biopolitical Roots of U.S. Immigration Control." In *Placing the Border in Everyday Life*, ed. R. Jones and C. Johnson, 33–63. Farnham, UK: Ashgate.

Comaroff, Jean, and John L. Comaroff, eds. 2012a. *Theory from the South: Or, How Euro-America Is Evolving toward Africa*. New York: Routledge.

Comaroff, Jean, and John L. Comaroff. 2012b. "Theory from the South: Or, How Euro-America Is Evolving toward Africa." *Anthropological Forum* 22 (2): 113–31.

Coronil, Fernando. 1996. "Beyond Occidentalism: Toward Nonimperial Geohistorical Categories." *Cultural Anthropology* 11 (1): 51–86.

Coronil, Fernando. 2004. "Latin American Postcolonial Studies and Global Decolonization." In *The Cambridge Companion to Postcolonial Literary Studies*, ed. Neil Lazarus, 221–40. Cambridge: Cambridge University Press.

Coronil, Fernando. 2008. "Elephants in the Americas? Latin American Postcolonial Studies and Global Decolonization." In *Coloniality at Large: Latin America and the*

Postcolonial Debate, ed. Mabel Moraña, Enrique D. Dussel, and Carlos A. Jáuregui, 396–416. Durham, NC: Duke University Press.

Corrunker, Laura. 2012. "'Coming Out of the Shadows': DREAM Act Activism in the Context of Anti-Deportation Activism." *Indiana Journal of Global Legal Studies* 19 (1): 143–68.

Coulthard, Glen Sean. 2014. *Red Skin, White Masks: Rejecting the Colonial Politics of Recognition*. Minneapolis: University of Minnesota Press.

Coutin, Susan B. 2000. *Legalizing Moves: Salvadoran Immigrants' Struggle for US Residency*. Ann Arbor: University of Michigan Press.

Coutin, Susan B. 2003. "Borderlands, Illegality and the Spaces of Non-Existence." In *Globalization under Construction: Governmentality, Law, and Identity*, ed. Richard Perry and Bill Maurer, 171–202. Minneapolis: University of Minnesota Press.

Coutin, Susan B. 2016. *Exiled Home: Salvadoran Transnational Youth in the Aftermath of Violence*. Durham, NC: Duke University Press.

Cox, Aimee Meredith. 2015. *Shapeshifters: Black Girls and the Choreography of Citizenship*. Durham, NC: Duke University Press.

Craven, Christa, and Dána-Ain Davis. 2013. *Feminist Activist Ethnography: Counterpoints to Neoliberalism in North America*. Lanham, MD: Lexington.

Crenshaw, Kimberlé. 1989. "Demarginalizing the Intersection of Race and Sex: A Black Feminist Critique of Antidiscrimination Doctrine, Feminist Theory and Antiracist Politics." *University of Chicago Legal Forum* 1989 (1): 139–67.

Dave, Naisargi. 2012. *Queer Activism in India: A Story in the Anthropology of Ethics*. Durham, NC: Duke University Press.

De Genova, Nicholas. 2002. "Migrant 'Illegality' and Deportability in Everyday Life." *Annual Review of Anthropology* 31:419–47.

De Genova, Nicholas. 2007. "The Production of Culprits: From Deportability to Detainability in the Aftermath of 'Homeland Security.'" *Citizenship Studies* 11:421–48.

De la Cadena, Marisol. 2006. "The Production of Other Knowledges and Its Tensions: From Andeanist Anthropology to *Interculturalidad*?" In *World Anthropologies: Disciplinary Transformations within Systems of Power*, ed. Gustavo Lins Ribeiro and Arturo Escobar, 201–24. New York: Berg.

Deloria, Vine, Jr. 1969. "Anthropologists and Other Friends." In *Custer Died for Your Sins*, chapter 4. Norman: University of Oklahoma Press.

Denzin, Norman K., Yvonna S. Lincoln, and Linda Tuhiwai Smith, eds. 2008. *Handbook of Critical and Indigenous Methodologies*. London: SAGE.

Diamond, Stanley, ed. 1979. *Towards a Marxist Anthropology*. The Hague: Mouton.

Dostal, Walter. 1972. "Declaration of Barbados." In *The Situation of the Indian in South America*, ed. Walter Dostal, 376–81. Geneva: World Council of Churches.

Du Bois, W. E. B. [1903] 1997. *The Souls of Black Folk*. Edited by Henry Louis Gates Jr. and Terri Hume Oliver. New York: W. W. Norton.

Dussel, Enrique. 1976. *Filosofía de la liberación*. Mexico City: Editorial Edicol.

Dussel, Enrique. 1996. *The Underside of Modernity*. Atlantic Highlands, NJ: Humanities Press.

Dussel, Enrique. 1998. "Beyond Eurocentrism: The World System and the Limits of Modernity." In *The Cultures of Globalization*, ed. Frederic Jameson and Misao Miyoshi, 3–31. Durham, NC: Duke University Press.

Dussel, Enrique. 2002. "World-System and 'Trans'-Modernity." *Nepantla: Views from South* 3 (2): 221–44.

Dussel, Enrique, Javier Krauel, and Virginia Tuma. 2000. "Europe, Modernity, and Eurocentrism." *Nepantla: Views from South* 1 (3): 465–78.

Ellison, Ralph. 1999. *Invisible Man*. Philadelphia: Chelsea House.

Escobar, Arturo. 1991. "Anthropology and the Development Encounter: The Making and Marketing of Development Anthropology." *American Ethnologist* 18 (4): 658–82.

Escobar, Arturo. 1995. *Encountering Development: The Making and Unmaking of the Third World*. Princeton, NJ: Princeton University Press.

Escobar, Arturo. 2004. "'Worlds and Knowledges Otherwise': The Latin American Modernity/Coloniality Research Program." *Cuadernos del CEDLA* 16:31–67.

Escobar, Arturo. 2007. "Worlds and Knowledges Otherwise." *Cultural Studies* 21 (2–3): 179–210.

Etienne, Mona, and Eleanor Burke Leacock. 1980. *Women and Colonization: Anthropological Perspectives*. Westport, CT: Praeger.

Fals Borda, Orlando. 1979. "Investigating Reality in Order to Transform It: The Colombian Experience." *Dialectical Anthropology* 4 (1): 33–55.

Fals Borda, Orlando. 2001. "Participatory (Action) Research in Social Theory: Origins and Challenges." In *Handbook of Action Research: Participative Inquiry and Practice*, ed. Peter Reason and Hilary Bradbury, 27–37. London: SAGE.

Fanon, Frantz. [1952] 1967. *Black Skin, White Masks*. New York: Grove Press.

Fanon, Frantz. 1991. *The Wretched of the Earth*. Trans. Constance Farrington. New York: Grove.

Fassin, Didier. 2007. "Humanitarianism as a Politics of Life." *Public Culture* 19 (3): 499–520.

Fassin, Didier. 2013. "Why Ethnography Matters: On Anthropology and Its Publics." *Cultural Anthropology* 28 (4): 621–46.

Feminist Africa. 2016. *The Politics of Fashion and Beauty in Africa*. Cape Town: African Gender Institute.

Fine, Janice, Anastasia Mann, David Tulloch, and F. Scott Bentley. 2014. "Meet the Neighbors: Organizational and Spatial Dynamics of Immigrant New Jersey." Rutgers Immigrant Infrastructure Mapping Project, Eagleton Program on Immigration and Democracy, Eagleton Institute. New Brunswick, NJ: Rutgers University.

Fluehr-Lobban, Carolyn, ed. 2003. *Ethics and the Profession of Anthropology: Dialogue for Ethically Conscious Practice*. 2nd ed. Walnut Creek, CA: Altamira.

Forte, Maximilian C. 2014. "Anthropology: The Empire on Which the Sun Never Sets." *Anthropological Forum* 24 (2): 197–218.

Forte, Maximilian C. 2016. *Canadian Anthropology or Cultural Imperialism?* Montreal: Zero Anthropology.

Foucault, Michel. 1977. *Discipline and Punish: The Birth of the Prison*. Translated by Alan Sheridan. New York: Vintage.

Foucault, Michel. 1978. *The History of Sexuality: An Introduction.* Vol. 1. New York: Vintage.

Frank, Andre Gunder. 1969. "Liberal Anthropology vs. Liberation Anthropology." In *Latin America: Underdevelopment or Revolution,* 137–45. New York: Monthly Review Press.

Gans, Herbert J. 2010. "Public Ethnography: Ethnography as Public Sociology." *Qualitative Sociology* 33 (1): 97–104.

Glaser, Barney G., and Anselm L. Strauss. 1967. *The Discovery of Grounded Theory: Strategies for Qualitative Research.* New Brunswick, NJ: Aldine Transaction.

Goldstein, Daniel M. 2000. "Names, Places, and Power: The Politics of Identity in the Miss Oruro Pageant, Cochabamba, Bolivia." *Political and Legal Anthropology Review (PoLAR)* 23 (1): 1–24.

Goldstein, Daniel M. 2004. *The Spectacular City: Violence and Performance in Urban Bolivia.* Durham, NC: Duke University Press.

Goldstein, Daniel M. 2012. *Outlawed: Between Security and Rights in a Bolivian City.* Durham, NC: Duke University Press.

Goldstein, Daniel M. 2014. "Laying the Body on the Line: Activist Anthropology and the Deportation of the Undocumented." *American Anthropologist* 116 (4): 839–42.

Goldstein, Daniel M. 2016. *Owners of the Sidewalk: Security and Survival in the Informal City.* Durham, NC: Duke University Press.

Goldstein, Daniel M., and Carolina Alonso-Bejarano. 2017. "E-Terrify: Securitized Immigration and Biometric Surveillance in the Workplace." *Human Organization* 76 (1): 1–14.

Gomberg-Muñoz, Ruth. 2010. *Labor and Legality: An Ethnography of a Mexican Immigrant Network.* Oxford: Oxford University Press.

Gomberg-Muñoz, Ruth. 2016. *Becoming Legal: Immigration Law and Mixed-Status Families.* New York: Oxford University Press.

Gomberg-Muñoz, Ruth, and Laura Nussbaum-Barberena. 2011. "Is Immigration Policy Labor Policy? Immigration Enforcement, Undocumented Workers, and the State." *Human Organization* 70 (4): 366–75.

González Casanova, Pablo. 1969. *Sociología de la explotación.* Mexico City: Grijalbo.

Gordon, Edmund T. 1991. "Anthropology and Liberation." In *Decolonizing Anthropology,* ed. Faye Harrison. Washington, DC: American Anthropological Association.

Gordon, Lewis R. 2004. "Philosophical Anthropology, Race, and the Political Economy of Disenfranchisement." *Columbia Human Rights Law Review* 36 (1): 145–72.

Gordon, Lewis R. 2013. "Race, Theodicy, and the Normative Emancipatory Challenges of Blackness." *South Atlantic Quarterly* 112 (4): 725–36.

Gough, Kathleen. 1968. "Anthropology and Imperialism." *Monthly Review* 19 (11): 12–27.

Gough, Kathleen. 1990. "'Anthropology and Imperialism' Revisited." *Economic and Political Weekly* 25 (31): 1705–8.

Graeber, David. 2009. *Direct Action: An Ethnography.* Oakland, CA: AK Press.

Grosfoguel, Ramón. 2005. "The Implications of Subaltern Epistemologies for Global Capitalism: Transmodernity, Border Thinking and Global Coloniality." In *Critical*

Globalization Studies, ed. Richard P. Appelbaum and William I. Robinson, 283–92. New York: Routledge.

Grosfoguel, Ramón. 2007. "The Epistemic Decolonial Turn." *Cultural Studies* 21 (2–3): 211–23.

Grosfoguel, Ramón, and Roberto Almanza Hernandez, eds. 2012. *Lugares descoloniales: Espacios de intervención en las Américas.* Bogotá: Editorial Pontificia Universidad Javeriana.

Guha, Ranajit. 1982. "On Some Aspects of the Historiography of Colonial India." *Subaltern Studies* 1 (1): 1–8.

Guha, Ranajit. 1999. *Elementary Aspects of Peasant Insurgency in Colonial India.* Durham, NC, and London: Duke University Press.

Guha, Ranajit. 2001. "Subaltern Studies: Projects for Our Time and Their Convergence." In *The Latin American Subaltern Studies Reader*, ed. Ileana Rodríguez, 35–46. Durham, NC: Duke University Press.

Gupta, Akhil, and James Ferguson. 1997. "Discipline and Practice: 'The Field' as Site, Method, and Location in Anthropology." In *Anthropological Locations: Boundaries and Grounds of a Field Science*, ed. Akhil Gupta and James Ferguson, 1–47. Berkeley: University of California Press.

Hale, Charles R. 2006. "Activist Research v. Cultural Critique: Indigenous Land Rights and the Contradictions of Politically Engaged Anthropology." *Cultural Anthropology* 21 (1): 96–120.

Hale, Charles R. 2008. "Introduction." In *Engaging Contradictions: Theory, Politics, and Methods of Activist Scholarship*, ed. Charles R. Hale, 1–28. Berkeley: University of California Press.

Hale, Charles R., and Lynn Stephen. 2014. *Otros Saberes: Collaborative Research on Indigenous and Afro-Descendent Cultural Politics.* Santa Fe, NM: SAR Press.

Haraway, Donna J. 1988. "Situated Knowledges: The Science Question in Feminism and the Privilege of Partial Perspectives." *Feminist Studies* 14 (3): 575–99.

Haraway, Donna J. 1991. *Simians, Cyborgs, and Women: The Reinvention of Nature.* New York: Routledge.

Harding, Susan. 1991. *Whose Science? Whose Knowledge? Thinking from Women's Lives.* Ithaca, NY: Cornell University Press.

Harding, Susan. 2008. *Sciences from Below: Feminisms, Postcolonialities, and Modernities.* Durham, NC: Duke University Press.

Harrison, Faye V., ed. 1991a. *Decolonizing Anthropology: Moving Further toward an Anthropology of Liberation.* Washington, DC: American Anthropological Association.

Harrison, Faye V. 1991b. "Anthropology as an Agent of Transformation: Introductory Comments and Queries." In *Decolonizing Anthropology: Moving Further toward an Anthropology for Liberation*, ed. Faye V. Harrison, 1–14. Washington, DC: American Anthropological Association.

Hemment, Julie. 2007. "Public Anthropology and the Paradoxes of Participation: Participatory Action Research and Critical Ethnography in Provincial Russia." *Human Organization* 66 (3): 301–14.

Heyman, Josiah McConnell. 1998. "State Effects on Labor Exploitation: The INS and Undocumented Immigrants at the Mexico–United States Border." *Critique of Anthropology* 18 (2): 157–80.

Heyman, Josiah McC. 2016. "Unequal Relationships between Unauthorized Migrants and the Wider Society: Production, Reproduction, Mobility, and Risk." *Anthropology of Work Review* 37 (1): 44–48.

Holmes, Seth. 2013. *Fresh Fruit, Broken Bodies: Migrant Farmworkers in the United States*. Berkeley: University of California Press.

Horton, Sarah. 2015. "Identity Loan: The Moral Economy of Migrant Document Exchange in California's Central Valley." *American Ethnologist* 42 (1): 55–67.

Horton, Sarah. 2016. "Ghost Workers: The Implications of Governing Immigration through Crime for Migrant Workplaces." *Anthropology of Work Review* 37 (1): 11–23.

Howe, Cymene. 2013. *Intimate Activism: The Struggle for Sexual Rights in Postrevolutionary Nicaragua*. Durham, NC: Duke University Press.

Huffer, Elise, and Ropate Qalo. 2004. "Have We Been Thinking Upside-Down? The Contemporary Emergence of Pacific Theoretical Thought." *Contemporary Pacific* 16 (1): 87–116.

Huizer, Gerrit, and Bruce Mannheim, eds. 1979. *The Politics of Anthropology: From Colonialism and Sexism toward a View from Below*. The Hague: Mouton.

Hunt, Sarah, and Cindy Holmes. 2015. "Everyday Decolonization: Living a Decolonizing Queer Politics." *Journal of Lesbian Studies* 19:154–72.

Hurston, Zora Neale. 1935. *Mules and Men*. Philadelphia: J. B. Lippincott.

Hurston, Zora Neale. 1937. *Their Eyes Were Watching God*. Philadelphia: J. B. Lippincott.

Hymes, Dell, ed. 1972. *Reinventing Anthropology*. New York: Pantheon.

Inda, Jonathan Xavier. 2006. "Border Prophylaxis: Technology, Illegality, and the Government of Immigration." *Cultural Dynamics* 18 (2): 115–38.

James, Wendy. 1973. "The Anthropologist as Reluctant Imperialist." In *Anthropology and the Colonial Encounter*, ed. Talal Asad, 41–69. Reading, UK: Ithaca.

Jameson, Frederic. 1991. *Postmodernism, or the Cultural Logic of Late Capitalism*. Durham, NC: Duke University Press.

Jimeno, Myriam. 2005. "La vocación crítica de la antropología en Latinoamérica." *Antípoda* 1:43–66.

Jones, Alison, with Kuni Jenkins. 2008. "Rethinking Collaboration: Working the Indigene-Colonizer Hyphen." In *Handbook of Critical and Indigenous Methodologies*, ed. Norman K. Denzin, Yvonna S. Lincoln, and Linda Tuhiwai Smith, 471–86. Thousand Oaks, CA: SAGE.

Jones, Delmos. 1988. "Toward a Native Anthropology." In *Anthropology for the Nineties*, ed. Johnetta Cole, 30–41. New York: Free Press.

Juris, Jeffrey S. 2007. "Practicing Militant Ethnography with the Movement for Global Resistance (MRG) in Barcelona." In *Constituent Imagination: Militant Investigations, Collective Theorization*, ed. Stevphen Shukaitis and David Graeber, 164–76. Oakland, CA: AK Press.

Juris, Jeffrey S. 2008. "Performing Politics: Image, Embodiment, and Affective Solidarity during Anti-Corporate Globalization Protests." *Ethnography* 9 (1): 61–97.

Juris, Jeffrey S. 2012. "Reflections on #Occupy Everywhere: Social Media, Public Space, and Emerging Logics of Aggregation." *American Ethnologist* 39 (2): 259–79.

Juris, Jeffrey S., and Alex Khasnabish. 2013. *Insurgent Encounters: Transnational Activism, Ethnography, and the Political.* Durham, NC: Duke University Press.

Kant de Lima, Roberto. 1992. "The Anthropology of the Academy: When We Are the Indians." *Knowledge and Society: The Anthropology of Science and Technology* 9:191–222.

Katz, Matt. 2017. "ICE Arrests in N.J. Courthouses Surging, Lawyers Say." *WNYC News,* December 11. https://www.wnyc.org/story/ice-arrests-nj-courthouses-surging -lawyers-say/. Accessed December 14, 2017.

King, Cecil. 1977. "Here Come the Anthros." In *Ethnographic Fieldwork: An Anthropological Reader,* ed. Antonius C. G. M. Robben and Jeffrey A. Sluka, 207–9. 2nd ed. Malden, MA: Wiley-Blackwell.

Kirsch, Stuart. 2002. "Anthropology and Advocacy: A Case Study of the Campaign against the Ok Tedi Mine." *Critique of Anthropology* 22 (2): 175–200.

Kirsch, Stuart. 2010. "Experiments in Engaged Anthropology." *Collaborative Anthropologies* 3:69–80.

Kirsch, Stuart. 2014. *Mining Capitalism: The Relationship between Corporations and Their Critics.* Berkeley: University of California Press.

Kovach, Margaret. 2009. *Indigenous Methodologies: Characteristics, Conversations and Contexts.* Toronto: University of Toronto Press.

Krotz, Esteban. 1993. "La producción antropológica en el Sur: Características, perspectivas, interrogantes." *Alteridades* 3 (6): 5–12.

Krotz, Esteban. 1997. "Anthropologies of the South: Their Rise, Their Silencing, Their Characteristics." *Critique of Anthropology* 17 (3): 237–51.

Kuper, Adam. 1983. "Anthropology and Colonialism." In *Anthropology and Anthropologists: The Modern British School,* 99–120. London: Routledge and Kegan Paul.

Lamphere, Louise. 2003. "The Perils and Prospects for an Engaged Anthropology: A View from the United States." *Social Anthropology* 11 (2): 153–68.

Lassiter, Luke Eric. 2005. *The Chicago Guide to Collaborative Ethnography.* Chicago: University of Chicago Press.

Lassiter, Luke Eric. 2008. "Moving Past Public Anthropology and Doing Collaborative Research." *NAPA Bulletin* 29:70–86.

Lazarus-Black, Mindie. 2000. "Review of Colonizing Hawai'i: The Cultural Power of Law." *Political and Legal Anthropology Review (PoLAR)* 23 (2): 141–45.

Lévi-Strauss, Claude. 1961. "Today's Crisis in Anthropology." *UNESCO Courier* 11:12–17.

Levins Morales, Aurora. 2001. "My Name Is This Story." In *Telling to Live: Latina Feminist Testimonios,* ed. Latina Feminist Group, 88–103. Durham, NC: Duke University Press.

Lewis, Diane. 1973. "Anthropology and Colonialism." *Current Anthropology* 14 (5): 581–602.

Lewis, Herbert. 2013. "Was Anthropology the Child, the Tool, or the Handmaiden of Colonialism?" *In Defense of Anthropology: An Investigation of the Critique of Anthropology,* 73–105. New Brunswick, NJ: Transaction.

Lins Ribeiro, Gustavo. 2014. "World Anthropologies: Anthropological Cosmopolitanisms and Cosmopolitics." *Annual Review of Anthropology* 43:483–98.

Lins Ribeiro, Gustavo, and Arturo Escobar, eds. 2006. *World Anthropologies: Disciplinary Transformations in Systems of Power*. Oxford: Berg.

Loomba, Ania. 2015. *Postcolonialism*. 3rd ed. New York: Routledge.

Low, Setha M., and Sally Engle Merry. 2010. "Engaged Anthropology: Diversity and Dilemmas." *Current Anthropology* 51 (supplement 2): S203–S226.

Lugones, María. 2007. "Heterosexualism and the Colonial/Modern Gender System." *Hypatia* 22 (1): 186–209.

Lugones, María. 2010. "Toward a Decolonial Feminism." *Hypatia* 25 (4): 742–59.

Lugones, María. 2012. "Interseccionalidad y feminismo descolonial." In *Lugares Descoloniales: Espacios de Intervención en las Américas*, ed. Ramón Grosfoguel and Roberto Almanza Hernandez, 119–24. Bogotá: Editorial Pontificia Universidad Javeriana.

Lurie, Maxine N., and Richard F. Veit, eds. 2012. *New Jersey: A History of the Garden State*. New Brunswick, NJ: Rutgers University Press.

Lyon-Callo, Vincent. 2008. *Inequality, Poverty, and Neoliberal Governance: Activist Ethnography in the Homeless Sheltering Industry*. Toronto: University of Toronto Press.

Maese-Cohen, Marcelle. 2010. "Introduction: Toward Planetary Decolonial Feminisms." *Qui Parle* 18 (2): 3–27.

Mafeje, Archie. 2001. *African Social Scientists' Reflections. Part 1, Anthropology in Post-Independence Africa: End of an Era and the Problem of Self-Redefinition*. Nairobi: Heinrich Böll Foundation.

Magubane, Bernard M., and James C. Faris. 1985. "On the Political Relevance of Anthropology." *Dialectical Anthropology* 9:91–104.

Maldonado-Torres, Nelson. 2006. "Césaire's Gift and the Decolonial Turn." *Radical Philosophy Review* 9 (2): 111–37.

Maldonado-Torres, Nelson. 2007. "On the Coloniality of Being." *Cultural Studies* 21 (2–3): 240–70.

Maldonado-Torres, Nelson. 2008. *Against War: Views from the Underside of Modernity*. Durham, NC: Duke University Press.

Maldonado-Torres, Nelson. 2011. "Thinking through the Decolonial Turn: Post-Continental Interventions in Theory, Philosophy, and Critique: An Introduction." *Transmodernity* 1 (2): 1–15.

Maldonado-Torres, Nelson. 2012. "Thinking at the Limits of Philosophy and Doing Philosophy Elsewhere: From Philosophy to Decolonial Thinking." In *Reframing the Practice of Philosophy: Bodies of Color, Bodies of Knowledge*, ed. George Yancy, 251–70. Albany: State University of New York.

Malkki, Liisa H. 1996. "Speechless Emissaries: Refugees, Humanitarianism, and Dehistoricization." *Cultural Anthropology* 11 (3): 377–404.

Marcus, George, and Michael M. J. Fischer. 1986. *Anthropology as Cultural Critique: An Experimental Moment in the Human Sciences*. Chicago: University of Chicago Press.

Mascia-Lees, Frances E., Patricia Sharpe, and Colleen B. Cohen. 1989. "The Post-Modernist Turn in Anthropology: Cautions from a Feminist Perspective." *Signs* 15 (1): 7–33.

Maurer, Bill. 2005. *Mutual Life, Limited: Islamic Banking, Alternative Currencies, Lateral Reason*. Princeton, NJ: Princeton University Press.

Mbembe, Achille. 2003. "Necropolitics." Translated by Libby Meintjes. *Public Culture* 15 (1): 11–40.

McClintock, Anne. 1995. *Imperial Leather: Race, Gender, and Sexuality in the Colonial Contest*. New York: Routledge.

Mead, Margaret. 1928. *Coming of Age in Samoa*. New York: Morrow.

Merry, Sally Engle. 2000. *Colonizing Hawai'i: The Cultural Power of Law*. Princeton, NJ: Princeton University Press.

Mertz, Elizabeth, and Mark Goodale. 2012. "Comparative Anthropology of Law." In *Comparative Law and Society*, ed. David S. Clark, 77–91. Cheltenham, UK: Edward Elgar.

Middleton, Townsend, and Jason Cons. 2014. "Coming to Terms: Reinserting Research Assistants into Ethnography's Past and Present." Introduction to Fieldwork(ers). Special Issue. *Ethnography* 15 (3): 279–90.

Mignolo, Walter D. 2000. *Local Histories/Global Designs: Coloniality, Subaltern Knowledges and Border Thinking*. Princeton, NJ: Princeton University Press.

Mignolo, Walter D. 2002. "The Geopolitics of Knowledge and the Colonial Difference." *South Atlantic Quarterly* 101 (1): 57–96.

Mignolo, Walter D. 2007a. "Delinking." *Cultural Studies* 21 (2–3): 449–514.

Mignolo, Walter D. 2007b. "Introduction." *Cultural Studies* 21 (2–3): 155–67.

Mignolo, Walter D. 2011a. *The Darker Side of Western Modernity: Global Futures, Decolonial Options*. Durham, NC: Duke University Press.

Mignolo, Walter D. 2011b. "Epistemic Disobedience and the Decolonial Option: A Manifesto." *Transmodernity* 1 (2): 44–66.

Minh-ha, Trinh. 1989. *Woman, Native, Other*. Bloomington: Indiana University Press.

Mohanty, Chandra Talpade. 1988. "Under Western Eyes: Feminist Scholarship and Colonial Discourses." *Feminist Review* 30:61–88.

Mohanty, Chandra Talpade. 2004. *Feminism without Borders: Decolonizing Theory, Practicing Solidarity*. 5th ed. Durham, NC: Duke University Press.

Moraña, Mabel, Enrique D. Dussel, and Carlos A. Jáuregui, eds. 2008. *Coloniality at Large: Latin America and the Postcolonial Debate*. Durham, NC: Duke University Press.

Morgensen, Scott Lauria. 2011. *Spaces between Us: Queer Settler Colonialism and Indigenous Decolonization*. Minneapolis: University of Minnesota Press.

Nader, Laura. 1972. "Up the Anthropologist: Perspectives Gained from Studying Up." In *Reinventing Anthropology*, ed. Dell Hymes, 284–311. New York: Pantheon.

Nandy, Ashis. 1989. *The Intimate Enemy: Loss and Recovery of Self under Colonialism*. Oxford: Oxford University Press.

Ndlovu-Gatsheni, Sabelo J. 2013. "Why Decoloniality in the 21st Century?" *Thinker* 48:10–15.

Nossel, Suzanne. 2016. "On 'Artivism,' or Art's Utility in Activism." *Social Research: An International Quarterly* 83 (1): 103–5.

Nzimiro, Ikenna. 1988. "Liberation Anthropology for the Year 2000." *International Social Science Journal* 40 (2): 221–29.

Okongwu, Anne, and Joan Mencher. 2000. "The Anthropology of Public Policy: Shifting Terrains." *Annual Review of Anthropology* 29:107–24.

Osterweil, Michal. 2013. "Rethinking Public Anthropology through Epistemic Politics and Theoretical Practice." *Cultural Anthropology* 28 (4): 598–620.

Overing, Joanna. 2006. "The Backlash to Decolonizing Intellectuality." *Anthropology and Humanism* 31 (1): 11–40.

Paris, Django, and Maisha T. Winn, eds. 2014. *Humanizing Research: Decolonizing Qualitative Inquiry with Youth and Communities.* Thousand Oaks, CA: SAGE.

Pels, Peter. 1997. "The Anthropology of Colonialism: Culture, History, and the Emergence of Western Governmentality." *Annual Review of Anthropology* 26:163–83.

Pels, Peter. 2014. "After Objectivity: An Historical Approach to the Intersubjective in Ethnography." HAU: *Journal of Ethnographic Theory* 4 (1). Accessed November 17, 2017. https://www.haujournal.org/index.php/hau/article/view/hau4.1.009/650.

Perez, Emma. 1999. *The Decolonial Imaginary: Writing Chicanas into History.* Bloomington: Indiana University Press.

Perez, Emma. 2003. "Queering the Borderlands: The Challenges of Excavating the Invisible and Unheard." *Frontiers: A Journal of Women's Studies* 24 (2–3): 122–31.

Perry, Keisha-Khan Y. 2013. *Black Women against the Land Grab: The Fight for Racial Justice in Brazil.* Minneapolis: University of Minnesota Press.

Pierre, Jemima. 2012. *The Predicament of Blackness: Postcolonial Ghana and the Politics of Race.* Chicago: University of Chicago Press.

Powers, Nicholas. 2016. "How to Topple a Wall with a Heartbeat." *The Moon Magazine.* Accessed February 15, 2017. http://moonmagazine.org/nicholas-powers-how -to-topple-a-wall-with-a-heartbeat-2016-12-31/.

Pratt, Mary Louise. 1992. *Imperial Eyes: Travel Writing and Transculturation.* New York: Routledge.

Prentki, Tim, and Sheila Preston. 2009. "Applied Theater: An Introduction." In *The Applied Theatre Reader,* ed. Tim Prentki and Sheila Preston, 9–15. London: Routledge.

Quijano, Aníbal. 1993. "'Raza,' 'etnia' y 'nación' en Mariátegui: Cuestiones abiertas." In *José Carlos Mariátgui y Europa: El otro aspecto del descubrimiento,* ed. Roland Forgues, 167–87. Lima, Peru: Empresa Editora Amauta S.A.

Quijano, Aníbal. 2000. "Coloniality of Power, Ethnocentrism, and Latin America." *Nepantla: Views from South* 1 (3): 533–80.

Quijano, Aníbal. 2001. "Globalización, colonialidad y democracia: Utopías, nuestra bandera." *Revista de debate político* 188:97–123.

Quijano, Aníbal. 2007. "Coloniality and Modernity/Rationality." *Cultural Studies* 21 (2–3): 168–78.

Radin, Paul. 1933. *The Method and Theory of Ethnology: An Essay in Criticism.* New York: McGraw-Hill.

Razsa, Maple. 2015. *Bastards of Utopia: Living Radical Politics after Socialism*. Bloomington: Indiana University Press.

Reason, Peter, and Hilary Bradbury, eds. 2008. *The SAGE Handbook of Action Research: Participative Inquiry and Practice*. 2nd ed. London: SAGE.

Redfield, Peter. 2012. "Humanitarianism." In *A Companion to Moral Anthropology*, ed. Didier Fassin, 451–67. Malden, MA: Blackwell.

Reiter, Bernd, and Ulrich Oslender, eds. 2014. *Bridging Scholarship and Activism: Reflections from the Frontlines of Collaborative Research*. East Lansing: Michigan State University Press.

Restrepo, Eduardo. 2007. "Antropología y colonialidad." In *El giro decolonial: Reflexiones para una diversidad epistémica, más allá del capitalismo global*, ed. Santiago Castro-Gómez and Ramón Grosfoguel, 289–304. Bogota: Siglo del Hombre Editores.

Restrepo, Eduardo, and Arturo Escobar. 2005. "'Other Anthropologies and Anthropology Otherwise': Steps to a World Anthropologies Framework." *Critique of Anthropology* 25 (2): 99–129.

Rivera Cusicanqui, Silvia. 2010. "The Notion of 'Rights' and the Paradoxes of Postcolonial Modernity: Indigenous Peoples and Women in Bolivia." *Qui Parle* 18 (2): 29–54.

Rivera Cusicanqui, Sylvia. 2012. "Ch'ixinakax Utxiwa: A Reflection on the Practices and Discourses of Decolonization." *South Atlantic Quarterly* 111:95–109.

Robbins, Joel. 2013. "Beyond the Suffering Subject: Toward an Anthropology of the Good." *Journal of the Royal Anthropological Institute* 19:447–62.

Rodd, Michael. 1988. *Theatre for Community, Conflict and Dialogue: The Hope Is Vital Training Manual*. Portsmouth, NH: Heinemann Drama.

Rodriguez, Robyn. 2017. *In Lady Liberty's Shadow: The Politics of Race and Immigration in New Jersey*. New Brunswick, NJ: Rutgers University Press.

Rosaldo, Michelle, and Louise Lamphere, eds. 1974. *Women, Culture, and Society*. Stanford, CA: Stanford University Press.

Rosaldo, Renato. 1989. "The Erosion of Classic Norms." In *Culture and Truth: The Remaking of Social Analysis*, 25–45. Boston: Beacon.

Rylko-Bauer, Barbara, Merrill Singer, and John van Willigen. 2006. "Reclaiming Applied Anthropology: Its Past, Present, and Future." *American Anthropologist* 108 (1): 178–90.

Said, Edward W. 1978. *Orientalism*. New York: Vintage.

Said, Edward W. 1989. "Representing the Colonized: Anthropology's Interlocutors." *Critical Inquiry* 15 (2): 205–25.

Said, Edward W. 1993. *Culture and Imperialism*. New York: Vintage.

Saldívar, José David. 1997. *Border Matters: Remapping American Cultural Studies*. Berkeley: University of California Press.

Sandoval, Chela. 2000. *Methodology of the Oppressed*. Minneapolis: University of Minnesota Press.

Sanford, Victoria, and Asale Angel-Ajani, eds. 2006. *Engaged Observer: Anthropology, Advocacy, Activism*. New Brunswick, NJ: Rutgers University Press.

Sanjek, Roger. 1993. "Anthropology's Hidden Colonialism: Assistants and Their Ethnographers." *Anthropology Today* 9 (2): 13–18.

Santos, Boaventura de Sousa. 1995. *Towards a New Common Sense: Law, Science and Politics in the Paradigmatic Transition*. New York: Routledge.

Santos, Boaventura de Sousa. 2006. *The Rise of the Global Left: The World Social Forum and Beyond*. London: Zed.

Santos, Boaventura de Sousa, João Arriscado Nunes, and Maria Paula Meneses. 2007. "Introduction: Opening Up the Canon of Knowledge and Recognition of Difference." In *Another Knowledge Is Possible: Beyond Northern Epistemologies*, ed. Boaventura de Sousa Santos, xix–lxii. London: Verso.

Scharrón-Del Río, María R., and Alan A. Aja. 2015. "The Case FOR 'Latinx': Why Intersectionality Is Not a Choice." *Latino Rebels*, December 5. Accessed June 15, 2016. http://www.latinorebels.com/2015/12/05/the-case-for-latinx-why-intersectionality-is-not-a-choice/.

Scheper-Hughes, Nancy. 1995. "The Primacy of the Ethical." *Current Anthropology* 36 (3): 409–20.

Scheper-Hughes, Nancy. 2009. "Making Anthropology Public." *Anthropology Today* 25 (4): 1–3.

Schiwy, Freya. 2007. "Decolonization and the Question of Subjectivity." *Cultural Studies* 21 (2–3): 271–94.

Sefa-Boayke, Jennifer. 2015. "Kenyan Animated Short Film 'Yellow Fever' Explores Colorism and Self-Image among African Girls and Women." *OkayAfrica*, March 25. Accessed December 22, 2017. http://www.okayafrica.com/yellow-fever-kenyan-animated-short-film-ngendo-mukii/.

Seth, Suman. 2009. "Putting Knowledge in Its Place: Science, Colonialism, and the Postcolonial." *Postcolonial Studies* 12 (4): 373–88.

Shore, Chris, and Susan Wright. 1999 "Audit Culture and Anthropology: Neoliberalism in British Higher Education." *Journal of the Royal Anthropological Institute* 5 (4): 557–75.

Simpson, Audra. 2014. *Mohawk Interruptus: Political Life across the Borders of Settler States*. Durham, NC: Duke University Press.

Simpson, Audra, and Andrea Smith, eds. 2014. *Theorizing Native Studies*. Durham, NC: Duke University Press.

Singer, Merrill. 2008. "Applied Anthropology." In *A New History of Anthropology*, ed. Henrietta Kulick, 326–40. London: Blackwell.

Sistren, with Honor Ford-Smith. 2005. *Lionheart Gal: Life Stories of Jamaican Women*. Kingston, Jamaica: University of the West Indies Press.

Smith, Andrea. 2006. "Heteropatriarchy and the Three Pillars of White Supremacy." In *The Color of Violence: The INCITE! Anthology*, ed. INCITE! Women of Color against Violence, 66–73. Boston: South End Press.

Smith, Joshua J. 2015. "Standing with Sol: The Spirit and Intent of Action Anthropology." *Anthropologica* 57 (2): 445–56.

Smith, Linda Tuhiwai. 2012. *Decolonizing Methodologies: Research and Indigenous Peoples*. 2nd ed. London: Zed.

Speed, Shannon. 2006. "At the Crossroads of Human Rights and Anthropology: Toward a Critically Engaged Activist Research." *American Anthropologist* 108 (1): 66–76.

Speed, Shannon. 2007. *Rights in Rebellion: Indigenous Struggle and Human Rights in Chiapas*. Stanford, CA: Stanford University Press.

Speed, Shannon. 2008. "Forged in Dialogue: Toward a Critically Engaged Activist Research." In *Engaging Contradictions: Theory, Politics, and Methods of Activist Scholarship*, ed. Charles R. Hale, 213–36. Berkeley: University of California Press.

Spivak, Gayatri C. 1988. "Can the Subaltern Speak?" In *Marxism and the Interpretation of Culture*, ed. Cary Nelson and Lawrence Grossberg, 271–313. Urbana: University of Illinois Press.

Spivak, Gayatri C. 1999. *A Critique of Postcolonial Reason: Toward a History of the Vanishing Present*. Cambridge, MA: Harvard University Press.

Spurlin, William J. 2001. "Broadening Postcolonial Studies/Decolonizing Queer Studies: Emerging 'Queer' Identities in Southern Africa." In *Postcolonial, Queer: Theoretical Intersections*, ed. John C. Hawley, 185–206. Albany: SUNY Press.

Steele, Abby. 2016. "Why I'm Ditching Western Beauty Standards and Embracing My Afro." *The Tab*, n.d. Accessed December 22, 2017. https://thetab.com/uk/2016/08/03/ditching-western-beauty-standards-embracing-afro-12017.

Steinmetz, George, ed. 2013. *Sociology and Empire: The Imperial Entanglements of a Discipline*. Durham, NC: Duke University Press.

Stilltoe, Paul. 2007. "Anthropologists Only Need Apply: Challenges of Applied Anthropology." *Journal of the Royal Anthropological Institute* 13:147–65.

Stocking, George W., Jr. 1992. "Anthropology as Kulturkampf: Science and Politics in the Career of Franz Boas." In *The Ethnographer's Magic and Other Essays in the History of Anthropology*, 92–113. Madison: University of Wisconsin Press.

Stocking, George W., Jr., ed. 1993. *Colonial Situations: Essays on the Contextualization of Ethnographic Knowledge*. Madison: University of Wisconsin Press.

Stocking, George W., Jr. 2001. *Delimiting Anthropology: Occasional Essays and Reflections*. Madison: University of Wisconsin Press.

Stoler, Ann L. 1989a. "Making Empire Respectable: The Politics of Race and Sexual Morality in 20th-Century Colonial Cultures." *American Ethnologist* 16 (4): 634–60.

Stoler, Ann L. 1989b. "Rethinking Colonial Categories: European Communities and the Boundaries of Rule." *Comparative Studies in Society and History* 31 (1): 134–61.

Stoler, Ann L. 2008. "Imperial Debris: Reflections on Ruins and Ruination." *Cultural Anthropology* 23 (2): 191–219.

Stoler, Ann L. 2016. *Duress: Imperial Durabilities in Our Times*. Durham, NC: Duke University Press.

Strathern, Marilyn. 2000. *Audit Cultures*. London: Routledge.

Stuesse, Angela. 2010. "What's 'Justice and Dignity' Got to Do with It? Migrant Vulnerability, Corporate Complicity, and the State." *Human Organization* 69 (1): 19–30.

Stuesse, Angela. 2015. "Anthropology for Whom?: Challenges and Prospects of Activist Scholarship." In *Public Anthropology in a Borderless World*, ed. Sam Beck and Carl Maida, 221–46. New York: Berghahn.

Stuesse, Angela C. 2016. *Scratching Out a Living: Latinos, Race, and Work in the Deep South*. Berkeley: University of California Press.

Stuesse, Angela, and Mathew Coleman. 2014. "Automobility, Immobility, Altermobility: Surviving and Resisting the Intensification of Immigrant Policing." *City and Society* 26 (1): 51–72.

Svitak, Adora. 2014. "The Asian Beauty Problem." *Huffington Post*, May 5. Accessed December 22, 2017. https://www.huffingtonpost.com/adora-svitak/teen-body-image_b_5251604.html.

TallBear, Kim. 2014. "Standing with and Speaking as Faith: A Feminist-Indigenous Approach to Inquiry." *Journal of Research Practice* 10 (2): 1–7.

Taussig, Michael. 1991. *Shamanism, Colonialism, and the Wild Man: A Study in Terror and Healing*. Chicago: University of Chicago Press.

Taylor, Peter. 2003. *Applied Theatre: Creating Transformative Encounters in the Community*. Portsmouth, NH: Heinemann Drama.

Tlostanova, Madina V., and Walter D. Mignolo. 2012. *Learning to Unlearn: Decolonial Reflections from Eurasia and the Americas*. Columbus: Ohio State University Press.

Trask, H. 1991. "Natives and Anthropologists: The Colonial Struggle." *Contemporary Pacific* 3 (1): 159–67.

Trouillot, Michel-Rolph. 1991. "Anthropology and the Savage Slot: The Poetics and Politics of Otherness." In *Global Transformations: Anthropology and the Modern World*, 7–28. New York: Palgrave Macmillan.

Tuck, Eve, and K. Wayne Yang. 2014. "R-Words: Refusing Research." In *Humanizing Research: Decolonizing Qualitative Inquiry with Youth and Communities*, ed. Django Paris and Maisha T. Winn, 223–48. Thousand Oaks, CA: SAGE.

Visweswaran, Kamala. 1988. "Defining Feminist Ethnography." *Inscriptions* 3–4: 27–47.

Visweswaran, Kamala. 1994. *Fictions of Feminist Ethnography*. Minneapolis: University of Minnesota Press.

Viveiros de Castro, Eduardo. 2009. *Métaphysiques cannibales*. Paris: Presses Universitaires de France.

Walia, Harsha. 2013. *Undoing Border Imperialism*. Oakland, CA: AK Press.

Walsh, Catherine. 2007. "Shifting the Geopolitics of Critical Knowledge." *Cultural Studies* 21 (2–3): 224–39.

Weiner, Annette. 1976. *Women of Value, Men of Renown: New Perspectives in Trobriand Exchange*. Austin: University of Texas Press.

West, Paige. 2016. "Teaching Decolonizing Methodologies." *Savage Minds: Notes and Queries in Anthropology*, July 25. Accessed December 21, 2017. https://savageminds.org/2016/07/25/teaching-decolonizing-methodologies/.

Willis, William. 1974. "Skeletons in the Anthropological Closet." In *Reinventing Anthropology*, ed. Dell Hymes, 284–312. New York: Pantheon.

Wolf, Margery. 1972. *Women and the Family in Rural Taiwan*. Stanford, CA: Stanford University Press.

Wynter, Sylvia. 2003. "Unsettling the Coloniality of Being/Power/Truth/Freedom: Towards the Human, after Man, Its Overrepresentation; An Argument." *New Centennial Review* 3 (3): 257–337.

Wynter, Sylvia. 2006. "On How We Mistook the Map for the Territory, and Reimprisoned Ourselves in Our Unbearable Wrongness of Being, of Désêtre: Black

Studies toward the Human Project." In *Not Only the Master's Tools: African American Studies in Theory and Practice*, ed. Lewis R. Gordon and Jane Anna Gordon, 85–106. Boulder, CO: Paradigm.

Zong, Jie, and Jeanne Batalova. 2017. "Frequently Requested Statistics on Immigrants and Immigration in the United States." *Migration Policy Institute*. Accessed January 3, 2018. https://www.migrationpolicy.org/article/frequently-requested-statistics -immigrants-and-immigration-united-states#ChangeOverTime.

Index

indigenism, 26

indocumentados. *See* undocumented immigrants

inequality, 1–4, 17–20, 26, 32, 34, 51, 53, 76

injury. *See* work accidents

Institutional Review Board (IRB), 75, 154n26, 159n45

interdisciplinarity, 19, 21, 139, 150n11. *See also* transdisciplinarity

intersectionality, 25, 152n15. *See also* decolonial theory

Jameson, Frederic, 159n1

jornalero, 14, 39, 53, 56, 62–66, 73, 75, 139, 143

King, Martin Luther, Jr., xiii, 103

Lassiter, Luke Eric, 3, 33, 70

Latin America, 26, 41–44, 56, 62, 156n30. *See also* Bolivia; Guatemala; Mexico

Latinx, 6, 53, 62, 64, 139

Levins Morales, Aurora, 159n1

Lévi-Strauss, Claude, 35, 156n29

López Juárez, Lucia, xii–xiii, 10–15, 40, 60–61; development of undocumented activist theory, 90–100; fieldnotes, 78–106; life as immigrant and organizer, 54–58; personal journey toward decolonial ethnography, 137–46; role in research and book project, 73–77. *See also* Undocumented Activist's Theory of Undocumentation

Lugones, María, 23, 25, 147

Maldonado-Torres, Nelson, 22, 28, 147, 151n3, 152n17, 160n2, 160n10

Mead, Margaret, 32, 155n29

Merry, Sally Engle, 25, 150n13

mestiza consciousness, 159n1. *See also* Anzaldúa, Gloria

Mexico, 55–57, 62, 78–79, 88–89, 96, 106, 115, 129, 131, 133

Mignolo, Walter, 26, 36, 136, 146, 152nn10–11, 154n18

Mijangos Garcia, Mirian A., xi–xiii, 10–15, 60–61, 67, 78, 106; development of undocumented activist theory, 90–100; fieldnotes, 79–105; life as immigrant and organizer, 39–45; personal journey toward decolonial

ethnography, 137–44, 145; role in research and book project, 73–77.
See also Undocumented Activist's Theory of Undocumentation

minors, undocumented. *See* immigrants' rights movement: undocumented youth and

modernity, 17, 29–30; coloniality and, 21–23, 25, 36, 138. *See also* science; trans-modernity

Mohanty, Chandra Talpade, 25, 154n22

music, xi, 73, 75, 85, 119, 131, 139–42, 144; "The Injured" (song), 133–34; "Sin Fronteras" [No Borders] (song), 102–3. *See also* artivism

National Science Foundation, 13, 68, 69, 76

neoliberalism, 49, 94; and capitalism, 19; and the university, 4. *See also* Western hegemony

New Jersey, xii, 6, 10, 12, 41–44, 50–51, 54–68, 73–74, 85, 87, 91, 109, 115, 125, 144; central, 13, 35, 64. *See also* Hometown, NJ

nongovernmental organizations (NGOs), 29, 46, 48–50

non-Western epistemologies, 4, 17–18, 20–21, 23, 27–30, 33–34, 147–48. *See also* alternative anthropologies: indigenous anthropology; alternative anthropologies: world anthropology; border thinking; science: Western epistemologies; Western hegemony

North American Free Trade Agreement (NAFTA), 62

nuclear family: and marriage, 154n20

Obama, Barack, 89n22; deportation machine of, xii, 54

objectification, 8

objectivism, 2, 32. *See also* anti-objectivism

Occupational Health and Safety Administration (OSHA), 113, 131, 135, 143. *See also* workers' rights

Office of Research and Sponsored Programs (ORSP), 154n26

organizer, xi, 51, 54, 71, 73–77, 87, 98–99, 144. *See also* community organizing

Participatory Action Research (PAR), 3, 33

patron, 44, 92, 102, 119, 133, 143, 145

poetry, xi–xii, 43; "Broken Poem," ix. *See also* artivism

CPSIA information can be obtained
at www.ICGtesting.com
Printed in the USA
FSHW010512040920
73563FS

9 781478 003953